Transforming Engage
and Well-l

William Scott-Jackson
Andrew Mayo

Transforming Engagement, Happiness and Well-Being

Enthusing People, Teams and Nations

palgrave
macmillan

William Scott-Jackson
Cass Business School
City University London and
    Oxford Strategic Consulting
London and Oxford
UK

Andrew Mayo
Middlesex Business School
Middlesex University
London
UK

ISBN 978-3-319-56144-8   ISBN 978-3-319-56145-5   (eBook)
DOI 10.1007/978-3-319-56145-5

Library of Congress Control Number: 2017939891

Cover credit: Beaubelle/Alamy Stock Vector

Printed on acid-free paper

This Palgrave Macmillan imprint is published by Springer Nature
The registered company is Springer International Publishing AG
The registered company address is: Gewerbestrasse 11, 6330 Cham, Switzerland

Acknowledgements

This book, and especially the research and practical experience that informs it, would not have been possible without the cooperation and advice from our many colleagues, including clients and workmates at Oxford Strategic Consulting and academic colleagues in the University of Oxford, University of Middlesex and Cass Business School. Needless to say, my co-author Prof. Andrew Mayo has contributed enormously to every conceivable aspect of the research, the writing and our combined enthusiasm!

One significant but peripheral finding from our research is that the so-called emerging countries often provide much better examples of advanced or new thinking than the, sometimes tired, developed economies of the west. No-where is this more true than some of the dynamic economies of the Arabian Gulf, where our colleagues in Oxford Strategic Consulting have worked for many years, advising governments and the private sector.

I would particularly like to acknowledge the 'active committed enthusiasm' of H.E. Dr. Ali al Jawad of the Omani Royal Diwan, who has always stimulated challenging discussions combining his exceptional practical and academic knowledge. He has been a great friend and advisor for many years.

His Highness Sheikh Mohammed bin Rashid Al Maktoum, ruler of Dubai and Prime Minister of the UAE, is famous for thinking 'outside-the-box' and is one the first government leaders to focus on the happiness of the people as a key objective of government. I would like to thank H.E. Ohood Al Roumi, Minster of Happiness; H.E. Dr. Aisha bin Bishr, Director General of Smart Dubai Office for the opportunity to contribute to this agenda; and my dear colleague Dr. Ali Al-Azzawi, City Experience Advisor, Smart Dubai Office for our valuable discussions and his most welcome contribution in Chap. 7.

H.E. Sultan bin Saaed Al Mansouri, UAE Minister of Economy, was one of the first people to support my wife and I in our research in the UAE, and our work has only been possible due to his hospitality, humour, help and advice.

The Kingdom of Saudi Arabia is, of course, engaged in a significant journey to move away from oil and to develop the capabilities, well-being and engagement of its people and I would thank HE Adel Fakieh, one of the smartest government leaders I know, for his support and good advice over the period of this research.

In Qatar, also enjoying an amazing transformation, I must thank H.E. Sheikh Khalifa Al Thani, Chairman of Qatar Chamber, who has long supported my work in developing Qatari talent, as well as providing great advice and guidance as needed.

My thanks especially to my wife, Dr. Julie Scott-Jackson, whose worldwide reputation in Palaeolithic Geoarchaeology has allowed us rare access to places and people we would otherwise never have experienced and whose unstinting support has allowed this unwilling author to slog through to produce more research outputs than he would have ever thought possible!

William Scott-Jackson

Contents

List of Figures

List of Tables

1

Engagement, Happiness and Well-Being: Why Bother?

1.1 Purpose of the Book

This book aims to provide the tools by which leaders of any organisation, from a small company to a nation state, can maximise the engagement, happiness and well-being of their people.

Leaders of any organisation, whether it be government or a commercial enterprise, have an obligation to not only create, but also maximise, the well-being of those they are responsible for. In addition, high levels of engagement lead to numerous beneficial outcomes, as we shall see. There have been many examples, both at national and at company level, where an absence of properly developed and nurtured well-being has resulted in friction of some sort, sometimes with catastrophic results, and similarly, a lack of engagement leads to significant issues in organisations.

There is also a recent surge in interest in 'happiness', another related concept, particularly at country level with Bhutan leading the way in defining Gross Domestic Happiness as the goal of government and countries like the UAE and India appointing Ministers of Happiness to reflect this wider goal. More recently, organisations have also begun to consider employee and customer happiness as a key issue with, for example, Dubai Smart City facilitating happiness projects to make Dubai the happiest city on earth (see Chap. 7). We will suggest that in many cases, what is required is a more active form of happiness (closer to engagement) rather than the relatively passive concepts of happiness and well-being as commonly defined.

Although it is a bit of a truism to say that individuals perform better when

© The Author(s) 2018
W. Scott-Jackson and A. Mayo, *Transforming Engagement,
Happiness and Well-Being*, DOI 10.1007/978-3-319-56145-5_1

they feel good not only about themselves, but about those who control or manage their destiny, it is still surprising how many governments, as well as those involved in commercial leadership/management, forget this very simple rule.

We consider well-being, happiness and engagement to be highly related, with high well-being/happiness contributing to high engagement and vice versa. Unfortunately, theory and practice have tended to be completely separate for all these concepts (with the notable exception of Ulrich and Ulrich (2010) who also combined research from psychology and management to explore the 'why of work'), whereas we see them as simply reflecting different dimensions of a common issue. If we think of the dimensions of active versus passive, happy versus unhappy and short term versus long term, then we arrive at Fig. 1.1.

This shows that, for example, the passive short-term high-level state is summed up as 'contentment', and indeed, it could be said that many 'happiness' programmes tend to aim for and result in contentment. But for the leaders of organisations and indeed nations, is short-term contentment what we need? We propose that a better goal is on the top right—an active high-level long-term state which we describe as *active committed enthusiasm (ACE)*. This definition allows us to include the excellent research and practice in all these related areas to arrive at one model whose goal is to maximise ACE in employees and citizens.

National and organisational success is much more easily created when there is a general sense of well-being and engagement, and where there are well-being and engagement, there will be success: a virtuous cycle.

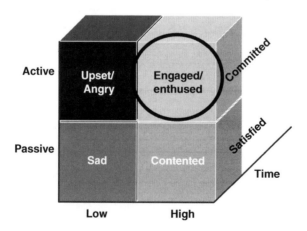

Fig. 1.1 Dimensions of happiness, well-being and engagement

We will be examining how leaders, whether at national or organisational level can help to improve both the well-being and engagement of their people in order to create benefits not only to the people themselves, but also to the organisation or nation itself.

Our research has adopted a multidisciplinary perspective to investigate how strategy and policy, individual psychology and management thinking can together not only create but also drive these beneficial outcomes.

Well-being and engagement levels worldwide are extremely low, and this is at least partly because they are both parts of an extremely complex process with a myriad of factors, causal relationships and parameters which need to be considered. So we are going to break down and model this complex process in order to make it easier to assess how individual factors can contribute to ACE.

We have developed a single framework which pulls all of these concepts together and we have named it a *process of active committed enthusiasm* (PACE, see Fig. 1.2). We are going to use PACE to distinguish between causes, constructs and outcomes.

It should also be recognised that individual and organisational contexts and needs change over time, which means that the PACE model is a dynamic tool rather than a one-off fixed model.

Our objective is to provide new ideas, models and clarity to help leaders of any type to maximise individual active committed enthusiasm (ACE). It is not only about measurement, but also, more importantly, the improvement, implementation and development of a truly engaged and happy workforce or citizenry enjoying high levels of well-being.

The principles outlined are valid no matter what the organisation is or its purpose. Whether it is a government or a charity, the principles outlined are exactly the same, but we have written the book from the very specific perspective of the organised body, rather than from the individual's perspective. In fact, we are looking on how the creation of ACE is necessary in order to contribute to the goals of any organised body of people:

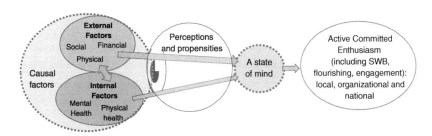

Fig. 1.2 A process for active committed enthusiasm

Of course, engagement, happiness and well-being are desirable states in themselves, but specifically, we are going to be looking at achieving high levels of ACE with beneficial outcomes, not just for the individual, but also for the organisation or nation.

It is a self-evident truth that an organisation or a nation exists (or should exist) to serve its population, which means that the achievements of both individuals and the organisation or nation are interdependent in the sense that active committed enthusiasm (ACE) among citizens or employees helps to achieve organisational/national goals and the achievement of organisational/national goals will also create ACE among the people.

We refer to this as bidirectional causality—a chicken and egg situation. In other words, the citizens of the country experience well-being because of that country's success, and the engagement and well-being of the citizens create that very success in the first place.

Engagement and well-being have been researched and interpreted in many different ways, and as we shall see, other authors have also introduced distinct but related concepts. For instance, Seligman (2012) refers to 'flourishing', whilst Stein and Sadana (2015) see well-being as a product or outcome of health. Macey and Schneider (2008) see the term engagement as referring to 'psychological states, traits and behaviours, as well as their antecedents and outcomes'.

The above three examples are just a few of the range of definitions that we have to contend with, so this may be a good point at which to clarify what we mean by well-being and engagement in the context of this book so it is clear where they fit in the PACE.

We see well-being as being a sustained, positive, perceived state of satisfaction with life (often referred to as subjective well-being). This is not to be confused with short-term happiness or even the absence of 'ill-being'.

Engagement, on the other hand, is an active state of committed enthusiasm towards an organisation, nation or government and its goals.

Engagement resides within the disciplines of management and organisation, and well-being is more a product of national policy and individual psychology.

Nevertheless, and despite the fact that the formal definition of well-being and engagement considers two separate standpoints, there is little doubt that well-being and engagement are highly related to both being identified as causal factors for the other.

We have applied the PACE model to both constructs, and through the model, we aim to demonstrate that the principles which we put forward apply to any sort of organisation, from the smallest group all the way through formal organisations and ultimately nation states.

In recent years, the Sultanate of Oman, for example, has been developing rapidly as a result of a government focus on well-being, from basic provision through to the current focus on intrinsically positive factors.

The Omani experience illustrates quite clearly how any leader can utilise the process model and compare the likely impacts of possible interventions in a systematic and structured manner.

The PACE model is therefore an aid to leaders of organised bodies to achieve national and organisational goals through maximising the engagement and well-being of their citizens and staff. It also provides a useful framework not only for practical application, but also for academic research.

1.2   Why Is It Important?

We have completed extensive research into the associations, and complex and often bidirectional causal links, between well-being and engagement, as well as outputs such as productivity, revenue, sick days, participation, Gross Domestic Product and shareholder value, as well as retention, emigration and a whole raft of other outputs.

Engagement and well-being as related concepts have very significant impacts on the personal, social and economic lives of individuals, organisations and societies. Largely due to their different academic foundations, one perceived difference between the two is that well-being, from the perspective of psychology, is seen as a desirable outcome in its own right with engagement, as a management issue, being viewed as a causal factor for increased productivity, success, effort, motivation, etc.

It is self-evident that such outcomes could also apply to well-being at national level.

Well-being is regarded as a fairly passive state, whereas the concept of engagement carries with it a degree of action and is closely aligned to enthusiasm and commitment.

Over 40 years ago, H.M Sultan Qaboos, the ruler of Oman, stressed that the aim of his national plan was not just the well-being of the citizens but also their active participation. You often hear politicians as well as chief executives say something along the lines of ... 'And our most important asset ... Is our people!' That particular phrase has been trotted out on so many occasions that it has become somewhat of a cliché, but the approach by the Omani government in recognising the importance of focusing on the well-being of its citizens clearly demonstrates that once that particular principle is applied properly, it does have a very positive effect on outcomes, specifically the active participation of Omani nationals.

The concepts of well-being and engagement, and more recently happiness, have been the subject of extensive theory, research and practice, so you may be thinking what can possibly be the practical purpose of this work?

- It has been shown consistently over the years through various studies that a lack of well-being can have a considerable net negative impact on everything from mental disorders such as anxiety, to more serious physical disorders such as diabetes and hypertension. Looking at a corporate scenario, it is understood that say, a sudden increase in sick days being taken and an increase in staff attrition are classic signs of a lack of well-being among individuals and ultimately lack of well-being among staff in general. Although well-being is defined as a personal thing and a function of an individual's state of mind, in a tight corporate environment an individual not feeling very good about themselves or about the company, and especially if he or she is a centre of influence, can very quickly create a sense of lower well-being among previously satisfied staff. On a larger scale, this can also apply at national level where, for instance, even a small issue can be picked up by the (social) media, and very soon, previously satisfied citizens suddenly realise that they weren't as happy as they thought they were. Well-being cannot be assumed to stay high, but it is a fluid and dynamic state which both companies and politicians need to be aware of and nurture on a continuous basis.

- You have probably heard the visitor to a company asking the question 'How many people work here?' Quick as a flash, the answer comes back, 'About half of them'. There are grains of truth in that, because real-world engagement continues to remain elusive with many studies and surveys indicating that only about 25% of people in work are fully engaged (e.g. Towers Watson 2014). Similarly, less than one-third of American workers were found to be engaged in their jobs (Fig. 1.3), and a Gallup survey (2015) found that just over half of employees were not engaged, with about 17.5% being 'actively disengaged'. Those studies were primarily at corporate level, but there is nothing to suggest that similar figures don't apply at national level, especially with recent political upsets (e.g. Brexit, Trump) seeming to reflect general states of active disengagement with political establishments. The state of engagement and well-being is much more difficult to assess globally, especially given the wide variety of definitions and measures. Nevertheless, a 2014 Gallup survey of over 130,000

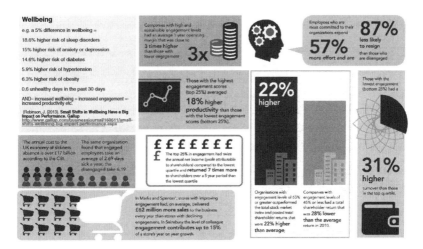

Fig. 1.3 Impacts of engagement and well-being

respondents suggested that globally only 17% of the population are 'thriving' in three or more elements (out of five). That could mean that the so-called best practice is either failing to be implemented or if it is being implemented, it is failing. This book will merge useful findings from two separate disciplines to provide insights for both researchers and policy-makers as well as leaders for all organisations, ranging from the smallest charity to national governments.

- In spite of much debate and discussion, as well as measurement and research, the definitions of well-being, happiness and engagement remain ambiguous to many. This book will attempt to define the main constructs in process terms and will help the reader to decide for themselves. The weighing of the various causal factors will help with decisions on impactful, relevant and effective interventions.

- The focus of this book is not on measurement for its own sake, or even for the sake of league tables, but on the practicalities of creating improvement. This focus has been chosen in order to give the leader or manager a clear view of when and where to intervene in the PACE as well as helping to determine which causal factors have the most significant impact. It would also help to decide which agencies, such as organisations (Quick et al. 2014) or government (Halpern 2008), could or should carry out relevant interventions.

- It may surprise some to discover that 51 of the world's largest 100 GDPs belong to corporations rather than governments (Franke 2015: 5), and many employ over 1 million people. That means that large corporations

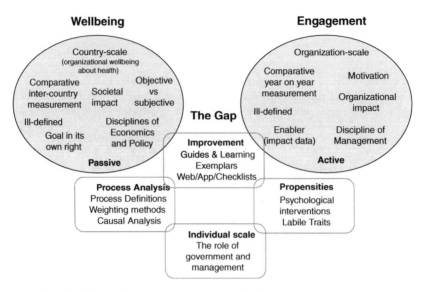

Fig. 1.4   The disciplines of engagement and well-being

have similar issues to consider as governments because they are effectively dealing with a 'population' as well as resources. Consequently, many of these large corporations are adopting an outlook similar to that of a government, and governments are increasingly looking to business models in order to optimise their economic success as well as the well-being of their citizens. HH Sheikh Mohammed Al Maktoum, ruler of Dubai, treats the country as if it were a business organisation (sometimes referred to as 'Dubai Inc') and has created high levels of economic and social success despite relatively low natural resources. A more recent (and certainly unproven!) example of this is the election of Donald Trump as President of the United States of America (USA), who is showing all the signs of running the USA as a large corporation. Whether he manages to engender a general sense of well-being among the population is something which still remains to be seen.

1.3   Integrating Well-Being and Engagement

Although well-being and engagement can be connected, one must not assume that one automatically follows the other.

Figure 1.4 above shows that both research and practice in the two fields have largely developed into distinct and apparently unrelated realms.

The next section explores the similarities and differences between the two constructs as well as related research and theory. We also explore how each set of research, practice and solutions can add to the understanding of the other.

The ultimate goal is not merely passive well-being or happiness, but the generation of active committed enthusiasm (ACE).

This will be achieved through:

- Understanding the process for active committed enthusiasm (PACE).
- Targeting individuals.
- The measurement and improvement of individual perceptions within PACE.

1.4 The Scope of the Book

For many years, the primary consideration when gauging the state of any nation has been related to economics and measures such as GDP. Unfortunately, although this approach does give an accurate snapshot of the state of an economy through the medium of numbers, it certainly does not assess either the well-being or the engagement of its citizens. In most economies, the wealth (and by implication) the well-being does not necessarily cascade down from the top or equally spread through society. That can mean that, although a government can be justifiably proud of its economic achievements, if these achievements are not being shared or perceived to be being shared by the population, then the levels of economic well-being experienced by the population will not be consistent. In addition, it has been clearly shown that above a certain level of economic development, more economic growth adds very little to overall well-being or ACE.

In fact, an unintended consequence of such a scenario can be the creation of negative social consequences as a large section of the population can be very aware that of the country's increase in wealth whilst also being fully aware that it is not fully participating or engaged in it. In order to be effective, any improvement has to be felt by the population at microlevel in order that individual fulfilment is experienced from the top to the bottom. Obviously, the same principle applies to organisations, and many companies have attempted to increase engagement of their staff by, for instance, communicating excellent financial results. If every individual within that business feels that he is not participating, then, paradoxically, those excellent financial results can unintentionally reduce individual engagement. Similarly, once individuals achieve a certain (high) level of income, then further increases add little to their ACE. Also, as we shall see, the effects of income on ACE are largely to do with perceptions of income equality or inequality rather than the income level itself.

You can see, therefore, that assessing well-being and engagement accurately is fraught with difficulties, as what appears to management or politicians to be an excellent measurable state of affairs from their perspective can be the opposite to others.

We are going to identify the key areas where the assessment of ACE and its development can be made more effective.

ACE, as an amalgam of well-being, happiness and engagement, is a multifaceted concept, which incorporates constructs ranging from individual health and psychological well-being all the way through to macroeconomic factors affecting the individual. This book is written primarily for those aiming to research, assess and improve well-being and engagement, and we feel that the following scope is appropriate:

- We recognise that well-being incorporates both subjective and objective factors, but as causal factors in the process (PACE). What is defined as objective well-being is no more than a factual state and independent of what the individual may be feeling. For instance, if the population is healthier, well fed with an increasing life expectancy we may assume (objectively) that there will be a certain element of well-being. On the other hand, subjective well-being is a perceptual matter and measured by some kind of assessment of the feelings of individuals or groups.
- We are focusing on improvement of ACE as an amalgam of well-being, happiness and engagement, but are very conscious of the fact that they can only be assessed as part of a general improvement strategy. In the scope of this book, the purpose of measuring well-being and engagement is to improve.
- We will show that it is individuals who are a critical factor in the PACE model and that both governments and organisations have a perfectly legitimate role in helping individuals to maximise their well-being and engagement, but that in order to achieve this, both organisations and governments must be willing to adjust their own perspectives and characteristics.

The function of the PACE model is to determine the most significant factors and times when interventions by 'management' can have a maximum possible impact, and to reinforce this, the final chapter provides a practical toolkit to assist in transforming well-being and engagement.

1.5 The Objectives of the Book

The objective of this book is to provide a toolkit and process framework to allow for practitioners and researchers to:

- Identify key areas of improvement of ACE and their likely outcomes.
- The key causal factors in the process and their relative impact.
- Individual and collective responses to specific initiatives.
- Analyse objective factors such as employment levels or pension provision with recommendations for specific functions of government and organisations.

In addition, we aim to:

- Provide a toolkit to help organisational and national leaders to maximise the active committed enthusiasm of their people and achieve the beneficial outcomes.
- Review all historical research on global best practice in order to generate recommendations based on a critique of the fundamental concepts in order not only to improve best practice but also to drive further research.
- Provide recommendations, with reference not only to global research, but to the varied cultural contexts and constraints.

References

Franke, A. (2015). Without purpose, you are nothing. *Professional Manager* (5). Chartered Management Institute.

Gallup. (2015). Majority of U.S. employees not engaged despite gains in 2014. *Gallup News*.

Halpern, D. (2008). An evidence-based approach to building happiness. In J. Wernick (Ed.), *Building happiness*. London: Black Dog Publishing.

Macey, W. H., & Schneider, B. (2008). The meaning of employee engagement. *Industrial and Organizational Psychology, 1*(1), 3–30.

Quick, J. Q., Bennett, J., & Hargrove, M. B. (2014). Stress, health and wellbeing in practice: Workplace leadership and leveraging stress for positive outcomes. In P. Y. Chen & C. L. Cooper (Eds.), *Wellbeing: A complete reference guide* (Vol. III, pp. 175–204). Chichester: Wiley Blackwell.

Seligman, M. E. (2012). *Flourish: A visionary new understanding of happiness and well-being*. Simon and Schuster.

Stein, C., & Sadana, R. (2015). The World Health Organization—The case for measuring wellbeing in Europe. *Global handbook of quality of life* (pp. 763–769). Netherlands: Springer.

Towers Watson. (2014). The 2014 global workforce study. Towers Watson.

Ulrich, D., & Ulrich, W. (2010). The why of work. Tata McGraw-Hill Education.

2

What are Engagement, Happiness and Well-Being?

2.1 Engagement

In recent years, both national and organisational leaders have realised the importance of enhancing performance outcomes (such as GDP or productivity), citizenship and satisfaction by improving the engagement of the population of the nation or workforce of an organisation.

The concept of engagement has developed over a long period from work such as Douglas McGregor's (1960) theory in which he postulated that many people enjoy meaningful and stimulating work and if engaged will work harder than the bare minimum. Certainly, in developed societies, the idea that the best performance from people is obtained through coercion is largely dead, as many jobs and roles are less procedural and where performance depends on active committed enthusiasm.

Engagement increases discretionary effort and is certainly the antithesis of the industrial relations view of a shifting balance and conflict of interest between management and workers.

The continued interest in engagement since the 1990s reflects the changing perception of management/worker relations. This has been augmented by the gradual disappearance of the traditional hierarchical management structures towards 'modern organisations' (Schaufeli 2013), which require much more flexible, responsible and self-managed workers and where discretionary effort is a major component of productivity. The modern informality of relationships between management and workers has accelerated these trends and increased the importance of engagement.

© The Author(s) 2018
W. Scott-Jackson and A. Mayo, *Transforming Engagement,*
Happiness and Well-Being, DOI 10.1007/978-3-319-56145-5_2

These changes require greater personal investment and motivation by the individual, rather than simply following instructions.

Ulrich (1997) suggested that these changes result from organisations needing to produce more with fewer human resources, but they may also reflect the wider social change towards individual freedom and expression which may itself result in greater productivity. So, both the new informality and the social change towards individual freedom result in a far greater potential for more engaged workers and citizens to exert more discretionary effort, resulting in greater productivity.

There are at least 50 different definitions of engagement as noted by MacLeod and Clarke (even back in 2011!). Some of the more widely accepted definitions follow:

- Engagement is about creating opportunities for employees to connect with their colleagues, managers and organisations. It is also about creating an environment where employees are motivated to want to connect with their work and really care about doing a good job. It is a concept that places flexibility, change and continuous improvement at the heart of what it means to be an employee and an employer in the twenty-first-century workplace (Gatenby et al. 2009).
- A positive attitude held by the employee towards the organisation and its values. An engaged employee is aware of the business context and works with colleagues to improve performance within the job for the benefit of the organisation. The organisation must work to develop and nurture engagement, which requires a two-way relationship between employee and employer (Robinson et al. 2004).
- Employee engagement, also called commitment or motivation, refers to a psychological state where employees feel a vested interest in the company success and perform to a high standard that may exceed the stated requirements of the role (see http://www.mercer.com).

Of course, people can be 'engaged' within any kind of organisation, from a football club to a nation, and can be directed at any role identity within the person's life, from their work–life to charitable activities to their role as a citizen. In an occupational context, engagement can be directed at:

- The organisation.
- The work.
- The profession.
- The social environment.

Engagement is not viewed as a valuable and desirable state purely for the individual's benefit. In management terms, it is viewed as something to be 'harnessed', and as a potential cause of valuable outcomes, ranging from increased productivity to reduced absenteeism and attrition. Engagement becomes a node in a process which can be measured, not just of the level of engagement itself, but also of its outcomes. Therefore, engagement differs from well-being, where well-being itself has tended to be seen as a beneficial outcome in its own right and where the antecedents and outcomes of well-being are often contemplated within the construct itself.

Academically, the interest in engagement has paralleled developments in positive psychology, originally described by Seligman (see Seligman and Csikszentmihalyi 2000). They suggested that individuals would lead better and more fulfilling lives by adopting optimistic views of the world and by modifying their world, including their working lives, to be more positive. Global interest in engagement has risen dramatically since the 1990s and continues to be a much discussed and researched topic.

The whole idea of engagement has been developed from two very different but highly relevant perspectives: the first is organisations wishing to harness more discretionary effort from their staff; and secondly, psychologists wishing to help people become more positive. This divergence is useful in providing perspectives but as with research into well-being, engagement research has been plagued by inconsistent construct definitions and operationalisations (Christian et al. 2011).

Truss et al. (2014: 1) identified that there was an 'increasing divergence between an academic focus on engagement as a psychological state and practitioner focus on engagement as a workforce strategy'.

For example, Heger (2007) found that there was a body of literature from business academics which focuses on engagement as a workforce strategy in contrast to practitioners for whom engagement was an aspect of individual psychology (Bridger 2015).

Towers Watson (2014: 3) defines engagement as *'employee's willingness to expand discretionary effort on their job'…* with the main causal factors being leadership, clear goals and objectives, workload and work/life balance, organisational image and empowerment.

Meanwhile, 'engagement for success' is a well-known and widely applauded UK initiative to encourage and facilitate engagement in the workplace. Its definition of employee engagement is 'a workplace approach designed to ensure that employees are committed to their organisation's goals and values, motivated to contribute to organisational success and are able at the same time to enhance their own sense of well-being'.

It is interesting that this definition encompasses employee's well-being in the same way that many definitions of subjective well-being (SWB) incorporate engagement.

The Chartered Institute of Personnel and Development (CIPD) defines engagement as: 'being positively present during the performance of work by willingly contributing intellectual effort, experiencing positive emotions and meaningful connections to others'. Once again, the definition of engagement includes SWB in the form of experiencing positive emotions and meaningfulness.

Shuck (2011) identified four types of definition of engagement:

- Needs satisfying—the person is engaged in expressing themselves and their needs.
- Burnout antithesis—where engagement is seen as a positive opposite to burnout.
- Satisfaction engagement—one of the most widely used engagement instruments, within organisations is the Gallup Q^{12}, which has been the subject of considerable analysis and testing. It is based on this definition of engagement, combining satisfaction with enthusiasm and involvement.
- Multidimensional—consisting of cognitive, emotional and behavioural components associated with role performance, as well as distinguishing between different objects of engagement. For example, job engagement or organisational engagement (Saks 2006).

Guest (2014) and others have criticised academic and practitioner interest in engagement as a fashionable fad or a concept developed in order to sell consultancy (Keenoy 2013).

Although there is little doubt that various models and theories of management and administration do tend to arrive in waves and many disappear over time, but as far as engagement is concerned, there is little doubt that 'one of the attractions of engagement is that it is clearly a good thing' (Guest 2014).

It is recognised that there are some potential issues with engagement:

- It could be perceived that only 'engaged' people are valuable and possibly that only engageable people should be recruited.
- Engagement is a panacea and is all that management needs to focus on.
- People have a duty to be engaged and that discretionary effort is the expected (and ever-increasing) norm.
- If managers are assessed and targeted on the amount of 'engagement' they can instil in their subordinates, there is a danger of that particular aspect of

management becoming a KPI or focus, leading to apparent compliance with no substance.

Guest also criticised engagement as lacking practices or a method. In other words: What do you do about it? What does a manager do in order to engage people? He also pointed out that there could be a dark side to engagement. The increased discretionary effort could be to such a high level as to possibly create burnout. That is, assuming that burnout is linked to engagement or *extreme* engagement.

If a certain level of engagement is achieved among staff, this quickly becomes the norm. In order to 'stretch' the staff, the expected levels of engagement will be increased with new exceptional levels being demanded. That could quite easily produce a medium- to long-term self-amplifying problem.

The focus of this book is to define well-being and engagement in terms of process, comprising causal factors, the construct and its outcome, with the addition of some strategies on how to engender well-being, commitment and engagement.

Schaufeli (2013) proposed a basic model in which job resources and personal resources impact on the experience of any engagement, which in turn results in organisational consequences.

Christian et al. (2011) define work engagement operationally, in order to carry out a study of antecedents and consequences, as 'a relatively enduring state of mind', referring to the simultaneous investment of personal energies in the experience of performance of work'. In a process framework, they described consequences of engagement (including performance); antecedents of engagement (e.g. autonomy); and proximal factors (e.g. job satisfaction). This approach helps to clarify the various concepts involved and their interrelationships and is developed within our PACE model.

Is engagement the same as job satisfaction, organisational commitment, job involvement or organisational citizenship?

This is not simply a question of semantics, but in order to be useful, engagement has to be distinct from the other similar concepts, and it needs to be measurable.

Some have suggested that engagement is simply a redefinition of job satisfaction, organisational commitment or job involvement. For instance, Newman et al. (2010) demonstrated correlations between these factors and engagement, but the correlations only suggest an overlap of around 15–29%, which may well suggest some kind of causal relationship, rather than identical nature.

'Job satisfaction', for example, is generally defined as a passive state of satisfaction, in contrast to engagement being active enthusiasm for performance. That is the crucial difference between the two: one is passive and the other active. That is why engagement is the factor which will have the greatest impact on productivity.

Schaufeli et al. (2008) indicate various components of engagement (such as energised and enthused), satisfaction (such as content and relaxed), workaholism (such as irritated and tense) and burnout (such as dejected and lethargic). The components shown reflect this book's key distinctions between active and passive constructs and include the similarly negatively related passive factor of 'boredom'.

Schaufeli suggests that engagement could be described as a mild form of workaholism, but workaholics tend to be less productive than engaged people because of all the negative connotations associated with workaholism.

Unlike workaholism, engagement has been found to correlate with various positive personality factors such as emotional stability and more energised forms of extraversion and consciousness (Inceoglu and Warr 2012). Studies have also found links between extraversion and high engagement, as well as high neuroticism and low engagement (Langelaan et al. 2006). Another study (Kim et al. 2009) has shown a link between conscientiousness and high engagement.

It has been suggested that engagement differs from 'organisational commitment' (Christian et al. 2011) because engagement directs an individual at his or her own performance, whereas organisational commitment refers to the organisation itself rather than the individual's part in it. It is also useful to point out that organisational commitment does not necessarily imply active enthusiasm.

'Job involvement' is another phrase which is worth looking at more closely. Job involvement is about a sense of identity or self-esteem in relation to a job, whereas engagement is about enthusiastic performance. For instance, an individual may take a great sense of pride and enjoy an elevation of self-esteem and promotion to an important or important-sounding job, but that does not necessarily follow that this will create engagement and, through that, enthusiastic performance.

Meta-analyses have found that leadership, personal dispositions and job factors are all related to engagement. The model developed by Christian et al. (2011) also suggests causal factors (such as conscientiousness and transformational leadership) and outcomes (performance) of work engagement and demonstrates the potential of the causal process and the value from the

Table 2.1 Similarities in components of engagement as defined by May et al. (2004) and Schaufeli et al. (2002)

May et al. (2004)	Schaufeli and Bakker (2004)
Physical engagement: 'I exert a lot of energy performing my job'	Vigour: 'At my job, I feel I am bursting with energy'
Emotional engagement: 'I really put my heart into this job'	Dedication: 'I am enthusiastic about my job'
Cognitive engagement: 'Performing my job is so absorbing that I forget about everything else'	Absorption: 'When I am working, I forget anything else around me'

practitioner perspective of truly understanding the causal significance of various factors.

It is also interesting to consider the *object* of an individual's engagement, that is to say at *what* the engagement is directed. The table below illustrates two examples where the defined object is 'my job'. You can also see that the principle of engagement when applied to other activities and other contacts is also expressed in that table: for instance, for 'job', substitute: a cause, my country, my sport, my hobby, etc. (Table 2.1).

For a nation, therefore, engagement with 'my country' would be a much more active strategic objective than the more passive, 'well-being'.

There is a basic difference in the nature of well-being and the nature of engagement. Well-being is inwardly focused, and, although it can be a function of external factors as well as internal ones; it is all about the individual, whereas engagement always has an external object, such as 'job' and 'country'.

This takes us to the concept of citizenship, which is generally defined differently depending on the context. Organisational citizenship is usually defined as a more active construct (Arthaud-Day et al. 2012) than citizenship at a national level, which is mostly about identity and belonging (Ichilov 2013). Many make the distinction between just 'citizenship' as passive and 'engaged citizenship' as the more active construct (Flinders 2014). The UN describes the active participation of citizens as 'civic engagement' (Hoffman et al. 2008).

Another distinction is that of organisational citizenship behaviour (OCB). This is seen as opposite to workplace deviant behaviour (Lee and Allen 2002) and is defined as 'employee behaviours that, although not critical to the task or job, facilitate organisational functioning'. Activities such as helping co-workers or attending functions that promote the organisation and generally expressing approval about the organisation and its goals are all examples of OCB.

OCB and engagement have an obvious relationship, but the two constructs are different in that engagement includes discretionary effort towards productivity and organisational effectiveness, but within the general remit of the individual's role. The five dimensions belonging to OCB are altruism, courtesy, sportsmanship, civic virtue and general compliance (Ariani 2013).

Engaged employees will likely increase the frequency of their organisational citizenship behaviours and also reflect individual behaviour that is discretionary and which is not subject to either that individual's job description or even recognised by the organisation's formal reward system.

Our extension of engagement at organisational level, being developed through this book, is a process of active committed enthusiasm (PACE), which will similarly result in OCB.

OCB is therefore to be viewed as an outcome of engagement, within the PACE framework.

At both organisational and country levels, what might be termed active disengagement or disaffection should be a concern. At opposite ends of the scale, we have citizens who won't vote (Echebarria Echabe 2014), and at the other end, activities such as striking or even revolt are the ultimate expression of active disaffection (Warkotsch 2015).

However, if a government is ruling legitimately and for the benefit of its citizens (and the same applies to an organisation), then any disaffection should not only cause some concern but should also be viewed positively as an opportunity for feedback, resulting in improved management and leadership decision-making as well as an opportunity to communicate with staff or citizens.

2.1.1 Models of Engagement

2.1.1.1 Personal Engagement/Needs Satisfying

This model of engagement was developed by Kahn in (1990) and has been further developed by May et al. (2004). It suggests that engagement comprises the following elements (which, however, we would describe as *inputs* to engagement): meaningfulness, psychological safety and availability.

Meaningfulness. '*The effort required to be engaged for a purpose which is worthwhile to me*'. May et al. concluded that meaningfulness has the strongest impact on engagement, which in turn is impacted by the fit between the person's aspirations, motivations and their role.

Psychological Safety. This refers to an individual being able to express feelings without fear of negative outcomes. May et al. found that in order for psychological safety to be present, supportive leadership is essential and has the greatest impact.

Availability. In other words, having the resources required to be engaged. May et al. found this factor to have the least impact on engagement.

2.1.1.2 Job Demands-Resources Model

The Job Demands-Resource model (JD-R) proposes that engagement and burnout are opposite, and engagement occurs as a result of:

- Sufficient job resources which allow achievement of goals.
- Balanced demands through mechanisms such as job control and support from colleagues.
- Personal resources which provide resilience such as optimism, self-efficacy and emotional stability.

In this model, if both the job and personal resources are exceeded by job demands, then burnout can occur. Schaufeli (2013) also highlighted the possibility of high levels of engagement, resulting in high perceptions of personal resources (Reverse Causality).

Studies have also shown the existence of a feedback loop, whereby greater engagement leads to greater job and personal resources and vice versa (Weigl et al. 2010). This study also confirms that personal resources are developed through engagement and experience.

2.1.1.3 Self-determination Theory

Deci and Ryan (2012) suggest that all human beings have a fundamental psychological need to be competent, autonomous and related to others and that satisfaction of these needs results in engagement. Failure to satisfy the psychological needs will tend to reduce engagement through lack of motivation. Proximal and distal factors also impact engagement well-being and whether goals become intrinsic or extrinsic. This model confirms the interrelationship between SWB and engagement, and their common antecedents.

2.1.1.4 Affective Shift Model

In this model, engagement is viewed as a short-term phenomenon which is influenced by how happy or unhappy one is (Bledow et al. 2011). This suggests that engagement will change during the day, depending on the mood and that negative and positive effects will have the corresponding impact on engagement. Although it is difficult to imagine an individual who is both unhappy and engaged, this type of situation can be interpreted as one which will create either burnout or workaholism.

2.1.1.5   Social Exchange Model

The social exchange model takes a transactional view, whereby employees reciprocate and give their time and engagement in return for a decent salary, but more importantly, recognition. This model might well apply at national level where, provided that the organisation or government supplies the resources then employees and citizens will be engaged. The converse is also true. Alfes et al. (2013) confirmed this when they found that engaged employees who felt supported and had a good relationship with the management had less intention to quit and demonstrated more citizenship behaviour. Income or material reward appears to have limited impact on daily behaviour, whereas recognition and leaders support and quality seem to have a positive effect.

2.1.1.6   Organisational Versus Job Engagement

Purcell (2014) drew the distinction between jobs/work engagement and organisational engagement. The latter recognises the social membership aspects which reflect the relationship between the organisation and the employee and at national level between the government and the citizen. In contrast, the job/work engagement focuses on the task. For instance, an employee could be highly engaged with the organisation, but not with a specific task, or alternatively, highly engaged with the specific task, but not with the organisation.

2.1.1.7   Commitment and Behaviour

Continuant commitment (CC) is where an employee is committed to such an extent that he feels no motivation to leave an organisation in the foreseeable future. Normative Commitment (NC) is transactional and is based on a cost–benefit analysis. Affective Commitment (AC) is an emotional commitment similar to the emotional aspects of engagement. This three-component model was devised by Meyer et al. (2012) and demonstrates the impact of commitment as a causal factor in well-being and engagement, as well as being one of its outcomes.

2.1.2 Antecedents and Causes of Engagement

There have been various attempts to categorise the causes of engagement. For example, Crawford et al. (2014) found that antecedents for engagement included job design, leadership, organisational support and HR practices. Stankiewicz and Moczulska (2012) stated that causes of engagement could be grouped as work, interpersonal and organisational factors, to which we would certainly add personal characteristics of optimism, resilience, extraversion, conscientiousness and neuroticism. See Fig. 2.1.

From the perspective of the individual, Kahn's (1990) proposition was that engagement is founded on meaningfulness, safety and availability, and we have used this model to group likely antecedents as follows:

2.1.2.1 Meaningfulness Antecedents

Job Challenge

The general term 'job challenge' includes broad scope, high workload, mastering personal growth and high responsibility enabling a potential for accomplishment. Engagement is positively associated with these factors. A meta-analysis found that job responsibility and workload have significant and positive relationships with engagement. Crawford et al. (2010) and Christian et al. (2011) found significant relationships between job complexities, problem-solving and engagement.

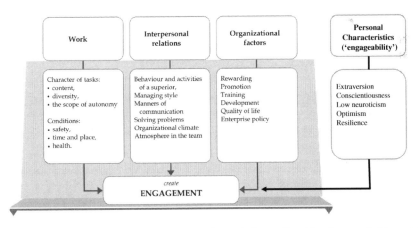

Fig. 2.1 Antecedents of engagement. Adapted from Stankiewicz and Moczulska (2012: 75) with personal characteristics added

Autonomy

Freedom, independence and discretion, plus a certain amount of responsibility when scheduling and planning work, lead to a sense of both ownership and control. This again was shown to have a positive relationship with engagement (Crawford et al. 2010; Christian et al. 2011).

Variety

Once again Crawford et al. (2010) and Christian et al. (2011) demonstrated that employees who are allowed to use many different skills and talents in their work will feel a positive impact on engagement.

Feedback

Whether through appraisal or continuous feedback, individuals who receive direct and clear information about their performance, thus enabling them to evaluate their progress, make them feel valued and acknowledged with a positive effect on engagement (Christian et al. 2011).

Fit

An individual's self-perception is all important within the work environment. An individual feels pride in his or her role when there are appropriate levels of status and influence. This leads to a positive impact on engagement (Crawford et al. 2010).

Opportunities for Development

The level of fulfilment felt by an employee with the corresponding effect on engagement is heavily influenced by their personal and professional development through training, as well as various pathways which give the opportunity for growth.

Reward and Recognition

Non-financial rewards, such as praise, recognition and so on, have a much more profound effect on engagement than simple financial reward (Bakker and Demerouti 2007). It is often argued that material rewards have a completely different motivational function to socio-psychological reward, such as recognition, and should be treated differently in research. For instance, Herzberg et al. (1959) describe pay as a 'hygiene factor' which was not a great motivator, but one of the most powerful demotivators if it was missing or at an inappropriately low level. A low income would decrease engagement, whereas a reasonable income would only increase engagement up to a 'normal' level. On the other hand, a psychological factor such as recognition would be a definite 'satisfier' which would increase engagement.

2.1.2.2 Psychological Safety Antecedents

To an individual, his or her work 'situation' is of paramount importance in that the preference is always for secure trustworthy situations with predictable behavioural consequences. Work situations feel more risky to the individual if they are unclear and threatening. This 'psychological safety' allows an individual to invest in a task or role without fear of adverse consequences for self-image, status, career progression, social networks, etc.

Social Support

Social support is the degree to which a government or an organisation is perceived not only to care about the individual, but also to value that individual. These perceptions are created and developed by many types of interaction, including concepts such as brand value. This perception of social support increases psychological safety whilst at the same time creating a feeling of obligation to the organisation. Both Saks (2006) and Crawford et al. (2010) found significant relationships between social support and degree of engagement.

Transformational Leadership

Transformational leadership is all about creating change in individuals as well as social system, organisations, etc. A transformational leader seeks to maximise the potential of each of his team members after the same time providing high levels of support and psychological safety. Aryee et al. (2012) found strong positive relationships between transformational leadership and engagement among telecommunications engineers in China. Chapter 5 of this book talks about leadership in some detail, but in general it is believed that leaders should be recruited and developed to '*offer clarity and appreciation of employees, effort and contribution, who treat their people as individuals and to ensure that workers are organised efficiently and effectively so that employees feel they are valued and equipped and supported to do their job*' MacLeod and Clarke (2009).

Leader–Member Exchange (LMX)

LMX refers to the relationships generated by the exchange of effort, resources and support between leaders and followers. Various studies suggest a positive relationship between LMX and engagement (Christian et al. 2011).

Workplace Climate

Workplace climate is all about the individual's perceptions of the organisational 'environment' in which he or she carries out their activities. Crawford et al. (2010) found positive relationships between workplace climate and engagement.

Organisational Justice, Equity

Fairness of outcome has an impact on engagement, as experienced by an individual or a group. Zhu et al. (2015) found a relationship between emotional intelligence and engagement with organisational justice as a strong mediating factor. Both Saks (2006) and Strom et al. (2014) found the perceptions about distributions and fair processes linked positively to engagement plus a relationship between organisational justice and engagement.

Job Security

It is generally accepted that the absence of job security will impact negatively on engagement. However, this does not necessarily mean that the presence of job security will cause a positive effect on engagement. One could hypothesise that complacency might be the result.

An individual's perception that they will be able to stay in their jobs for the foreseeable future would obviously be a factor in psychological safety. Various studies have established negative correlations between job security and engagement.

Barrick et al. (2015) defined a positive relationship between job security and engagement, but only when job security was measured as part of a range of 'best practice' human resource management procedures, which together reinforced employees' perceptions of the organisation cared about them.

2.1.2.3 Psychological Availability Antecedents

Psychological availability is the individual's sense of being ready to engage, capable and prepared to invest in the physical, cognitive and emotional resources.

Role Overload

Very often, individuals are set targets designed to 'stretch' them. The challenge can certainly increase productivity and even have a positive effect on engagement. However, there does come a certain point when a feeling of role overload can occur, triggering negative factors such as anxiety and anger. This will result in the individual becoming demotivated unless engaged. Many studies confirm a negative correlation between work overload and engagement. See meta-analysis by Crawford et al. (2010).

Work-Role Conflict

Crawford et al. (2010) found that where expectations of behaviour are inconsistent between superiors colleagues or clients, engagement will suffer because it is not possible to meet conflicting demands.

Family–Work Conflict

This is a very common issue and is quite simply the conflict in priorities and time between work and family. Several studies found a negative relationship between family–work conflict and engagement (e.g. Simbula 2010). However, other studies (e.g. Halbesleben et al. 2010) found a positive relationship between engagement and family, where high engagement causes family tensions rather than family tensions causing low engagement.

Resourcing Inadequacies

Crawford et al. (2010) found negative relationships between resource inadequacies and engagement.

Time Urgency

Time urgency and role overload are related factors, although a certain amount of time pressure may well enhance engagement and be very motivating. But this has to be within limits; otherwise, it begins to have a negative effect on engagement. The concept of 'too much' is a function of the individual and his perception, but obviously, the effect will be less for an individual who is effective at time management and self-organisation or who is generally optimistic.

Off-work Recovery

Off-work recovery refers to an employee's ability to 'switch off' by not working. In 2015, Sonnentag and Fritz found that the ability to disengage was related to engagement. They also found that high cognitive demands as well as emotional demands led to problems in being able to 'switch off'. This supports the suggestion that there can be such a phenomenon as 'too much engagement', leading to burnout or workaholism (Schaufeli et al. 2008).

Dispositions

Dispositions are tendencies to experience preferential affective states, for instance, dispositional optimism. Attitudes are formed by a combination of disposition and life experiences (Eschleman et al. 2015). Until the 1950s, attitudes towards jobs and decisions to leave were thought to be largely situational, but in 1952, Weitz proposed a dispositional component.

General optimism represents positive expectations of the future (regardless of the means by which they are met). In 2004, Carver and Scheier found that optimistic people exert more effort than pessimistic people and have better social relationships and higher levels of well-being.

There is a whole array of dispositions which include conscientiousness and positive activity. Conscientious individuals are hard-working, focused on positive affect which creates enthusiasm and alertness. These types of disposition would typically enhance engagement.

Personal resources are perceived aspects of self, relating to resilience and ability to control and impact the environment, including self-efficacy, self-esteem and optimism. In 2009, Xanthopoulou et al. found positive relationships between the three factors and engagement.

The Relational Context

One of the important factors to be taken into consideration when considering engagement is that of relationships. Whether these are knowledge sharing, belonging to a team in order to achieve tasks that could not be achieved by an individual or even creating a supportive and encouraging social atmosphere, these are all positive factors which encourage positive engagement (Kahn and Heapy 2014). This focus also introduces the notion that a group could demonstrate high or low engagement with its associated implications.

Social Meaningfulness

Meaningfulness derives in part from feeling part of an enterprise. This can be amplified by transformational leaders (see Chap. 5) who create engagement through social interaction with both the individual and the team. Then, this is further enhanced by contact with the recipients or beneficiaries of the work.

In 2001, Wrzesniewski and Dutton suggested that individuals can further enhance the work by increasing what is known as the relational context. For instance, hospital cleaners form relationships with patients that enrich their jobs and give them more meaning than would be gained from the job itself. In general terms, therefore, individuals can experience meaningfulness through confirmation of social identity and belonging, and the perception of social support.

Freedom to Express

Individuals should be allowed to freely express themselves without fear of sanction or any negative reaction from their leaders. Therefore, a supportive team environment increases their sense of psychological safety.

Energising Social Environment

Energising interactions are things such as competition, joking and supportive decision-making, which combine both the needs of the individual and that of the team. This enhances psychological safety. Highly pressurised teams such as firefighters or soldiers very often develop a culture of banter and joking so as to create and energise their social environment in order to counter the high pressure of their work.

Emotional Relief

Being able to share thoughts and emotions with one's peers in a supportive environment can have a very strong effect on both the individual and team.

2.1.3 Positive Psychology and Engagement

An individual's personal characteristics and propensities, as well as emotions, play a large part in mitigating or amplifying impacts of all other causal factors for engagement with some characteristics making some individuals more 'engageable' than others and vice versa.

When considering our PACE model, this becomes of paramount importance because this suggests that personal characteristics are a fundamental 'filter' through which all causal stimuli will flow. As this book is about intervention by government and organisational leaders, we feel that it is important to highlight how these propensities can be modified rather than merely noted and observed.

We agree that engagement is a psychological state, and it is recent research into 'positive psychology' which has helped to clarify our thinking rather than the traditional approach to psychology, which has tended to focus on the treatment or mitigation of disorders.

Organisational and business psychology has for many years concentrated mainly on solving what can only be termed as negatively oriented problems: for instance, poor performance, absenteeism, stress and burnout, with many still viewing well-being as no more than the absence of stress, rather than a positive state in its own right. We therefore are treating positive psychological concepts as being on their own scale or continuum rather than at the opposite end of the scale of negative psychological concepts.

The separation of positive improvement from disorder is of paramount importance and is demonstrated by Flink et al. (2015), where, for example, pain is treated by focusing on mood improvement rather than focusing on the pain itself.

In simple terms, therefore, we approach positive constructs such as engagement as entities to be studied in their own right, rather than treating them as outcomes as a result of removing negativity.

This especially applies to engagement which is a unique positive concept and cannot be manipulated by simply intervening to reduce burnout, stress or discontent. In recent years, engagement has become increasingly important as the psychological contact between employers and employees has become less transactional. Technology may suggest that individuals will be available to work 24/7, but of course this is going to require very different levels of engagement, willingness to deploy discretionary effort and changing our understanding of work–life balance (Rothbard and Patil 2012).

Born and Drori (2015) imply that modern work practices are going to require high levels of individual engagement rather than merely 'being there' or 'attending'.

With many individuals now, for instance, working from home and certainly not 'being there', what we have understood for many years that the traditional workplace is gradually being eroded and the signs are that, in the not too distant future, it will disappear (Chin 2014). That requires a complete rethink, with engagement becoming a crucial factor in this new environment.

Positive psychology is reflected in much management literature, for example:

- Job design: Job dimensions such as significance and autonomy could result in positive outcomes such as meaningfulness (Hackman and Oldham 1976).
- Job satisfaction: Job satisfaction is determined by 'motivators' (for example, recognition), whereas dissatisfaction is caused by hygiene factors, such as working conditions (Herzberg et al. 1959).
- Positive reinforcement: Reward, such as positive feedback, results in positive behaviour (Watson and Skinner 2001).
- Motivation: Maslow's (1955) hierarchic model shows self-actualisation as the pinnacle of human motivation and 'deficiency motivation' being clearly distinguished from 'growth motivation'.
- Positive affect: The high energy, full concentration and pleasurable engagement of positive aspect are not simply the opposite of the sadness and lethargy of negative aspect (Watson et al. 1988).

It is also worth highlighting that well-being is considered a passive state, whereas engagement is an active state.

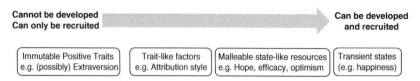

Fig. 2.2   Malleability continuum of positive traits and states

It is crucial for organisations to aim to intervene through positive psychology and understand the stability and malleability in the relevant traits, as in the malleability continuum of positive traits and states shown below. Traits that are immutable or impossible to change can only be recruited for (i.e. by getting new people), whereas traits that are malleable can be developed and trained (Fig. 2.2).

The outcomes of positive emotions enable the vigour, dedication and absorption required for engagement, whereas the outcomes of negative emotions, such as exhaustion, indifference or cynicism, are not amenable for engagement. But their removal will not automatically create engagement. Fredrickson (2013) found that positivity thresholds need to be exceeded before the individual flourishes in a work setting with an approximate ratio of at least three positive encounters for every negative.

'Being in the zone' is now a well-known modern phrase which was identified formally by Csikszentmihalyi (2014). He described it as a state of 'flow', in which the individual enters a state of low self-consciousness and energises their focus on high concentration and enjoyment on an intrinsically motivating task. It is characterised by complete absorption in the task. This concept is similar to engagement, although the 'flow' generally relates to a specific activity, which is more temporary or transient rather than the more general 'engagement' with the complete role or organisation.

The JD-R model requires a balance between the task at hand and the personal resources available. Youssef-Morgan and Bockorny (2013) note that neither flow nor engagement can take place where the job is too easy and that repeated short-term experiences of 'flow' could promote longer-term engagement.

Within the positive psychology model, Peterson and Seligman (2004) describe six core virtues: Wisdom and Knowledge, Courage and authenticity, Humanity, Justice, Temperance and Transcedence, with 24 related strengths.

2.1.3.1   Organisational Virtuousness

Organisational virtuousness is considered to have beneficial impacts for both the individual and the organisation (Youssef-Morgan and Bockorny 2013). On occasions when there are potential moral conflicts between the individual and organisational goals, the level of organisational virtuousness will reduce any conflicts. Virtuousness is also considered to be a great driver of energy and dedication when the individual considers the moral value of the work that he or she is engaged in rather than pure financial gain.

2.1.3.2   Positive Deviance

This refers to the behaviour of individuals with high self-determination and autonomy but with a desire to help others (Lavine 2012). Positive deviance is viewed as an uncommon but socially desirable behaviour that differs from norms and expectations. There are certain industries (for instance, investment banking), which prefer to hire this type of individual, the so-called corporate entrepreneur. This type of individual is very highly engaged and helpful to his or her peers and very often creates changes in corporate thinking as well as corporate culture.

2.1.3.3   Appreciative Enquiry

Cooperrider et al. (2013) propose appreciative enquiry as an organisational change methodology, which adopts a positive, strength-based approach. The methodology consists of a collaborative process where the company looks at its strengths, where it would like to be and then plans to accomplish the change followed by implementing the plan under the headings: Discovery, Dream, Design and Destiny. Its effect on engagement is through involvement and trust between the individuals participating in the process, plus the intrinsically motivational nature of being involved in creating change.

2.1.3.4   Positive Psychological Resources That Could Be Linked to Engagement

Hope

Hope can be defined as a determination to reach a goal with an optimistic perception of the pathway to achieve it. Sweetman and Luthans (2010) suggested that hope may be a necessary condition for engagement. Ouweneel et al. (2012) found that positive emotions from a previous day created greater engagement through feelings of positivity.

Self-efficacy

This is defined as an individual's self-perception of their ability to execute a particular task. Ma et al. (2014) found a clear relationship between self-efficacy, engagement and organisational commitment. Kok et al. (2014) found that efficacy is developed over time through task mastery, learning, social persuasion and encouragement as well as physiological and psychological arousal plus attribution style.

Resilience

Resilience is an individual's ability to deal with stress, pressure or some kind of 'threat'. It is the ability to rebound from adversity, conflict or any other negative event. Resilient individuals will remain engaged, even in the most difficult situations and that trait also appears to be linked to attribution style.

Optimism

There is a body of research which suggests that slightly unrealistic optimism, up to a certain level, is more functional in terms of engagement than realistic pessimism or depressive realism. Optimism is a positive outlook and a positive exclamatory style as suggested by attribution style theory.

Bortolotti and Antrobus (2015) questioned the simplistic view that depressive realism versus unrealistic optimism represents a choice between truth and well-being, where unrealistic optimism is better for well-being. People with depression have more realistic judgements about their own abilities, illnesses, etc., but realistic judgements of capability may be a bar when attempting new challenges or facing challenges that have previously failed. On the other hand, unrealistic optimism can be functional in attempting challenging tasks, exuding confidence and minimising the impact of negative events. However, in some contexts, unrealistic optimism is counter-productive. For instance, an unrealistically optimistic attitude about one's health can be dangerous. Although of course the counter argument is that an unrealistically positive or optimistic attitude can contribute to better health outcomes, risk-taking is also another area where optimists can deliver worse results than expected. Therefore, optimism is a positive trait as long as it does not prevent learning or caution.

Unrealistic optimism has a positive effect on well-being and engagement, but excessive optimism can lead to risky behaviour, poor planning and disillusionment.

Psychological Capital (PsyCap)

PsyCap is viewed as a higher-order construct combining elements of self-efficacy, hope, optimism and resilience (Luthans et al. 2007). It enables 'positive appraisal of circumstances and probability of success, based on motivated, effort and perseverance'. Studies have confirmed a significant positive relationship between PsyCap and job satisfaction, organisational commitment, organisations, citizenship, behaviours and job performance, as well as negative relationship with turnover intent, cynicism, job stress and deviance (Dawkins et al. 2013).

Newman et al. (2014) found potential positive relationships between PsyCap and engagement. PsyCap can be developed by:

- Promoting positive emotions in the workplace.
- Increasing flow experiences by aligning roles and employees and ensuring they have adequate resources.
- Maximising hope through appropriate goals, involving employees in setting goals and helping people succeed.
- Maximising efficacy by providing resources and the opportunity to experience mastery, precarious learning and positive feedback.
- Resilience can be developed by eliminating unnecessary risks, providing resources to help success in teaching employees how to deal with risks and setbacks.
- Optimism can be maximised by teaching cognitive strategies for evaluating negative and positive events (e.g. attribution style) and encouraging leniency for the past, appreciation of the present and opportunity-seeking for the future.
- Also, the organisation can itself communicate and be seen as more positive.

Compassion and Passion

Compassion and passion have both been suggested as antecedents for engagement (Shuck and Rocco 2014).

2.1.4 Measuring Engagement

2.1.4.1 Measuring Engagement

Engagement is a dynamic, changeable stage, and therefore, in the context of the individual, it would need to be somehow measured continuously in 'real time'. Because of the abyss of difficulties of this type of approach, the focus of practitioners tends to be at organisational rather than individual level, probably due to their most likely role as HR or organisational leaders where any impact that they have on engagement or well-being can only be achieved at high level by organisational interventions.

For both engagement and well-being, most measures either consider causal factors or assumed components. The Utrecht Work Engagement Scale (UWES) (Schaufeli et al. 2006) assesses the three constituents of 'vigour', 'dedication' and 'absorption, whereas the Gallup Q^{12} (Wagner and Harter 2006) assesses assumed causal factors such as recognition and having a friend at work. This can lead to a tautology where these factors comprise the measure of engagement and, by comparing them with this measure, are then confirmed as the key factors!

Company-based engagement surveys are often simply opinion surveys described as engagement surveys in the same way that some well-being measures at the country level are actually straightforward surveys of government performance in different areas.

Surveys, such as Q^{12} are indirect measures of engagement where the aggregated construct of engagement appears highly similar to basic job satisfaction. Schaufeli (2013) makes a very important point in that these measures of engagement actually measure antecedents and therefore due to the complexity of process, might not always reflect engagement itself.

Youssef-Morgan and Bockorny (2013) proposed that 'positive managers, employees and organisations are necessary for engagement'. However, the recommendation that employers should therefore 'select for positivity' risks making a whole section of the population unemployable and assumes that positivity is more or less a fixed trait which cannot be modified. As previously discussed, it is possible for individuals to be to unrealistically optimistic, and Youssef-Morgan and Bockorny go on to suggest the usefulness of certain roles which, they suggest, do require a certain degree of negativity.

2.1.4.2   Burnout-Antithesis Measures

Originally, engagement was constructed as the opposite of burnout. Therefore, the measure was simply a reverse burnout scale. Since then, it has been identified that engagement is a distinct construct, leading to scales, such as the UWES and the Shirom-Melamed Vigour Measure (SMVM). The UWES attempts to assess individual vigour, dedication and absorption, whereas the SMVM assesses vigour, comprising physical energy, emotional energy and 'cognitive liveliness'.

The SMVM majors on asking questions based on frequency. For instance, questions are designed to ask 'how often', rather than all other approaches which tend to ask 'how much?'. This differing approach was highlighted by Fletcher and Robinson (2013).

2.1.4.3   Measures Derived from the 'Needs-Satisfying' Approach

Kahn (1990) considered three dimensions of engagement: meaningfulness, psychological safety and psychological availability. Scales based on this conceptualisation include several well-known measures.

The psychological engagement measure (May et al. 2004) asks to what degree respondents agree with various terms in the context of emotional engagement, cognitive engagement and physical engagement. Clearly, this instrument focuses on the job rather than engagement in relation to any wider concepts such as the organisation and a measure of agreement of various descriptions described to the subject. Studies using this scale have found that meaningfulness exhibits the strongest relationship with engagement, with psychological safety having the lowest relationship.

2.1.4.4   Satisfaction-Engagement Measures

Probably the most widely used survey by organisations globally is the Gallup Q^{12} (Harter et al. 2009). Measures reflecting the satisfaction-engagement approach tend to address the individual's emotional engagement with the organisation. A major issue with this method as a measure of engagement is that the questions asked are actually about factors which are assumed to cause engagement, rather than assessing engagement itself. For example, 'Do I know what is expected of me at work?' and 'Does my superior or someone at work seem to care about me as a person?' Although several studies confirm causality between the 12 items asked and organisational outcomes such as customer loyalty/engagement productivity, profitability, turnover, safety incidents, shrinkage, absenteeism, patient safety incidents and quality (Harter et al. 2009), these are actually demonstrating relationships between, for example, 'knowing what is expected of me' and customer loyalty, with no clear or necessary role for engagement itself.

Another measure, designed by the Institute of Employment Studies (Robinson et al. 2004), tests pride in the organisation, altruistic willingness and alignment. This instrument is based on the definition of engagement as:

'A positive attitude held by the employee towards the organisation and its values. An engaged employee is aware of business context and works with colleagues to improve performance within the job for the benefit of the organisation. The organisation must work to develop and nurture engagement, which requires a two-way relationship between employer and employee' (Robinson et al. 2004).

2.1.4.5   Multidimensional Measures

In 2006, Saks distinguished between engagement in relation to the job and engagement in relation to the organisation and developed a specific scale for each, suggesting that job and organisational engagement are different but related constructs.

Several engagement instruments, particularly those applied by organisations to improve engagement, suffer from ambiguous content in that they include potential antecedents for engagement, such as 'my job challenges me', and possible outcomes of engagement, such as 'I help my colleagues when they have a problem' and confounding variables such as 'I often work more than my contracted hours' (Fletcher and Robinson 2013).

This type of 'mixture' of questions makes retest reliability difficult to establish because whereas some factors will remain reasonably constant such as 'I try to help others', other questions such as 'I feel positive about my work' may vary considerably over time.

In 2013, Fletcher and Robinson suggested that many engagement instruments which contain mostly positively worded questions can encourage what is known as 'acquiescence bias'.

Many of these reports focus on positive responses and may give a result, such as '80% of our employees are engaged', but it is the remaining 20% which should be important to management because the goal is to improve engagement and not merely to confirm the ratio of employees which is engaged.

2.1.5 Outcomes of Engagement

Schaufeli suggests that engagement should be considered as a psychological state in conjunction with its behavioural expression. This suggests that a key area of research and practice should be on the causal link between the state of engagement and the required productive or high-performance behaviour.

Stairs and Galpin (2010) found that high levels of engagement lead to:

- Low absenteeism.
- Higher employee retention.
- Increased employee effort.
- Increased productivity.
- Improved quality and reduced error rates.
- Increase sales.
- Higher profitability, earnings per share and shareholder returns.
- Enhanced customer satisfaction and loyalty.
- Faster business growth and higher likelihood of business success.

In general, creating organisational engagement scores by averaging large numbers of individual scores may be convenient, but not reflect useful reality. Similarly, snapshot organisational/national surveys sometimes taken once can only reflect transient current levels of engagement rather than being representative of a longer time period or a general level of engagement.

At the team level, engagement has been shown to correlate positively with task and team performance, collective positive effect (which in turn improves SWB) and efficacy beliefs (Costa et al. 2014).

Rothman (2014) summarises the various outputs of employee engagement as productivity, job satisfaction, motivation, commitment, low turnover intentions, customer satisfaction, return on assets, profits and shareholder value, personal initiative and learning, discretionary effort and concerns of quality.

2.1.6 Improving Engagement: Organisational Approaches

2.1.6.1 Human Resource Management (HRM) and Engagement

Sparrow and Balain (2010) identified three distinct notions of how engagement impacts performance, which human resources practitioners tend to adopt when considering interventions to improve engagement:

- Process improvement: Employees who are in a 'reciprocal exchange relationship' with the organisation will payback organisation investments by working for the benefit of the organisation, its customers and other stakeholders, and if they are committed and satisfied with their desire to stay, they will exert discretionary effort.
- Predictive of performance models: These assume that positive attitude energises positive feelings which strengthen identification with the organisation, heightening motivation and leading to greater commitment and effort.
- Strategic narrative: This focuses on communications and messaging to align the organisation and the employee's motivations creating a sense of greater alignment. Performance is enhanced by the individuals identifying with organisational goals.

Sparrow (2014) suggests that engagement is predicted to affect performance in three ways:

- Proximal: task performance, commitment, satisfaction, intention to quit.
- Intermediate: customer service, innovation, lean management.
- Distal: quality or financial performance.

  Links to intermediate outcomes are under-researched. Issues include:

- Engagement may be caused by performance, for example, in a high-performing workgroup, so causality is likely to be bidirectional (Winkler et al. 2012).
- Engagement may not have a smooth linear relationship with performance.
- Engagement impacts performance, but may be mitigated by, for example, skill, knowledge or the right equipment.
- Sometimes engagement may only work at team level, but if one member is not engaged, it could adversely impact the team's performance.
- Survey responses, in particular, those which purport to measure engagement for individual outcomes such as satisfaction, will actually be influenced by all sorts of personal and situational factors.

MacLeod and Clarke (2009) in their report, 'Engage for Success', propose that the most effective strategies for engagement include:

- Visible and empowering leadership developing and disseminating a strong strategic narrative which answers the question 'engage with what...?' (Sparrow 2014).

- Engaging managers who focus, support and empower the people in support of the clear narrative.
- Facilitating 'employee voice' for challenging and reinforcing the narrative.
- Organisational integrity based on the narrative and the associated values.

Research into change management is moving from a focus on overcoming employees resistance to change, to how to elicit positive interpretations and engagement with change (Scott-Jackson 2002).

2.1.6.2 Human Resource Development (HRD) and Engagement

Shuck and Wollard (2010) defined engagement as the cognitive, emotional and behavioural energy an employee directs towards positive organisational outcomes. If we replace 'employee' with 'member', then a different definition could apply to any group, including a country. HRD has been proposed as an engagement-enhancing strategy in specific instances of, for example, reducing incivility (Reio and Sanders-Reio 2011), training to address adversity, conflict management and transformational leadership (Shuck and Heard 2012).

HRD interventions that could be used to increase engagement include organisation development (OD), which encompasses strategic change and wide-scale process improvement.

A key factor in maximising engagement is the behaviour of the leader, so a key HR intervention in relation to engagement must be leadership development.

2.2 Well-Being and Happiness

There have been many definitions of well-being and happiness, and the different nuances within those definitions have largely depended on the disciplinary background of the researcher, as well as the assumptions he or she may have made.

To the layman, well-being is an easily understood term about an individual feeling good about their life and their various environments: physical, psychological, political, environmental, etc. The myriad of factors which can affect well-being are what makes it so difficult to pin down a single generally accepted definition. Research therefore tends to be not into well-being per se, but into the factors which may affect it, both positively and negatively.

A great stumbling block to creating an overall definition of 'well-being' is the fact that the various definitions of the phrase are differently defined by various disciplines. For instance, a Treasury minister will define well-being very differently to the psychologist who in turn will define it very differently to the manager of a small factory who in turn will find himself defining it differently at home when he is considering his immediate family rather than his employees.

In our context, 'well-being' is a sustained, positive, perceived state of satisfaction with life rather than short-term happiness, or the absence of 'ill-being'.

On the other hand, 'engagement' is all about 'doing' or 'wishing to contribute, take part or participate'.

As far as well-being is concerned, there is yet another subtle distinction to be made and that is the difference between objective well-being and subjective well-being. Objective well-being actually (and confusingly) refers to the causes of well-being specifically those that are factual and non-perceptual and can be measured directly. An objective well-being cause could be level of housing, for example. Subjective well-being again refers to the cause, which in this case is an individual's response to situations based on their subjective perception of that situation. Of course, not all individuals respond in the same way to any particular external stimulus (Varelius 2004).

It can be argued that well-being/happiness, without engagement, is a worthwhile outcome in itself although Bryson et al. (2014) found associations between well-being and workplace performance and quality, but no association between short-term positive and negative work-related happiness (an emotion sometimes referred to formally as 'positive affect') on performance. Of course, it is quite easy to envisage that a perfectly contented person might not be the most engaged with their role or work.

In other words, well-being need not necessarily affect either engagement or performance.

As noted above, well-being is most often defined in terms of its supposed causes (objective or subjective), which doesn't particularly help us to understand well-being. Similarly, Allin and Hand (2014) point out that the specification of how well-being is measured is also used as a definition of what is meant by well-being; in other words, the definition of well-being and its measurement procedure are often described as one and the same.

Michaelson et al. (2012) suggest that well-being is an aggregate of purpose, autonomy, control, satisfaction with life and happiness. Veenhoven (2014) also describes four 'qualities of life' which taken together produce one overall definition of well-being.

Life chances comprise livability of the environment, which is quite straightforward and is a factor outside the subject's control, and life-ability of the individual, which is very much to do with the subject's adaptive potential to deal with external factors such as challenges and opportunities. This factor tends to be a focus for therapists, psychologists and educators.

The results or outcomes of well-being are described as the usefulness of life —another external quality equivalent to meaningfulness in other definitions of well-being—and satisfaction with life, which is a primary measure included in most well-being studies. Veenhoven (2014) suggests that:

- Pleasures are temporary, which means that they are very much short-term sources of positive impact.
- Part satisfaction refers to a specific part of one's life, for example, working life or personal life.
- Peak experience is all about intense happiness about every aspect of life, similar to Maslow's (1955) 'self-actualisation' or Seligman's (2012) 'flourishing'.
- Life satisfaction which Veenhoven saw as 'an overall appreciation of one's life as a whole'.

Taylor (2015), on the other hand, defined well-being within the following much broader perspectives:

- Hedonistic or mental state.
- Desire satisfaction, with well-being being measured in terms of the degree of satisfaction of perceived or actual preferences.
- Objective well-being. This assumes well-being roughly in line with Herzberg's (1959) 'hygiene factors'.
- Capabilities, which are the individual's own abilities and coping mechanisms enabling the subject to lead a satisfactory life. We will return to the individual's capabilities or propensities later in the book as a primary factor in ACE.

Taylor goes on to suggest that because of the plethora of definitions, policymakers have to choose a particular definition, against which to measure or use something, such as the capability-based UN human development index, or even adopt a mix. He also suggests that there are areas which appear to moderate societies' well-being and he set out an array of markers which are common across a range of theories, making them useful for policymakers.

Assume X is a marker of well-being, so according to mainstream series of well-being, it is either:

- A generally accepted part of well-being or
- Something that could be regarded as reliably productive of well-being at the individual level or
- Something that can be regarded as a reliable indicator of well-being at the individual level.

Taylor's markers include factors such as happiness, health, life satisfaction, success, relationships, leisure, adequate income and job satisfaction.

Income and employment may well be regarded as hygiene factors (Hertzberg 1959), which in themselves are not often regarded as motivators, but the lack of them certainly can represent a demotivational force.

Taylor's markers certainly provide a useful set of potential inputs for a process model of well-being.

2.2.1 Objective Well-Being

Objective well-being describes the factors that are assumed to cause well-being rather than well-being itself. In addition, they have nothing at all to do with an individual's perception or his feelings.

Objective factors can be directly measured, and it is often assumed that such external factors can then be possibly adjusted in order to improve well-being.

For instance, the Happy Planet Index (Abdallah 2012) includes 'ecological footprint' as a key component of the well-being formula. As this is assumed to be a causal factor, the argument follows that an adjustment of one's ecological footprint will directly affect well-being. However, there are some flaws in this supposition.

- Many statistical studies demonstrate an association between (an enormous number of) objective factors and various definitions of well-being. However, there have been few studies demonstrating the causal link between the various factors and well-being. That is primarily because it is very difficult to carry out studies to prove causal links.
- Factors which cause well-being vary widely and are assumed according to the model of well-being. That can give rise to cause and effect problems because, for instance, it can be assumed that exercise causes well-being. But then again well-being may cause a positive attitude to health, which can then lead to taking exercise.

- The contribution of individual factors to a feeling of well-being is even more difficult to prove or demonstrate as the causal linkages themselves remain unproven. For instance, which contributes more to well-being? A long life or a good education? You can see that in order for an accurate model of well-being to be created, it would be very useful to arrive at various weightings between causal factors but also bearing in mind that they will vary according to the individual.
- One individual may be motivated by money, the other may be motivated by having a strong family life, whereas yet another may find that the most important factor in his or her life is having a large and close group of friends. These motivations will also, of course, change over time, even daily!

2.2.2 Subjective Well-Being

It is generally accepted that the impact of objective factors such as wealth do not have a measurable or predictable impact on well-being or happiness either across societies or individuals once a certain level has been achieved. That must mean that there are other 'internal' factors which have an impact on well-being. In 1984, Diener introduced the concept of subjective well-being (SWB). This represents an individual's *perception* of their own well-being. Diener postulated that this subjective well-being is a tripartite structure comprising of:

- Life satisfaction.
- Frequent positive experiences.
- Infrequent negative experiences.

This, once again, defines well-being in terms of its causes rather than defining well-being itself. Life satisfaction is a perceptual evaluation of one's overall life and may include comparative evaluations with others' experiences.

Subjective well-being can be related to factors such as socio-economic advantages, higher income, better education, as well as positive psychological, interpersonal and physical functioning, but these causes are all filtered through the individual's perception. SWB has been measured at national and pan-national levels, usually through surveys suggesting links to high standards of living, better health (mental and physical) and greater peace.

Once again, we look at the causal effect argument because, for instance, peace could cause SWB or SWB could cause peace or some other unknown variable could cause both. There have been other studies which have demonstrated that SWB can be altered in the short to medium term by changes in circumstances Luhmann (2012).

It could also be argued that SWB can be a function of an individual's disposition (either genetic or conditioned) and can therefore be regarded as stable and trait-like. That would mean that if an individual or a group were subject to negative input, those with a predisposition to optimism or feeling of well-being would eventually return to that state because they were genetically programmed to be naturally positive, whereas others may be either permanently affected for varying lengths of time (Lucas and Donnellan 2012).

In 2014, Busseri argued against this three-factor model of SWB. He suggested that it was not clear how the three components related to each other or even if they are causally related. He introduced the following alternative models:

- Model 1: tripartite: Life satisfaction, positive and negative effects of the components of the tripartite model of SWB. Any of the components could separately impact SWB.
- Model 2: hierarchic: In this model, the three factors come together to form the overall higher-order factor of SWB. That means that both their commonalities and variations are all important in the definition. For instance, the factors maintain their relative relationships with population: across gender, age and ethnicity (Linley et al. 2009).
- Model 3: causal system: This model closely mirrors the main theme of this book. We assume that well-being and engagement are related to factors within a complex set of sub-factors and that so far practice in the field of well-being has suffered by confusing components and causes. It is often assumed that positive and negative factors influence life satisfaction, but not vice versa. In the causal model, SWB seems to be referring to life satisfaction alone with positive and negative affect being causal factors. Schimmack (2008) found differences between East and West Germany based on unemployment and regional differences, whereas Busseri (2014) found that SWB was a function of age, higher income, being in a relationship, investment of thought and effort into work and finances, which all contributed to greater life satisfaction. He also found that life satisfaction remained stable, even when positive and negative effect varied.
- Model 4: composite: This model assumes that a calculation of the levels of the three factors leads to an overall figure for SWB. This is often confused with the higher-order approach within model 2. This approach exposes the

crucial but often ignored question of weightings, although in much of the research a large number of variables are mostoften given equal weights.

Busseri's causal model number 3 above aligns more or less with the principles adopted in this book. That is to say, it assumes that life satisfaction, positive and negative affect are all separate parts of a causal model.

Subjective well-being is a function of the individual and is what is perceived and assessed by that individual. Therefore, it is impossible for any external observer to measure an individual's subjectivity. All that the observer can do is ask an individual to assess his or her own perceptions and most surveys will include questions such as '*All things considered, how satisfied are you with your life as a whole these days?*' (from the World Values Survey: http://www.worldvaluessurvey.all/WBS.asp).

Inevitably, that brings us to another question, and that is how does an individual objectively assess what can best be described as 'a feeling'.

Evaluative: An evaluative approach can include objective factors that impact on an individual's life. For instance, an individual may consider his or her well-being or how satisfied they are with wealth or health. They can also evaluate their life relative to others. Emotional factors can be evaluated as well as an inclination towards negativity or positivity as a result of genetic make-up or life-experiences.

Hedonic criteria: These are the sort of positive criteria which are transient in nature and have a very short-term effect on well-being. This phenomenon by its very nature can vary widely over very short periods and yet impact quite substantially on an individual's state of mind. As the effect of this type of factor can be quite profound, we may need to isolate any sustained causes of negative or positive affect, which are independent of objective factors. This has been the subject of much research in the field of positive psychology.

Eudemonic criteria: These relate to Maslow's 1943 model and the self-actualisation peak of the motivational hierarchy. That is to say that sustained well-being is increased, not just short-term happiness, but also more eudemonic factors such as positive relations with others, autonomy, purpose in life as well as personal growth (Ryff 1989: 1071); this involves change, development, 'stretch', etc.

Hicks (2013) makes the point that whilst effective factors are transient, eudemonic criteria may be more sustained. Nevertheless, these are often seen as less amenable to measurement or improvement.

Comparative evaluation (an individual's separate self-assessment and perception of SWB) is often a function of the individual pairing himself or herself with other people or groups which they consider as benchmarks.

Therefore, factors such as a perceived inequality of income will have a greater impact on subjective well-being than income per se.

The PACE framework positions the components of objective and subjective well-being more correctly as potential causal factors. The model shows that objective and subjective causal factors when combined with close group situations and individual socio-psychological factors can combine to result in well-being and engagement.

Interventions by leaders, whether national or organisational, tend to focus on the objective macrocauses of well-being and engagement. Although one could argue that this is the correct approach because it is easier for an organisation of any size to be able to focus on objective factors, we maintain that organisational and national leaders should indeed consider and intervene to modify socio-psychological factors which may well have more impact on well-being and happiness.

Both researchers and practitioners have become increasingly concerned when trying to identify the major factors associated with well-being and trying to identify causal directions. For instance, a manager's seniority might produce workplace well-being for that individual, but once again we have a chicken and egg situation. The question as to whether being promoted causes the well-being or whether high levels of well-being in the individual increases chances of promotion.

This search for a cause is doubtless a difficult one and suggests that well-being is best seen as a component of the process with causes and outcomes, many of which have a duality in the sense that many factors can be both causes and outcomes.

2.2.3 Well-Being as the Absence of Disorder

Originally, well-being was regarded as essentially the absence of mild or severe mental disorder or stress. Cooper (2014) introduced a major series entitled 'Well-being: the Complete Reference Guide' which stated *'we know that one in 4–6 people in most countries in the world suffer from a common mental disorder… The cost of low productivity due to lack of mental well-being represents a significant proportion of gross domestic product'.*

Such a theory might suggest that at organisational level, the focus might be on reducing occupational stress, whereas at country level the focus might be on avoiding or curing mental disorders such as depression.

In this model, nearly every element of life is a potential contributor to or causes the depletion of mental capital. Therefore, one of the components of well-being is mental resilience. The UK government's major 2-year review on well-being states:

'The relentless demands for increased competitiveness will combine with changing family commitments, such as the two-earner family and the increasing need to care for older adults. These demands will have major implications for work–life balance and the well-being of workers and have knock-on effects for their families and communities' Foresight Mental Capital and Well-being Project (2008: 12).

This perspective can obviously affect policymakers by encouraging a misunderstanding of the relationship between well-being and ill-being. In the same way that the absence of disease does not necessarily suggest health, a lack of ill-being does not necessarily suggest well-being (Huppert 2014).

This particular viewpoint results in causal antecedents, covering every life circumstance that could possibly cause stress or damage well-being, including learning difficulties, maternal diet, maternal mental ill-health, alcoholism, poverty, stress or work and negative stereotypes of older people. As a result, recommendations include parental coaching, targeting of vulnerable groups and use of drugs for cognitive enhancement (Foresight Mental Capital and Well-being Project 2008).

These interventions attempt to achieve no more than a 'small change in the average level of well-being across the population that would produce a large decrease in the percentage with mental disorder, and also in the percentage who have subclinical disorder' (Foresight Mental Capital and Well-being Project 2008).

Theoretically, outcomes would include, for businesses, more productive employees and greater competitiveness.

However, this perspective produces interventions which have the primary outcome of the reduction in symptoms of depression, anxiety and conduct disorders, whereas the intended effect is an improvement in pro-social behaviour, interpersonal relations or subjective well-being (Huppert 2014).

2.2.4 Positive Psychology Perspective

It has been recognised for some time that wellness is not simply an absence of illness and this has led to research to define the distinct components of psychological or subjective well-being and happiness. Huppert and So (2013), for example, derived a comparative list of components of SWB as defined by some major studies.

Seligman (2012), for example, defines psychological well-being—he calls it 'flourishing'—as consisting of positive emotion, engagement, relationships, meaning and accomplishment. Note that 'engagement', the other main focus of this book, is seen as a component of SWB. The four main conceptualisations of 'flourishing' are shown in Table 2.2.

This positive view of well-being is sometimes labelled 'flourishing' and is often contrasted with 'languishing' as defined by Keyes (2002) with the midpoint of 'moderately mentally healthy'.

Many authors see well-being as no more than the absence of disorder, whereas some define positive well-being as not even being on the same continuum as mental disorder. Keyes (2002), for example, distinguished this SWB continuum from mental disorder so that, for example, conceivably, someone could be flourishing whilst suffering from schizophrenia. However, in 2002, despite describing SWB as not simply the absence of ill-being, Keyes derived his SWB components by identifying positive versions of symptoms described in the internationally agreed diagnostic manual (DSM) for mental ill conditions (American Psychiatric Association 2003) and developed the Mental Health Continuum-Short Form scale which uses the question 'how often in the past month did you feel …' against items such as 'interested in life'.

The Keyes (2002) model is based on the definition of well-being as comprising emotional (hedonic), psychological (eudemonic) and social (eudemonic) components.

In his research, Keyes used the scope of episodic frequency. That is to say, he would ask questions phrased in the manner of *how often in the last month, did you?* Needless to say, such an approach might include recall inaccuracies, and of course, if the perception of SWB is not being in taken into consideration, then this may not matter. This type of questioning research also does not consider the intensity of experiences. For instance, extreme happiness

Table 2.2 Four conceptualisations of flourishing

Jahoda (1958)	Ryff (1989)	Antonovsky (1985)	Ryan and Deci (2001)	Seligman (2012)
Autonomy	Autonomy	Comprehensibility	Autonomy	Positive emotion
Environmental mastery	Environmental mastery	Manageability	Competence	Engagement
Self-actualisation	Personal growth	Meaningfulness	Relatedness	Relationships
Self-attitude	Self-acceptance			Meaning
Integration	Purpose in life			Accomplishment
Perception of reality	Positive relationships			

may be easier to remember than slight sadness. Keyes scoring is based on adding the various scales without any weighting. This means that it is assumed that all factors scored have the same weighting and therefore the same contribution to well-being. The other aspect which is to be taken into consideration is that of culture.

Hone et al. (2014) report wide international variations, with, for instance, Koreans reporting a rate of flourishing of 8% and, at the other end of the scale, US college students reporting a rate of 49%. It is altogether possible that Koreans may believe that perceiving high scores would be immodest and would allow that innate attitude to affect their responses.

Keyes also found correlations between flourishing or well-being and superior physical and psychological functioning.

In 2013, Huppert and So defined a continuum from ill-being through to well-being, with mental disorder at the opposite end to well-being. But, as we saw, Keyes (2002) states mental disorder is distinct and not part of the continuum with 'languishing' as the polar negative flourishing. Huppert and So, on the other hand, treated mental disorder as a negative pole with *languishing* as a slightly more positive dimension.

So far, the Huppert and So scale does not seem to have been very widely applied, but they did identify the opposite symptoms to those described in the DSM (American Psychiatric Association 2003) and the international classification of diseases (World Health Organisation 1990), resulting in the following 'features of flourishing', which are assessed by the European social survey (DSS round three: European social survey 2014; Table 2.3).

Diener et al. (2010) created the flourishing scale (FS) and attempts to add some eudemonic aspects to the previous emotional/hedonic focus scale, such as satisfactory life and positive and negative effect. Diener develops the scale through review of literature, suggesting dimensions of well-being which are important for positive functioning and comprising confidence, self-acceptance, meaning, relatedness, optimism, giving and engagement. All items are phrased as positives (which can lead to bias) from strongly disagree to strongly agree.

In spite of the bias issue, several studies have confirmed the scale's validity, reliability and structure (Hone 2014).

In 2012, Seligman developed the PERMA scale to assess positive emotions, engagement, positive relationships meaning and accomplishments. The scale was developed from hundreds of potential items in studies of over 11,000 individuals. This was then refined to produce the 16-item PERMA-Profiler (Table 2.4).

Table 2.3 Features of flourishing and indicator items from the ESS. Adapted from Huppert and So (2013)

Component of flourishing	ESS indicator item
Competence	Most days I feel a sense of accomplishment from what I do
Emotional stability	(In the past week) I felt calm and peaceful
Engagement	I love learning new things
Meaning	I generally feel that what I do in my life is valuable and worthwhile
Optimism	I am always optimistic about my future
Positive emotion	Taking all things together, how happy would you say you are
Positive relationships	There are people in my life who really care about me
Resilience	When things go wrong in my life it generally takes me a long time to get back to normal (reverse score)
Self-esteem	In general, I feel very positive about myself
Vitality (In the past week)	I had a lot of energy

Table 2.4 Components of flourishing and indicator items from the PERMA-Profiler. Derived from Seligman (2012)

Component of flourishing	PERMA-P indicator item
Positive emotion	In general, how often do you feel joyful?
	In general, how often do you feel positive?
	In general, to what extent do you feel contented?
Engagement	How often do you become absorbed in what you are doing?
	In general, to what extent do you feel excited and interested in things?
	How often do you lose track of time whilst doing something you enjoy?
Positive relationships	To what extent do you receive help and support from others when you need it?
	To what extent have you been feeling loved?
	How satisfied are you with your personal relationships?
Meaning	In general, to what extent do you lead a purposeful and meaningful life?
	In general, to what extent do you feel that what you do in your life is valuable and worthwhile?
	To what extent do you generally feel that you have a sense of direction in your life?
Accomplishment	How much of the time do you feel you are making progress towards accomplishing your goals?
	How often do you achieve the important goals you have set for yourself?
	How often are you able to handle your responsibilities?
General well-being	Taking all things together, how happy would you say you are?

Hone (2014) suggests that the various models which have been developed are all slightly different purposes, but agree that open 'flourishing' refers to high levels of SWB and that SWB itself cannot be adequately measured by a single-item assessment.

All four studies agree that flourishing includes both hedonic and eudemonic attributes.

There is some overlap with engagement appearing in all four studies and all four models with positive relationships and meaning also appearing in all four. All four models are short and easy to administer and produce data useful for individuals, policymakers and health professionals.

Only Keyes (2002) includes life satisfaction as an item, but both Huppert and So, as well as Hone, recommend the inclusion of a life satisfaction question alongside the measures of flourishing as shown in Seligman's PERMA-Profiler.

All four models also agree that well-being is not simply the absence of ill-being (depression), and Keyes suggests that mental disorder is a separate concept and not on the same continuum.

Researchers have attempted to show the differences in these constructs and point out that it is possible for individuals to present aspects of well-being and be suffering from a mental disorder at the same time. Nevertheless, it appears to be generally accepted that the languishing–flourishing continues as a separate construct from mental disorder. In 2002, Keyes proposed two continuums: one for mental disorder and one for mental health, on the perfectly reasonable assumption that the two are not mutually exclusive.

Considering causal factors, high national wage, higher education, being in a relationship and paid employment, affect psychological well-being. Education, income and employment status all relate to social well-being, being married and aged between 45 and 54 and with more than 16 years of education seem to relate to flourishing (Schotanus-Dijkstra 2015).

The strongest predictive value on the languishing–flourishing scale is personality or personality traits, especially low neuroticism, high extraversion and high conscientiousness. Lyubomirsky et al. (2005) suggested that each individual has a genetically fixed stable happiness level which is unlikely to change and that genetics contribute up to 50% to this long-term happiness.

This 'hedonic treadmill' theory suggests that there is a happiness baseline, to which individuals may return after positive or negative events which affect their well-being (Mancini 2015).

2.2.5 Comparability and Equity in Subjective Well-Being

It has been shown that well-being is a function of comparability as well as fairness.

Comparability is a straightforward comparison by the subject of his or her circumstances relative to a close group such as family, neighbours, workmates. Therefore, people living in comparatively impoverished circumstances can still experience well-being because they are no better off or worse off than their peers. This phenomenon is more powerful at a 'local level' than at national level. However, this can change very quickly when modern media and communications allow such people to see that people outside the immediate sphere are materially better off than they are. Country comparison studies show a weak relationship between wealth and SWB in poor countries. This is primarily a result of human adaption theory to factors such as poverty, discrimination, unhealthy conditions.

Equity is all about 'fairness'. The perceptions and well-being can be very strongly influenced by an individual believing that they are not receiving fair treatment from an employer, a government or friends.

So, in general terms, well-being, flourishing and all other perceived states are not merely a function of objective assessments of, for example, income and health, but also an individual's perception of his 'place' relative to others (Fig. 2.3).

Imagine an individual earning a high income, but living amongst many poor people. Both his/her self-perception and feeling of well-being may well be high. However, if you transplant that individual into an environment where his/her high income compared to his friends and neighbours is lower than theirs, there may well be a negative shift in both self-perception and well-being.

Allin and Hand (2014) describe subjective well-being as simply one component pillar of overall well-being. However, they did recognise a paradox within the model, best explained as follows: 'since subjective well-being is

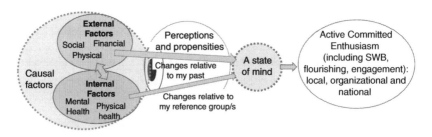

Fig. 2.3 Relativities in the PACE node of subjective well-being

regarded as a component of quality-of-life, at first glance it might look as if they've rather circular definition results'. This logical dilemma was not resolved by Allin and Hand, who suggest that well-being in itself is fundamentally subjective. It is a 'feeling' and that causal factors (factors which contribute to well-being or 'drive' well-being, for instance, health or wealth) are not 'well-being' in themselves.

That means that objective factors are important *components* of a causal process which contribute to an individual's building of a sense of well-being.

However, even subjective well-being is very often described in terms of psychological factors which are of course causes, rather than the construct itself. Statistically speaking, subjective well-being is the dependent or outcome variable and objective factors are independent or predictor variables.

Recent OECD work on subjective well-being supports this view and recommends assessment of 'a variety of objective well-being outcomes and how they combine to produce an overall perception of well-being'. The OECD recognises that objective causal factors are 'outcomes'. However, it also recognises that these outcomes combine to pass through a mitigating filter of personal factors and assessments, to produce the final subjective well-being.

2.2.6   Antecedents and Causes of Well-Being

One can argue that every single aspect of an individual's life and personal characteristics is going to have an effect on well-being—either directly or indirectly—especially if the definition of well-being also includes short-term affect. If, for instance, in a single day, an individual listens to a favourite piece of music which affects him or her emotionally and then receives a phone call from his or her daughter saying that the daughter has passed examinations, followed by a new story about possible flooding within their area closely followed by a phone call from a workmate indicating that the company is in trouble, these will all have an effect on well-being. The difficulty is twofold: firstly, deciding on which of those factors has the biggest effect (positive or negative) on well-being and secondly, which 'events' are going to have the longest or shortest effect on well-being.

There have been many studies and theories, and the following section discusses the most significant factors based on sound research. We have limited ourselves to the type of research which uses statistical association analyses to discover the degree of significance between a specific instrument assessing well-being and some devised measure of the variable in question. There are some flaws with this methodology, but the results have value. Some studies have used global data sources such as the World Values Survey and others use relatively small samples based on specific characteristics such as occupation in a dual-nationality.

At the beginning of this book, we have indicated that we are interested in helping organisational leaders to maximise organisational goals using the PACE, so our analysis has been made with this very pragmatic goal in mind. The factors below are organised into loose groups of convenience, although many will overlap:

- Policy-related factors (such as national/organisational income and governance).
- Work-related factors such as commuting.
- Environmental factors such as pollution.
- Social factors such as having friends.
- Individual factors such as gender and personality.

We also discuss *homoeostasis* (or hedonic adaptation as it's known in the happiness literature), which is the phenomenon of individuals having a well-being 'baseline' to which we all return no matter whether well-being has been affected negatively or positively.

Eger and Maridal (2015) carried out an analysis of causal factors, distinguishing between happiness (short-term affective state) and life satisfaction (a longer-term cognitive experience). The World Values Survey suggests that they are related but different concepts. Eger and Maridal described them as evaluative well-being (EWB) and affective well-being (AWB), and these are reflected in Dubai's ABCDE model (see Chap. 7), where A (Affective) equates to AWB and C (Cognitive) equates to EWB (Fig. 2.4).

Eger and Maridal describe the following factors causing EWB and AWB:

- Living standards: EWB is impacted considerably by living standards, but only up to medium income levels, whilst the effect on AWP is only short-lived. Living standards or wealth can also increase EWB indirectly, if, for example, it allows someone to help others and thereby gain more meaning in their own lives.

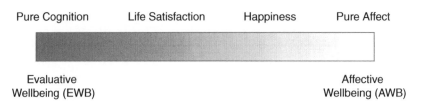

Fig. 2.4   Well-being—life satisfaction and happiness on the EWB–AWB

- Health and environment: objective indicators of health, identified in the literature, include life expectancy, undernourishment, suicide rates, positive experiences, mental and physical suffering and air, water and sanitation quality. It is interesting to note that EWB itself is also a *predictor* of future good health.
- Freedom: political, economic, civil and religious. This could be measured at microlevel or as perceived by any individual.
- Community and relationships, including social life and family.
- Peace and security: as indicated by levels of violence, corruption and crime.
- Opportunity: including access to education, employment and so on without discrimination.

The world database of happiness (http://worlddatabaseofhappiness.eur.nl) was developed by Veenhoven and colleagues (2014) in order to provide an overview of the huge and growing research and findings on the subject of happiness, whether measured in terms of SWB, flourishing and engagement. Currently, it contains about 9000 articles and books, which are organised and accessible through searching and indexes. Veenhoven uses this database to review the major themes and research findings, including a review of the measures in causal factors of SWB referred to in the following sections:

2.2.6.1   Policy-Related Factors

In each of the sections below, it is important to consider the likely causal direction. For instance, Bender (2005) suggests that the impact of income, health, social contacts and education increases along with increasing subjective well-being. That means that SWB is a cause of these phenomena rather than an outcome.

Inflation

At a national level, inflation would not appear to be associated with well-being (SWB). However, at the individual level, the effect of volatile, unpredictable, higher or lower inflation does have an effect on an individual and therefore SWB. Of course, one test to remember is that inflation is a function of the state of an economy, so therefore, inflation per se is not necessarily the main associated factor.

Income Levels

The Easterlin (1974) paradox suggests that rises in national income do not necessarily result in rises in SWB and in fact can sometimes result in what is termed 'unhappy growth', especially if it is perceived that national income is not distributed fairly and results in greater inequality and low aspirations. It has also been shown that increases in income only create an increase in life satisfaction, to a certain level (Andrada 2015; Eger 2015). Hence the phenomenon of rich and poor countries being able to have identical life satisfaction levels.

SWB does increase with income per capita, but the gains are smaller in higher income countries. Jorm and Ryan (2014) suggested income impacts life evaluation/satisfaction *more* than it influences measures of affect.

At an individual level, it could be that SWB as a perception is based on relative rather than absolute incomes. Or that the important impact of income increases to satisfy basic needs or that income is a hygiene factor (Hertzberg 1959) or that rich people adapt to high incomes, or that higher income is offset by hard work or other disadvantages (Di Tella and MacCulloch 2008).

This could suggest that if societal well-being is in the aim of government, then growth in national income would only be a valid policy goal up to a certain level and that is because eventually a rise in national income in developed economies will only be of value if it gives rise to more meaningful goals such as improving relationships or the quality of working life (Diener and Oishi 2000). The government's policy for growth in national income, leading to more meaningful work for the population, or if the policy focused on changing the population's reference groups for income comparison focused on SWB evaluation, would be another approach. As an example, this is one of the effects of the Bhutan happiness initiative (Biswas-Diener et al. 2015).

We have already discussed the fact that there is a strong relationship between gross domestic product, as well as individual wealth, and well-being, but only up to a certain level, with similar results for measures such as positive aspects/happiness.

The general consensus is that the relationship between income and well-being is logarithmic. That is to say that an equivalent income increase for two individuals with widely varying salaries will have a different effect; $1000 increase for somebody earning $1000 will have far more impact on their well-being than the same $1000 increase for someone earning $1 million.

Higher incomes equate to higher well-being until a certain level is reached after which the effect will tend to zero. Other factors such as social capital tend to increase in 'value' to an individual who may experience an income reduction.

If we look at the most affluent countries in the world, the USA and Germany, well-being levels appear to have risen very little over the past 30 years, having achieved a certain reasonably high level.

There is some danger in considering causal variables in isolation, and it has been shown that the effect of income changes is reduced if other factors such as quality of government, social capital, health and other factors are included (Abdallah 2012).

The interdependence of the various factors that we consider is illustrated by the fact that national income will impact on other variables, such as health, and other variables, such as quality of government will impact GDP. Hence the reference to complex causal interrelationships.

At the individual level, the relationship between income and SWB seems greater in middle age groups rather than the younger or older (Cummins 2003). This could be as a result of the aspirational and dynamic nature of the incomes of middle age groups relative to the comparatively static incomes of both the young and the old. This could be as a result of the perception in the middle group that effort, attention and competence all influence income.

Another important finding is that well-being does not appear to be highly related to relative income, for instance, compared to that of one's neighbours. Income is more strongly related to life satisfaction and Cantril's (1965) ladder (which compares how I feel with my expectations) than to happiness measures (Kahneman et al. 2004). This may be to do with what we refer to as relativities and certainly Cantril's ladder implies relative rather than absolute progress.

In 2014, Veenhoven and Vergunst analysed the world database of happiness over time periods from 10 to 40 years in 67 nations. They found a positive correlation between GDP and happiness, where happiness had increased more within countries which had achieved the greater economic success. As a result, they dismissed the Easterlin paradox, which suggests that economic growth does not create greater happiness.

Interestingly, though, Easterlin (2012) showed in a study of China from 1992 to 2010 that as China's GDP increased, the life satisfaction of the lowest socio-economic groups decreased and the life satisfaction of the top third of the population increased. This was more indicative of the growing income inequality in China with the lowest socio-economic groups being very aware of the fact that the new wealth was not cascading equally to their level.

Beja (2014) indicates that Easterlin's finding also suggests that short-term increases in wealth or income may increase happiness, but in the long term, it returns to a normal previous baseline. It is suggested that this could be as a result of psychological factors in human happiness (hedonic adaptation) and that any increase in happiness is a finite phenomenon. That is to say happiness cannot continue rising ad infinitum, and of course, if a population is scoring a measure at virtually maximum then it is numerically impossible to increase the score.

Healthcare, infrastructure, employment, pensions, common government excellence and income inequality are the 'visible' factors which individuals would expect to reflect any national rise in GDP. However, if these factors do not affect individuals in reasonably equal proportions that rise in GDP will not necessarily increase the well-being of the individual.

Beja (2014) found no substantive evidence of the long-term relationship between income growth and happiness, and there is therefore no guarantee that national income growth translates as individual happiness.

Therefore, the important question is not 'what is the national income?' but 'what is *done* with that income?'

That suggests that income growth in well-governed equitable societies will have a positive effect on SWB and badly governed, inequitable societies will experience a diametrically opposite impact. Having said that, a well-governed equitable society with a very low GDP will not have the means to realise those benefits. The opposite is also true. There are governments perhaps described as dictatorships or kingdoms which *do* provide social and material benefits to its population and in spite of that, still experience low levels of well-being.

Hence, the Easterlin paradox and the 'unhappy growth' paradox which suggest that if an increase in national income does not result in an increase in national happiness, then the pursuit of income might be the wrong goal for government.

Income Inequality

Let us look at two contradictory situations, although it is now generally accepted that income inequality does have a significant impact on SWB (Jorm and Ryan 2014).

If we look at former communist bloc countries after the collapse of the USSR, which had a relatively low level of the inequality, in general, the SWB was low. On the other hand, countries in Latin America, where there is high inequality, mostly enjoy high SWB.

Just those two situations suggest that other factors are often more signif-icant than inequality. For instance, in Latin American countries 'freedom in how the day spent' is significant. Meanwhile, in Russia and its former satellites, there may exist distinct factors such as a supposed innate Slav melancholy through to the overall low-income level, especially in terms of household wealth (Zavisca and Hout 2005).

However, Veenhoven (2014) found either no relationship between greater income inequality and greater SWB or in some cases a positive shift in SWB when there was income inequality.

It would appear, therefore, that income inequality, possibly perceived as a comparison with past and present situations, may be a key factor in SWB but other factors might mitigate its effect.

Veenhoven explains this by a balancing out of positive and negative effects. In 2004, Alesina found a negative relationship between inequality and SWB. That is to say, higher inequality equals lower SWB; this was among poor and politically left-leaning people in Europe. However, Oishi et al. (2011) found that the effects of income inequality were often mitigated by perceptions of fairness and trust.

As stated before, income inequality is a powerful factor if it is perceived as a result of a comparison in a local context: family, friends, workmates, etc. However, knowing that a celebrity is earning millions of pounds per annum does not appear to have a negative effect on SWB. This could be because at the national level, being aware of a large income differentiation between oneself and a stranger is more of an abstract than seeing one's next-door neighbour enjoying what is obviously a higher income.

Therefore, a reasonable strategy for government may be to target income inequality within various key groups rather than attempting to reduce income inequality overall.

Debt

The effect of debt on SWB very much depends on both context and the type of debt. For instance, an individual's largest debt is usually a mortgage which can be several multiples of annual income, and yet, this type of debt does not appear to have a negative impact on SWB, whereas credit card debt, or what appears to be unmanageable debt, can have a strong negative effect on SWB (Tsai 2014). Therefore, it is not the size of the debt, which affects SWB, but its nature. It is also worth mentioning that something like unmanageable or out-of-control debt is also a symptom of other personal and financial issues which will affect SWB. It is fair to say that any kind of debt will not necessarily be a problem which affects SWB unless paying it back becomes an issue. It is a self-evident truth that a delinquent debt will affect SWB.

Social Welfare and Taxation Regimes

On a national level, one study has shown that there is no relationship between national expenditure on social security and SWB (Di Tella 2013). However, on a microscale, there is little doubt that, for instance, unemployment benefits had a positive impact on tests on the SWB of the unemployed and welfare generosity also has a positive effect on SWB. This has been demonstrated by several studies. Once again, it is important to draw the distinction between life satisfaction, as opposed to happiness (Haller and Hadler 2006).

It can be said that higher public spending and benefits entitlement seem to be associated with higher SWB. For instance, Flavin (2011) and Kotakorpi and Laamanen (2010) completed studies which clearly showed associations between state spending, state intervention in markets on SWB and more, especially for middle-income individuals. Other studies have found no relationship, but suggest that a range of factors associated with modern living do have a positive impact on SWB; this has been described as 'modernity' by Veenhoven (2014).

Unemployment

Unemployment has always been associated with negative SWB as far as an individual is concerned, but it is very difficult to measure the effect at national level, because it is practically impossible for any statistical analysis to be sensitive to factors such as the black economy and various uses of time by the unemployed, which also have an impact on SWB.

Di Tella et al. (2013) suggest that unemployed people have a life satisfaction score of between 5 and 15% lower than employed people, although these effects vary across age, gender, nationality. For instance, the effect of unemployment in a modern first-world society can be far more devastating to the individual than in, say, a third world country for several reasons. For instance, it continues to be difficult to exactly define 'employed' in subsistence economies. As a matter of interest, the link between unemployment and SWB was at its highest in the UK. This, it is believed, is possible to do with comparability and in effect difficulties in 'keeping up with the Joneses'.

Returning briefly to the cause and effect argument, of course, it is possible that people with a negative SWB are more likely to be unemployed (Milner 2014).

As a comparatively transient phenomenon, SWB will return to its baseline after an individual becomes unemployed and suffers negative SWB although the effects of unemployment appear to linger and are greater than one would predict merely through loss of income.

For instance, Fryer and Payne (1984) suggest a whole range of negative well-being effects, ranging from feelings of inferiority and hopelessness to apathy and distrust. These are not always temporary effects and have been shown to linger. It is not merely the difference between becoming unemployed and long-term unemployment, but is a result of the impact of unemployment on attribution style and general optimism.

At the government level, the broad-brush policy is always to minimise unemployment, but it would be useful if both governments and organisations concentrated more on the consequences of unemployment, especially related to the individual, for instance, that loss of self-esteem and meaningfulness could be 'cushioned' by certain types of organisation sponsored activity. These can vary from outplacement programmes to targeted training and development. In fact, any activity that an organisation can provide to soften the blow of collateral damage caused by unemployment will have a positive effect on SWB, not just on the unemployed but also those remaining in work.

Unemployment Rate

In 2011, Helliwell and Huang suggested that the SWB of *employed* people is lower in areas of low employment, whereas interestingly, the SWB of unemployed people is at its highest in areas of high unemployment. Once again, it is the phenomenon of comparability which is affecting well-being. At the individual level, an unemployed person with an unemployed partner might have a higher SWB than an unemployed person with employed partner (Clark 2003).

Political System/Governance

Studies have shown that good governance has a positive association with SWB.

Abdallah (2012) found that there are several factors which demonstrate good governance, including things such as 'having a voice', accountability, political stability, government effectiveness, regulatory quality, rule of law, control of corruption. These all have a strong association with SWB.

These features (and others) are generally cited as the qualities of a democracy. However, SWB is certainly not a pure function of democracy as can be demonstrated in Russia, where individuals appeared to feel more positive, i.e. with higher SWB in the old communist days, before democratic structures were introduced to Russia.

Therefore, it would appear that labelling a system of government will not necessarily have a measurable impact on SWB, and in fact, several studies which have tried to demonstrate a relationship between democracy and SWB have had inconclusive results.

A change in political system will have an impact on SWB, although some suggest that a lowering of national SWB may cause political change, rather than vice versa (Inglehart and Klingemann 2000).

In addition, an increase in SWB has been shown to be associated with increases in free choice (Inglehart et al. 2008). Poland is an excellent example where there had been a very obvious change in SWB since Poland gained its independence from the USSR and it enjoyed what can only be described as the new national 'confidence'. That can be possibly attributed to not only the change, but also the new-found freedoms of expression which had then been accepted as the norm.

Veenhoven (2014) in his major review of previous research has identified the correlation as not so much with democracy and SWB but with institutional and government effectiveness such as rule of law and low levels of corruption which contribute to SWB. To put it generally, it is a predictable and secure environment which will have a positive impact on well-being.

Another phenomenon which has been identified (Frey and Stutzer 2005) in contributing to well-being is that of what they termed 'procedural utility'. That is a preference for clear and transparent rules and processes, even if they are not always to the individual's benefit.

2.2.6.2   Work-Related Factors

There is a distinction to be made between work-related well-being and the concept of engagement. Work-related well-being is usually defined with reference to the physical and mental health of employees.

In the context of this book, we are primarily focused on mental well-being. This has an affinity to SWB as defined in the national context, and with reference to the PACE framework, we consider that physical health, for instance, is a causal factor for SWB. In the organisational context, outcomes of physical well-being are factors such as increased productivity, less absenteeism, less attrition and more alertness. Therefore, work-related well-being stems from concern about employees' health (both physical and mental) and has generally taken a welfare perspective, with only some attention to performance or business outcomes.

In 2015, Karlsson considered the relationship between business outcomes and work-related well-being. He looked at it in terms of customer service and value creation through employee/customer interactions.

Once again, considering the cause–effect conundrum, Anderson et al. (2013) identified the reverse causality, where customer behaviour impacts on employee well-being with the result that the customer service process impacts on the well-being of both stakeholders.

This reinforces the theory that well-being in any setting can be viewed as a component in a process with outcomes as well as causes. The outcomes can be very valuable objectives for organisations of all sizes, from governments to small companies, leading to goal-driven well-being, which is an active state with similarities to engagement.

In 2015, Karlsson suggested that outcomes of this eudemonic well-being include better health, productivity, effectiveness, decision-making, respect, harmony and social networks plus outcomes of hedonic well-being (gratification), leading to productivity, engagement, better customer relations, etc.

Karlsson identified a range of antecedents to work-related well-being in customer-facing employees, which included workgroup factors such as team spirit and processes such as effective IT.

Fredrickson (2013) suggested that positive emotions do not arise in negative circumstances. Therefore, feeling positive enables a broadening and building of psychological resources which have implications for engagement. Negative or positive circumstances have been described as 'workplace climate', and this in turn has been shown to influence levels of engagement (Schaufeli 2013) and work-related well-being (O'Neil and Arendt 2008).

Work-related well-being has also been defined as comprising of three domains: levels of exhaustion, depersonalisation and personal accomplishment (Shuck and Reio 2014). All are impacted by psychological climate and engagement. All three of the above domains would be reduced in a positive climate.

One could surmise that these three domains are causes of psychological well-being, but Shuck and Reio also show that well-being can be a direct outcome of engagement.

Derived from the Schwartz Outcome Scale, Blais et al. (1999) defined psychological well-being as follows, on a 0–10 scale, ranging from 'never' to 'all the time':

- Given my current physical condition I am satisfied with what I can do.
- I have confidence in my ability to sustain important relationships.
- I feel hopeful about my future.
- I am often interested and excited about things in my life.
- I'm able to have fun.
- I am generally satisfied with my psychological help.
- I'm able to forgive myself for my failures.
- My life is progressing according to my expectations.
- I'm able to handle conflicts with others.

Shuck and Reio suggested that improvements in workplace climate, which is invariably created by leaders, will result in a positive impact on engagement, as well as psychological work-related well-being. They said: 'employers can significantly affect employee well-being by focusing on psychological work-place climate and engagement as antecedents'.

Veenhoven (2014) discovered two major correlations for work-based SWB:

Autonomy seems to be a strong work-related predictor of life satisfaction. He notes that this also fits well with the correlation of freedom in a national setting with life satisfaction. Perhaps freedom and autonomy are important in all domains.

Veenhoven also found that some of the data suggested that the size of organisation predicts life satisfaction, but that may be because of the fact that a large organisation is in a better position to provide facilities and support to its employees rather than a smaller organisation.

Jeffrey (2014) from the National Economic Forum (NEF) describes work-related well-being as individuals feeling happy, confident and satisfied in their roles. He goes on to suggest that people who achieve good standards of well-being are likely to be more creative, loyal and productive and also provide better customer satisfaction. He considered well-being and engage-ment as part of an overall rounded approach designed to help employees to:

- Strengthen their personal resources.
- Flourish and take pride in their roles.
- Function to the best of their abilities (as individuals and with colleagues).
- Have a positive experience of their work.

We have added some major causes to those identified by Jeffrey, as below (Table 2.5).

Table 2.5 Main causal factors for work-based well-being

Causal factor	Possible employer actions
Health (including sleep and vitality)	Provide health facilities, sponsor activities, allow exercise breaks, healthy canteen, avoid overwork and long hours
Work–life balance (well-being peaks at 55 h per week then drops rapidly)	Identify and facilitate employees' working preferences (hours, place and so on.)
Equitable pay (income affects well-being but mostly through comparison to others)	Set high minimums for pay levels (absolute pay affects well-being more for the lower paid). Institute fair, visible pay levels
Job security	Avoid redundancies, or at least manage fairly and supportively
Feedback on one's performance (but not too much)	Encourage two-way feedback, for example, on manager's style and an open atmosphere, rather than formal
Achievable, if challenging, jobs	Clarity, challenge, commitment, feedback and task complexity with self-determined goals
Leadership behaviour (listening, support, respect, care)	Select, develop and encourage transformational rather than transactional leadership
Working conditions	Need to be physically safe, comfortable and attractive
Perceived social value of the organisation's work and the job (meaningfulness)	Define and communicate the social contribution of the organisation and the jobs within it. Institute social programmes, especially in the local area
Match job to skills—do what you do best every day.	Recruit, develop and allocate people to roles that utilise and develop their strengths
Autonomy—control my work and the organisation of my day	Create management ethos of trust and delegation. Provide good support and allow mistakes if possible
Relations with colleagues	Create opportunities for social connection
Relations with manager	Ensure managers are personable and approachable
Experience positive feelings	Emphasise the positive, display optimism, recognise contributions
Occupation level	People at higher levels have higher SWB (which could be a reverse causality) but impacted by more meaningful work self-esteem and status. Create opportunities for everyone for meaningful work, status and self-esteem

(continued)

Table 2.5 (continued)

Causal factor	Possible employer actions
Self-employment (in rich countries)	This seems to be related to autonomy (see above).
Commuting	Reduce unnecessary travel through remote working

2.2.6.3   Environmental Factors

Not all environmental factors are going to be within the specific consideration of PACE. Many objective or material factors, including the general environmental factors, have a diminishing impact on SWB when their quality increases above a certain level. Therefore, all that government or employees need to provide is a good global standard. Having said that, many environmental factors can be impacted or affected by government as well as organisations.

In addition, environmental factors, in common with many other objective factors, are what is known as 'contextual'. This means that the 'requirement' in a poor country will be different to that in a richer country and would also change over time. For instance, the UN identifies this phenomenon by describing how a gap in expectations of public service can actually damage civic engagement (Hoffman et al. 2008). However, in this example, James (2009) discovered that the citizens' expectation levels about the quality of household waste removal were more strongly associated with satisfaction than the actual quality and level of performance.

Therefore, if an individual's expectations are low, they will be satisfied if those low expectations are met even though quality and performance are low. The converse is also true.

Physical Environment

Living in an area which is perceived as deprived reduces SWB (Abraham 2010), whereas SWB is enhanced where there is a positive perception of, for instance, the local landscape. That is where rural environments have a stronger positive effect than urban environments. Easterlin et al. (2011) showed that there were occasions, however, when the advantages of an urban context outweighed any rural landscape effect.

There are other anomalies. For instance, cul-de-sacs appear to be positively related to SWB, compared to through roads (Halpern 2008). These factors can be influenced by organisations, for instance, by the choices of location and governments can also create positive open environments through the choices of housing locations and other types of infrastructure.

Housing

The quality of housing is associated with SWB with low-grade housing increasing stress and lowering life satisfaction. Living in overcrowded conditions or in high-rise flats (Bond et al. 2012) has a negative effect on SWB as does living alone (Evans et al. 2003). On the other hand, homeownership has a positive effect on SWB (Tennant 2007).

Pollution

Pollution (whether atmospheric or acoustic) has a negative effect on SWB. Atmospheric pollution is based on perception, whereas noise pollution has a direct effect. However, an attempt to reduce pollution can also have a negative effect on SWB if, for instance, they restrict various freedoms of certain groups. For instance, the well-being of a cigarette smoker will be negatively affected if he or she is in a restaurant and told that they cannot smoke. Again, recent studies confirmed the role of perception and expectation where, for example, a smoker's SWB would not be impacted by not smoking on a long flight. Living by a noisy main road will have a negative impact on SWB, but without that noisy road and its traffic, the individual may have to live away from a convenient link to a town or airport (Croxford 2014).

Crime

General levels of crime do not appear to impact on SWB, but the perception of not living in a safe area can have a negative effect. Being a victim of crime certainly does have a negative effect on an individual's SWB, and very often, this is a powerful long-lasting effect (Lorenc et al. 2012).

Transport

Commuting (especially on crowded trains) has been shown to have a negative effect on SWB, whereas a journey by car can have a positive effect because of its association with self-esteem and the mastery aspects of well-being (Tyler

2014). Public transport can have both negative and positive impact on SWB. For instance, travelling on public transport, especially buses, implies a certain social standing, and although it may enable some social communication, generating positive SWB as well as giving access to amenities, on balance, its effect could be considered neutral.

Climate

In 2008, Van Prag and Ferrer-i-Carbonell suggested that extremes of weather, especially temperature, can have a profoundly negative effect on SWB. On the other hand, the perceived benefits and the feel-good factor of living in a hot climate can have a very positive effect on SWB.

2.2.6.4   Social Factors

Relationships and Social Capital

Relationships and social capital can have very positive impact on SWB. Both governments and organisations can affect this aspect of SWB through what are termed 'nudge' policies. Here citizens are encouraged towards certain behaviours through gentle coercion, such as the provision of community facilities such as clubs and events.

In order for a society or organisation to function effectively, there needs to be a network of relationships. This is referred to as social capital. This is most often measured by membership of voluntary bodies. This is a rather flawed definition because, for instance, there may be a network of relationships which have absolutely nothing to do with formal membership of voluntary bodies. The effect of voluntary bodies on SWB may be as a result of simply belonging, or taking part in meaningful activity, rather than the social capital effect itself.

Sarracino and Bartolini (2015) have shown that in spite of that, there is often a correlation between SWB and social capital as measured. They completed a study of China's growth between 1990 and 2007 and considered answers in the World Values Survey on trust of others, citizenship as well as the more traditional membership of associations. They found a high correlation between a reduction in social capital and lowering of SWB, despite a rapid increase in GDP.

The fact that individualism appears to have a positive effect on SWB, but that in this case a form of collectivism also had a positive effect on SWB, appears paradoxical. However, there may be other factors which affect SWB, such as the social aspect of collectivism being outweighed by, say, a decrease in the amount of freedom or possibly income variables having an effect.

It has been shown that social capital appears greater in individualistic societies where individuals who become more autonomous and seemingly liberated from social bonds actually become even more dependent on society in general (Allik and Realo 2004).

The relationship between individualistic societies and a degree of engagement was confirmed by Shantz et al. (2013). Individualistic components of autonomy and neutral dependence may facilitate social capital.

Beilmann and Realo (2012) describe this collectivism in terms of family (kinship), peers (companionship) and nation/society (patriotism) in which individuals could vary between these types.

Individualism is a mix of autonomy, self-responsibility and perception of uniqueness.

Correlations between collectivism, individualism and SWB also obscure reality as the positive association of individualism may well be due to the correlation of individualism with wealth, development and other factors found only in developed nations.

Let's have a look at the associations between particular facets of social capital and SWB:

Social Activity

Although there is a strong relationship between SWB and supportive social networks, this does not appear to be a function of the size of the network. Siedlecki (2014) has shown that older people, for instance, tend to prune or limit their networks and focus their time on close personal or emotional contacts. On a macrolevel or country level, nations with high social activity have a higher SWB. Those positive associations are a function of trust and deeper social connections.

Sarracino and Bartolini (2015) suggest that, for instance, in both China and the USA, there has been a general increase in wealth and well-being. But despite these positive factors, there has been a general decline in social activity. It is suggested that the lack of increase and well-being exists because the two factors have basically neutralised each other.

In fact, Huppert (2014) found that social activity mitigated the impact of stress on SWB.

Altruism

The question here is, does SWB cause altruism or does altruism have a positive effect on SWB? Nevertheless, there does appear to be a relationship between the frequency and scale of altruistic behaviour and SWB subject of course to the ever-present cause–effect conundrum. This relationship has also been proposed by proponents of positive psychology with 'helping others' being advised as a source of personal happiness.

Organisational Membership

Membership of an organisation, together with the associated feeling of 'belonging', has a positive association with SWB, except joining an organisation such as a trade union, which is viewed as a defensive response to a threat, where security is the perceived objective, rather than an augmentation of social presence or belonging. This principle also applies to membership of a religious group as well as attendance at religious services (Helliwell and Huang 2014). Positive Psychology also points to spirituality as a potential source of self-happiness.

Trust

Both trust in institutions and trust in other people are both positively associated with SWB (Helliwell and Huang 2014).

Personal Relationships

In general, a stable relationship, such as marriage, has a positive effect on SWB and in all likelihood mitigates against any negative impact on SWB. Being single, however, is associated with lower SWB.

Family Relationships

Family conflict is negatively associated with SWB (Carr et al. 2014). Separation or the break-up of relationships also has a negative effect on SWB, but it is mitigated by other factors such as having a meaningful occupation.

Work–Family Conflict

Work–family conflict (Winefield et al. 2014) often described as negative work–life balance is associated with lower SWB.

Social Status

Veenoven (2014) reports that several studies found a correlation between an advantage social status and satisfaction with life.

2.2.6.5   Health Factors

Both governments and organisations have realised their responsibilities for the health of their citizens and people in their employ, irrespective of the impact of health in the PACE framework, but once again we have a situation where circular causality can create a virtuous circle, that is to say where better health promotes higher SWB, which in turn leads to better health. As Helliwell showed in 2009, self-rated health is positively associated with SWB. Although disability has always been associated with a negative impact on SWB, recent events, including the 2012 Paralympics, have changed the self-image of many disabled people, resulting in a great change in SWB. This certainly confirms the roles of perceptions in SWB (Wood 2013). There is also one proven theory, which suggests that individuals do adapt to long-term conditions and there is also evidence that SWB may be a very positive factor which has a positive impact on general health.

Longevity

When health is measured in terms of life expectancy, it is correlated with life satisfaction, but not with affect. This leads to a question as to whether or not people experience fewer extremes of emotion as they age. In 2014, Veenhoven suggested an index of 'happy life expectancy' which combines life satisfaction and longevity measures at the country level. Looking at the individual, however, this does not suggest that individuals are living long and happy lives. A proportion of the population are happy and a proportion of them live a long life—but they might not be the same group.

Physical Activity

There is a positive association between physical activity and SWB, and as Malcolm et al. suggest in 2013, physical activity can reduce anxiety, lower the incidence of depression, improve mood and create greater psychological resilience.

Psychological Health

Mental disorders almost always result in lower SWB (Diener and Seligman 2004) although many have argued that the absence of disorder does not imply the presence of SWB or happiness. In 2002, Keyes suggested that mental disorder and SWB are related but independent constructs.

Smoking

Several studies have shown a correlation between smoking and lower SWB, but once again the causal direction is probably two-way (Lawrence et al. 2013). This particular view is countered by the fact that provision of smoking places promotes well-being, mainly through providing a social outlet for the smoker (Lawrence et al. 2013). This becomes less relevant as smoking becomes less prevalent in society of course.

Sleep

Kahneman et al. (2004) have shown an association between poor sleep or lack of sleep and lowered SWB. However, the causal direction is not yet clear.

Education

There is evidence that there is a positive association between a good education and SWB, both within countries and between countries (Stutzer and Frey 2012; Mellander 2012, respectively). Veenhoven (2014) indicates the correlation between education and life satisfaction is lower in rich nations.

Caring for Others

Caring for others has both a positive and negative effect on SWB. Ratcliffe et al. (2013) found that when carers were caring for spouses and caring for children, the effect on SWB was more positive than negative. It might also be that caring by choice has a positive effect compared to being forced by circumstances.

2.2.6.6   Individual Factors

There are certain individual factors which are impossible for governments and organisations to control. For instance, factors such as age are not modifiable. However, it is possible for governments as well as organisations to create an atmosphere in which positive outlooks can be developed in citizens and staff.

Age

The lowest pay-related SWB appears to be associated with middle age, that is to say, between the ages approximately 35 and 50 (Van Praag and Ferrer-i-Carbonell 2008). Other studies have suggested higher SWB in older people.

Gender

In 2015, Andrada found that women appeared to be less satisfied with their lives than men, although the impact of gender on SWB is still unclear. Studies tend to find different variations in different countries. This suggests that culture plays a part in the variations. The same may be found with ethnicity and perhaps sexual orientation.

Ethnicity

It is most likely that it is not ethnicity per se, which has an impact on SWB, but other people's or perhaps a state's response to ethnicity, which has the impact. So, for example, current reactions against migrants in the USA and Europe might well impact the SWB of certain ethnic groups, but this is because of hostility not due to ethnicity itself.

Materialism

Many studies reveal a negative association between materialist values and SWB and also between extrinsic (versus intrinsic) motivations and SWB (Dittmar 2014).

Personality

Many studies have shown strong positive links between extraversion, agreeableness, conscientiousness and 'openness to experience' with SWB. However, neuroticism has a negative association with SWB (Rietveld 2013).

If SWB is perceptual, it is a legitimate goal for governments as well as organisations to help their citizens/staff to improve their positivism and therefore their SWB and engagement, in exactly the same way that it is practical and legitimate to help improve physical health and well-being.

In 1989, Headey and Wearing proposed a 'dynamic equilibrium' model, where other events and changes in circumstances can influence an individual's SWB. Eventually, the individual will adapt and return to biologically determined 'set point' or level of the adaption.

More recent research, however, has shown that this 'set point', is not entirely determined biologically but with as much as 50% being as a result of other factors, either objective or non-genetic predispositions.

Even genetically predisposed tendencies such as extraversion and neuroticism can be modified (Diener et al. 1999). Optimism and a belief that one has control over one's life and self-esteem are all correlated significantly with SWB and are all modifiable.

Genetic Heritability

Heritability is a very important causal factor in SWB, but it is not modifiable by any means, either by governments or by organisations. So, for individuals, positivism explains a large part of their SWB, and if that particular personality is explained primarily by genetic factors, then there would be little room for governments or organisations to intervene. This section deals with research in this particular field.

Keyes et al. (2010) suggest that of all the effects impacting on life satisfaction, heritability contributes between 36 to 56%, with little evidence of strong mitigating effects of family environment. He completed a study of over 300 US twins in order to investigate measures of the three types of subjective well-being: hedonic (emotional well-being), eudemonic (psychological well-being) and social well-being.

For *emotional* well-being, the measure included questions such as '*How often in the last 30 days have you felt calm and peaceful/cheerful/extremely happy/in good spirit/satisfied/full of life?*' Subjects were asked to rate their life overall on a scale of 0–10. Then, the scales were added together.

For *psychological* well-being, the scales were once again simply added and the questions were in several specific categories:

- Self-acceptance: 'I like most part of my personality'.
- Positive relations: 'Maintaining close relationships has been difficult for me'.
- Personal growth: 'For me, life has been a continual process of learning, changing and growth'.
- Purpose: 'When I look at the story of my life, I am pleased with how things have turned out so far'.
- Mastery: 'I'm good at managing the responsibilities of daily life'.
- Autonomy: 'I have confidence in my own opinions, even if they are different to the way other people think'.

Social well-being was assessed on the basis of the subject's perception and interaction with both his or her macro- and microenvironment:

- Social acceptance: 'I believe that people are kind'.
- Social growth: 'Society is becoming a better place for everyone'.
- Social contribution: 'I have something valuable to give to the world'.
- Social coherence: 'I try to think about and understand what could happen next in our country'.
- Social integration: 'I feel close to other people in my community'.

Keyes et al. (2010) found that the impact of a heritable propensity towards mental well-being was of the order of 72% and over 50% heritable for each of emotional, psychological and social components with no evidence of environmental or familial influence overall, but substantial environmental influence on emotional and social well-being.

He stresses the interaction between heritability and environment, suggesting that the traits associated with social and emotional well-being (compassion altruism, extraversion, etc.) and the environmental qualities such as openness and trust which help with well-being could be investigated to help those with a low innate propensity for well-being.

In addition to the genetic aspect of SWB, a recent review of the evidence to date found that our emotions, cognition, behaviour and mental health are influenced by a large number of entities that reside in our bodies whilst pursuing their own interests, which need not coincide with ours. Such 'selfish' entities include microbes, viruses, foreign human cells and imprinted genes regulated by virus-like elements (Kramer and Bressan 2015). Their conclusions were that:

1. Gut and brain microbes can cause. 'Reckless behaviour (associated with workplace and traffic accidents -possibly because it renders one less careful and slows down reaction time), depression, suicides, changes in personality, and various mental and neurological diseases, including bipolar and obsessive-compulsive disorders' (Kramer and Bressan 2015).
2. Ancient viral DNA is implicated in some mental disorders.
3. Virus-like elements interfere with material and paternally inherited genes to cause opposite physical and behavioural effects.

These 'selfish entities' impact behaviour as shown below:

The major issue is that many genes appear to have small additive effects, rather than a few genes having large effects (Pluess 2015). This makes it difficult to devise psychological interventions based on an understanding of the interactions between heritable and environmental factors and/or how to mitigate heritable effects.

Pluess (2015) suggests that a greater understanding of the biological mechanisms involved will allow 'the development of psychological as well as pharmaceutical treatments aimed at promoting well-being, personalised suggestions aimed at maximising well-being based on an individual's genotype as well as taking an individual's genetic sensitivity to specific environmental influences or particular forms of psychological intervention into account'.

2.2.7 Homoeostasis

An interesting phenomenon is that across the world, most people rate themselves fairly similarly on life satisfaction. In developed countries, on a scale of 0–200, the mean score is about 75 and even countries with the lowest life satisfaction levels still rate themselves above 50 (Cummins 2003).

Homoeostasis is our ability to remain or achieve a relatively stable equilibrium, and that is why we often see SWB returning to a baseline, even after extreme positive or negative events. So, the question is whether or not self-rated life satisfaction is subject to a homeostatic process.

In 1971, Brickman and Campbell proposed that individuals adapt quickly to changes in their lives and return to their baseline levels of happiness on a 'hedonic treadmill', whereas Headey and Wearing (1989) suggest that happiness levels tend to return to a predetermined norm opposed to a theory of dynamic equilibrium where SWB is impacted by events that quickly return to a biologically determined norm.

These phenomena probably exist for two distinct reasons: the first is because humans have an underlying propensity to oscillate around a mean of happiness and secondly, because the scales used to assess happiness and life satisfaction are bounded Likert scales and the construct is related to expectations.

For instance, if I was experiencing a certain level of happiness today, my expectations of my level of happiness tomorrow would be based on today's level. Allin and Hind (2014) suggest that well-being and happiness follow such a homeostatic process.

2.2.8   Measuring Well-Being

2.2.8.1   Measures of Objective Well-Being

Objective measures of, for example, quality of housing, national income, do not directly measure well-being. They measure causal factors which have been demonstrated to have an association with some measure of SWB or sometimes assumed to have a relationship.

Nevertheless, these kinds of measures do have potential values. Firstly, a factor may reflect the delivery of some sort of government, organisational service, and it is good to understand how well it is delivered, whether or not it affects well-being. Secondly, if there is a causal link which can be demonstrated, compared to other factors, then this type of indirect measure may well indicate something about the resulting levels of well-being and more importantly, suggest further action.

2.2.8.2   Measures of Subjective Well-Being

The Cantril Ladder (1965) of Life Scale is a device which is still used to measure well-being and part of its value lies in its simplicity. The individual places him or herself on an imaginary ladder of 10 steps where the top represents the best possible life imaginable for the individual and the bottom represents the worst possible life. This model is useful because it appears to measure an individual's perception directly because that individual's opinion is not based on evidence, analysis or models.

However, as the objective is invariably to improve SWB, a single-item scale such as this does have limitations because it is so difficult to use it to drive actions, but these scales do certainly provide comparisons with other demographics.

The World Values Survey (http://www.worldsvaluesurvey.com) includes the question '*All things considered, how satisfied are you with your life as a whole these days?*' This type of question tends only to provide a 'snapshot' of a feeling of well-being, is subject to current mood and therefore does not indicate any sort of stable SWB. Anusic (2012) found that life satisfaction measures are influenced by mood or event changes every single week, with changes in effect being even more variable, whereas personality traits remain relatively stable.

The study suggested that personality measures appear to be trait-like over two months, whereas a retest in another one week would be appropriate for measures of life satisfaction and affect.

Huppert (2014) suggests that although life satisfaction scores appear relatively stable and trait-like, they reflect self-image or aspiration rather than real feelings. For instance, 'few people like to think that they are the sort of person who is generally dissatisfied'.

Anusic (2012) challenges this stable trait argument, but Huppert notes three further issues with comprehensibility, complexity and congruence.

Comprehensibility: Many people surveyed did not clearly understand what was meant by 'satisfied' and raised questions about comparativeness. In other words, they were not thinking 'in vacuo' but wanted to know who they were supposed to be comparing themselves with in order to gauge the level of their own 'satisfaction'. For instance, if they are comparing themselves to individuals who were deprived socially and materially, they might think that they should be registering a reasonable level of satisfaction, whereas if they were being asked to compare themselves to their peers, the level of satisfaction may not appear to be that great.

Complexity: In order to evaluate one's own life satisfaction, one should really take into account and evaluate all aspects of one's life, including the comparative weightings of each factor which one considers.

Huppert (2014) also highlights examples of the highly beneficial government intervention, which ultimately results in no change in satisfaction because expectations change in line with intervention. An example is, if ambulance response times improve, people's expectations will increase. That simply means that an individual's own perception of life satisfaction can remain static, even when conditions improve, because their expectation has changed or increased.

Congruence: In 2013, Huppert and So discovered that correlations between items such as 'having a sense of meaning in one's life' and 'good relationships' with life satisfaction. They also found some overlap between life satisfaction and 'flourishing', suggesting that they were related but not identical constructs.

Diener et al. (2013) found that single-item life satisfaction scales reflected:

- Differences between nations were different objective conditions.
- Differences between groups in different circumstances.
- Correlations with other non-self-report measures.
- Genetic and psychological associations, changes in the significant life events and
- Predictions of future actions, such as suicide.

They also acknowledged that life satisfaction scales content was by mood as well as question order, but also suggest that these influences can be controlled.

Life satisfaction scores can be used to assess specific policy decisions, for instance, investing in transport or local office provision where, for example, life satisfaction has been affected by people having to commute long distances (Diener et al. 2013).

The approach to well-being measurement varies depending on the situation. A single-item life satisfaction measure may be appropriate if the purpose of the measurement is to compare countries at a coarse level or correlate many different variables. However, if the objective is to help individuals to improve their own SWB, then a different measure would be more appropriate.

As Huppert (2014) highlights, there are many potential instruments developed by different researchers and all predicated on different and underlying conceptualisations of SWB or 'flourishing'. In other words, the measurement methods are all dependent on not only the understanding of SWB or 'flourishing' but also the use to which the measurement is to be put. Huppert suggests that a solution to this is to develop an objective method to define the key components and cites Huppert and So (2013) as such an attempt.

Huppert also suggests that an expert consensus should be reached and suggests the new economic foundation as being a possible facilitator. However, previous experience tells us that the history of academic theorists and researchers achieving a consensus is not always encouraging and both individuals and organisations are already free of a specific political or social agenda or theoretical perspective.

For instance, the NEF publishes the Happy Planet Index (Abdallah 2012). This combines life satisfaction with life expectancy, plus a calculation of ecological footprint to produce 'Happy Life Years' as a key measure of well-being at the national level. Of course, this model makes certain assumptions about what causes well-being and, for instance, could result in countries with the most inequality receiving the highest Happy Planet scores, whilst those with low inequality and, for instance, high military expenditure could find themselves with the lowest scores (Tausch 2011).

The above is an excellent example of scores being based on the factors which a particular organisation considers of interest but not meeting the needs and assumptions of others. Another example is that of Bhutan which does not measure happiness, but the assumed *causes* of happiness which are described as the four pillars: Sustainable Development, Cultural Values, the Natural Environment and Good Governance.

Seligman's (2012) PERMA scale takes a more general approach in providing a 'dashboard' of individual measures for specific components of SWB, arguing that there is no value in providing a composite scale as it would not provide actionable information or have any explamatory value and would depend on arbitrary weighting of the various factors.

Another recommendation (Huppert 2014) is to carry out factor analysis and other statistical tests such as item response theory (IRT) on very large population samples to establish a robust factorial structure and demonstrable reliability for the smallest sensible number of differentiating items. This type of approach assumes a consistency of factor influence across populations, whereas in actual fact, the strength and composition of key factors vary between individuals and change over time.

Huppert and So (2013) compared 10 components of open 'flourishing' across 22 European nations. France scored lower on life satisfaction indexes despite its relative prosperity. However, at a component level, it scored very high on engagement but very low on self-esteem, optimism and positive relationships. Spain, on the other hand, scored high on self-esteem, but low on confidence and vitality. The UK, with similar life satisfaction scores to Spain, scored high on positive relationships with low on engagement.

In these cases, the composite or 'dashboard' results are far more informative than the single-item life satisfaction score. Therefore, merely adding the scores to create a composite would make no real sense, as there is no way of knowing whether, for instance, a certain score for emotional stability has any relationship to a similar score for competence.

2.2.8.3   Issues with Measurement

There are certain red flags associated with measurement of responses. Here are some examples:

- On a Likert scale, an individual score of 4 is not necessarily equivalent to twice a score of 2.
- One individual's score of 4 may not be equivalent (mathematically) to another individual's score of 4. On a Likert scale, respondents will score the same level of intensity differently to each other.
- Although a set of Likert scales uses the same numbers, the actual units they are measuring are ill-defined and different to each other, for example, the level of agreement that 'my company looks after people' versus the level of agreement that 'life is good these days'. The different scales with their different units of interest should only be manipulated or formulated with great care, in the same way that it would not generally be appropriate to add a figure in miles to a figure in tonnes and express the answer in height.

2.2.8.4   Common Measures of Subjective Well-Being

These are some of the most common single-item SWB questions:

Single-Item Measures

Life Satisfaction
'All things considered, how satisfied are you with your life as a whole nowadays?' (Go from 1 dissatisfied to 10 satisfied).

Overall Happiness
'Taking all things together, would you say you are?' (1 very happy through to 10 for not at all happy).

Happiness in the Past
'How much of the time during the past week were you happy?' (On a scale of 1–4).

Cantril's Ladder
'Please imagine a ladder, with steps numbered from nought at the bottom to 10 at the top. The top of the ladder represents the best possible life and the bottom of the ladder represents the worst possible life for you. On which step

of the ladder would you say you personally feel you stand at this time?' This is an interesting question as it implies some kind of progression to ultimate happiness.

Multi-item Measures

Satisfaction with Life Scale

Developed by Diener (1984), comprising five questions, rated from 1 strongly disagree to 7 highly agree:

- In most ways my life is close to my ideal.
- The conditions of my life are excellent.
- I am satisfied with my life.
- So far I have gotten the important things I want in life.
- If I could live my life is over, I would change almost nothing.

Domain-Specific Well-Being

In these instruments, overall life satisfaction is deconstructed into satisfaction various specific domains. For example, from US General Survey:

Overall happiness: 'Taken altogether, how would you say things are these days-would you say that you are happy, pretty happy or not too happy?'

Financial: 'We are interested in how people are getting along financially these days. So far as you and your family are concerned, would you say that you are pretty well satisfied with your present financial situation, more or less satisfied, or not satisfied at all?'

Employment: Asked of person is currently working, temporarily not at work, or keeping house: "On the whole, how satisfied are you with the work you do-would you say you are very satisfied, moderately satisfied, a little dissatisfied, or very dissatisfied?'

Family life: 'Tell me the number that shows how much satisfaction you get from that your family life (ranging from one a very great deal through to 7 none)'.

Health: 'Tell me the number that shows how much satisfaction you get from your health and physical condition (ranging from one a very great deal, through to 7 none)'.

Day reconstruction method (DRM)

The DRM asks respondents to keep a diary about yesterday, describing episodes of about one hour duration (Kahneman 2004). The DRM starts with general questions, including overall and domain-specific life satisfaction questions:

- Taking all these things together, how satisfied are you with your life as a whole these days?
- Overall, how satisfied are you with your life at home?
- Overall, how satisfied are you with your present job?
- When you are at home, what percentage of the time are you: in a bad mood, a little low or irritable, in a mildly pleasant mood, in a very good mood?
- When you are at work what percentage of the time are you: in a bad mood, a little low or irritable, in a mildly pleasant mood, in a very good mood?

Then, the diary episodes are reviewed by the respondent to describe how they felt during each episode on a scale from 1 (not at all) to 6 (very much) under the following items:

- Impatient for it to end
- Happy
- Frustrated/annoyed
- Depressed/blue
- Competent/capable
- Hassled/pushed around
- Warm/friendly
- Angry/hostile
- Worried/anxious
- Enjoying myself
- Criticised/put down
- Tired

Scale of positive and negative experience (SPANE)

SPANE is a similar event recall method. Developed to measure the balance between experience positive and negative affect (Diener et al. 2010). SPANE is a 12-item Likert scale, with six items assessing positive experiences and six items assessing negative experiences over the previous four weeks, including three general and three specific items per subscale.

'Please think about what you have been doing and experiencing during the past four weeks then report how much you experience each of the following feelings':

- Positive
- Negative
- Good
- Bad
- Pleasant

- Unpleasant
- Happy
- Sad
- Afraid
- Joyful
- Angry
- Contented

Pemberton happiness index (PHR)

A 21-item scale evaluating remembered and experienced well-being in various life domains, including hedonic, eudemonic social and general well-being, as well as positive and negative affect (Hervás and Vázquez 2013; Table 2.6).

Table 2.6 Pemberton happiness index items. After Hervás and Vázquez (2013: 9)

Domains and subdomains	Item content
Remembered well-being	
General well-being	I am very satisfied with my life
	I have the energy to accomplish my daily tasks
Eudemonic well-being	
Life meaning	I think my life is useful and worthwhile
Self-acceptance	I am satisfied with myself
Personal growth	My life is full of learning experiences and challenges that make me grow
Relatedness	I feel very connected to the people around me
Perceived control	I feel able to solve the majority of my daily problems
Autonomy	I think that I can be myself on the important things
Hedonic well-being	
Positive affect	I enjoy a lot of little things every day
Negative affect	I have a lot of bad moments in my daily life
Social well-being	I think that I live in a society that lets me fully realise my potential
Experienced well-being	
Positive experiences	Something I did made me proud
	I did something fun with someone
	I did something I really enjoy doing
	I learned something interesting
	I gave myself a treat
Negative experiences	At times, I felt overwhelmed
	I was bored for a lot of the time
	I was worried about personal matters
	Things happened that made me really angry
	I felt disrespected by someone

Warwick-Edinburgh mental well-being scale (WEMWBS) asks:
'over the past two weeks'

- I've been feeling optimistic about the future (1 none of the time five, all of the time).
- I've been feeling useful.
- I've been feeling relaxed.
- I've been dealing with problems well.
- I've been thinking clearly.
- I've been feeling close to other people.
- I've been able to make up my own mind about things.

The General Health Questionnaire (GHQ)

This was developed to help detect psychiatric disorders in community and clinical settings. For well-being, the scores are inverted so that it is treated as a measure of well-being, assuming it is the opposite end of the continuum from mental disorder, and specifically, depression. The scoring is along a scale from 'better/healthier than normal', 'same as usual', 'worse/more than usual' to 'much worse/more than usual' on the following dimensions:

- Feeling Unhappy.
- Thinking of Self As Worthless.
- Losing Confidence.
- Feeling Unhappy and Depressed.
- Could Not Overcome Difficulties.
- Capable of Making Decisions.
- Face up Problems.
- Able to Concentrate.
- Enjoy Normal Activities.
- Play Useful Part in Things.
- Under Strain.
- Lost Much Sleep.

Centre for Epidemiological Studies-Depression (CES-D) Scale

This measures levels of depression, including positive and negative questions on affective scale in the following symptom groups:

Sadness (dysphoria): question numbers 2, 4, 6
Loss of Interest (anhedonia): question numbers 8, 10
Appetite: question numbers 1, 18
Sleep: question numbers 5, 11, 19

Thinking/Concentration: question number 3, 20
Guilt (worthlessness): question numbers 9, 17
Tired (fatigue): question numbers seven, 16
Movement (agitation): question numbers 12, 13
Suicidalideation: question numbers 14, 15.

Pan-National Comparative Surveys of Well-Being

The World Values Survey (WVS)

The WVS is taken every five years across 40 countries among a large number of items covering everything from religious affinity to family circumstances. It asks '*All things considered, how satisfied are you with your life as a whole nowadays?*' (Scale from 1, dissatisfied to 10 satisfied) and '*Taking all things together, would you say that you are?*' (1 very happy through to 4, not at all happy).

It is widely referenced and analysed because of its coverage and a large number of comparable items.

OECD: Better Life Initiative

The mission of the Organisation for Economic Co-operation and Development (OECD) is to promote policies that will improve the economic and social well-being of people around the world and is a forum for governments to share common problems and initiatives.

The OECD better life initiative is a new interactive web-based tool which allows individuals to set their own 'weight' on 11 dimensions of OECD well-being indicators and '*to see how countries average achievements compare, based on one's personal priorities in life and to show one's index and choices of weights with other people in their networks*'.

The OECD bases its method on a capabilities view (Sen 1993; Scott-Jackson et al. 2011). People's capabilities are combined with the degree to which they can choose which capabilities matter. This approach recognises the importance of the weightings applied to variables in calculating any aggregated measure of SWB and also recognises the SWB effects of allowing people to be engaged.

By 2013, 44,000 indices had been shared and these showed that overall, life satisfaction, health and education were the most important dimensions of life. The 11 dimensions included in the OECD Better Life Index are:

- Income and Wealth.
- Jobs and Earnings.

- Housing.
- Health Status.
- Work–Life Balance.
- Education and Skills.
- Social Connections.
- Civic Engagement and Governance.
- Environmental Quality.
- Personal Security.
- Subjective Well-Being.

The OECD also enables countries to modify the dimensions to suit their own needs, where, for example, Italy introduces the 12th dimension of 'culture'.

The ability of individuals to enter their own data provides an ever-increasing databank, but needs to be used with caution as, for example, 'jobs' is the most important dimension in a mine in Saudi Arabia, but with only 12 and 78 responses, respectively.

Overall, this is an extremely powerful methodology using modern data collection, big data techniques and providing an ever more useful body of data, as well as a good model for local, national and organisational well-being measures.

European Values Survey (EVS)

The EVS is taken every 9 years and covers over 20 European countries. Similar to the WVS, among a large number of items covering everything from religious affinity to family circumstances, it asks: *'all things considered, how satisfied are you with your life as a whole nowadays?'* (Scale from one dissatisfied to 10 satisfied) and *'taking all things together, would you say that you are?'* (1 = very happy through to 4 = not at all happy).

The Euro Barometer

A survey of 300,000 people in 12 European countries was based on home interviews and including the question: 'On the whole, are you very satisfied, fairly satisfied, not very satisfied, not at all satisfied with the life you lead?'

The Gallup World Poll

A worldwide survey, including Cantril's ladder: 'Please imagine a ladder, with steps numbered from zero at the bottom to 10 at the top. The top of the ladder represents the best possible life for you and the bottom of the ladder represents the worst possible life for you. On which step of the ladder would you say you personally feel you stand at this time?'

The International Social Survey Programme (ISSP)

The ISSPP is an annual set of national surveys covering 41 countries and focuses on social science research questions. That includes: *'if you were to consider your life in general, these days, how happy or unhappy, would you say you are, on the whole?'* (on the scale: 4 = very happy, 3 = fairly happy, 2 = not very happy and 1 = not at all happy).

The US General Social Survey (GSS)

The GSS survey is for about 30,000 US residents and is carried out annually. It includes the question *'taken altogether, how would you say things are these days? Would you say you are?'* (very happy = 3, pretty happy = 2, not too happy = 1).

The European Social Survey (ESS)

The ESS covers 20 countries by interview. It includes the question*: 'All things considered, how satisfied are you with your life as a whole nowadays?'* (0 = extremely dissatisfied and 10 means extremely satisfied). It also includes: *'taking all things together, how happy'.*

The German Socio-Economic Panel (GSOEP)

GSOEP is based on 24,000 members of 11,000 households by interview. Variables include household composition, employment, occupations, earnings and health and satisfaction indicators. It includes a wide-ranging question *'how satisfied are you with the following areas of your life?'* (including health, sleep, job, etc.). Also *'how often have you felt… (Angry, worried, happy, sad) in the past four weeks?'*

The British Household Panel Survey (BHPSS) now called 'understanding society'

This follows the same sample over time and is therefore suitable for longitudinal causal analysis, interviewing all members of households. It includes: *'how satisfied are you with your life overall?'* and *'would you say that you are more satisfied with life, less satisfied, or feel about the same that you did a year ago?'*

There are many more measures in use at national, pan-national and global levels, in addition to well-being questions included in many organisational annual surveys (which often also include engagement assessment and will be discussed further). There is a huge amount of data available for analysis and mostly freely available from the providers. Having analysed all the available instruments, we have developed the ACEq questionnaire which focuses on Active Committed Enthusiasm, rather than basic well-being. For details see www.PACEtools.org.

References

Abdallah, S., Michaelson, J., Shah, S., Stoll, L., & Marks, N. (2012). *The happy planet index: 2012 report. A global index of sustainable well-being.* London: The New Economics Foundation.

Abraham, A., Sommerhalder, K., & Abel, T. (2010). Landscape and wellbeing: A scoping study on the health-promoting impact of outdoor environments. *International Journal of Public Health, 55,* 59–69.

Alfes, K., Shantz, A. D., Truss, C., & Soane, E. C. (2013). The link between perceived human resource management practices, engagement and employee behaviour: A moderated mediation model. *The International Journal of Human Resource Management, 24*(2), 330–351.

Allik, J., & Realo, A. (2004). Individualism-collectivism and social capital. *Journal of Cross-Cultural Psychology, 35*(1), 29–49.

Allin, P., & Hand, D. J. (2014). *The wellbeing of nations: Meaning, motive and measurement.* Chichester: Wiley.

American Psychiatric Association. (2003). *Diagnostic and statistical manual of mental disorders: DSM-5.* ManMag.

Anderson, L., Ostrom, A. L., Corus, C., Fisk, R. P., Gallan, A. S., Giraldo, M., et al. (2013). Transformative service research: An agenda for the future. *Journal of Business Research, 66*(8), 1203–1210.

Andrada, D. (2015). On the trails of the gender 'life satisfaction' gap: A mixed level analysis. *Annals-Economy Series, 2,* 257–263.

Antonovsky, A. (1985). The life cycle, mental health and the sense of coherence. *Israel Journal of Psychiatry and Related Sciences, 22*(4), 273–280.

Anusic, I., Lucas, R. E., & Donnellan, M. B. (2012). Dependability of personality, life satisfaction, and affect in short-term longitudinal data. *Journal of Personality, 80*(1), 33–58.

Ariani, D. W. (2013). The relationship between employee engagement, organizational citizenship behavior, and counterproductive work behavior. *International Journal of Business Administration, 4*(2), 46.

Arthaud-Day, M. L., Rode, J. C., & Turnley, W. H. (2012). Direct and contextual effects of individual values on organizational citizenship behavior in teams. *Journal of Applied Psychology, 97*(4), 792.

Aryee, S., Walumbwa, F. O., Zhou, Q., & Hartnell, C. A. (2012). Transformational leadership, innovative behavior, and task performance: Test of mediation and moderation processes. *Human Performance, 25*(1), 1–25.

Bakker, A. B., & Demerouti, E. (2007). The job demands-resources model: State of the art. *Journal of managerial psychology, 22*(3), 309–328.

Barrick, M. R., Thurgood, G. R., Smith, T. A., & Courtright, S. H. (2015). Collective organizational engagement: Linking motivational antecedents, strategic implementation, and firm performance. *Academy of Management Journal, 58*(1), 111–135.

Beilmann, M., & Realo, A. (2012). Individualism-collectivism and social capital at the individual level. *Trames, 3,* 205–217.

Beja, E. L., Jr. (2014). Income growth and happiness: Reassessment of the Easterlin paradox. *International Review of Economics, 61*(4), 329–346.

Bender, K. A., Donohue, S. M., & Heywood, J. S. (2005). Job satisfaction and gender segregation. *Oxford Economic Papers, 57*(3), 479–496.

Biswas-Diener, R., Diener, E., & Lyubchik, N. (2015). Wellbeing in Bhutan. *International Journal of Wellbeing, 5*(2), 1–13.

Blais, M. A., Lenderking, W. R., Baer, L., deLorell, A., Peets, K., Leahy, L., et al. (1999). Development and initial validation of a brief mental health outcome measure. *Journal of Personality Assessment, 73*(3), 359–373.

Bledow, R., Schmitt, A., Frese, M., & Kühnel, J. (2011). The affective shift model of work engagement. *Journal of Applied Psychology, 96*(6), 1246.

Bond, L., Kearns, A., Mason, P., Tannahill, C., Egan, M., & Whitely, E. (2012). Exploring the relationships between housing, neighbourhoods and mental wellbeing for residents of deprived areas. *BMC Public Health, 12*(1), 48.

Born, N., & Drori, E. (2015). *What factors will transform the contemporary work environment and characterize the future of work?* Cornell University, ILR School. Retrieved June 14, 2015, from http://digitalcommons.ilr.cornell.edu/student/78.

Bortolotti, L., & Antrobus, M. (2015). Costs and benefits of realism and optimism. *Current Opinion in Psychiatry, 28*(2), 194.

Bridger, E. (2015). The Positive Psychology of Employee Engagement. Voice. Engage for Success. http://www.engageforsuccess.org/positivepsychology-employee-engagement/#.VWwp6kZB8as.

Busseri, M. A. (2014). Toward a resolution of the tripartite structure of subjective well-being. *Journal of Personality, 83*(4), 413–428.

Brickman, P., & Campbell, D. T. (1971). Hedonic relativism and planning the good society. In *Adaptation-Level Theory* (pp. 287–305). New York: Academic Press.

Bryson, A., Forth, J., & Stokes, L. (2014). *Does worker wellbeing affect workplace performance?* Department for Business, Innovation and Skills, UK Government, London, UK.

Cantril, H. (1965). *The pattern of human concerns.* New Brunswick.

Carr, D., Freedman, V. A., Cornman, J. C., & Schwarz, N. (2014). Happy marriage, happy life? Marital quality and subjective well being in later life. *Journal of Marriage and Family, 76*(5), 930–948.

Carver, C. S., & Scheier, M. F. (2014). Dispositional optimism. *Trends in Cognitive Sciences, 18*(6), 293–299. CBI-AXA (2007). *Annual Absence and Labour Turnover Survey.*

Chin, G. (2014). Working from home can work well. *Science, 346*(6215), 1339–1340.

Christian, M. S., Garza, A. S., & Slaughter, J. E. (2011). Work engagement: A quantitative review and test of its relations with task and contextual performance. *Personnel Psychology, 64*(1), 89–136.

Clark, A. E. (2003). Unemployment as a social norm: Psychological evidence from panel data. *Journal of Labor Economics, 21*(2), 323–351.

Cooperrider, D. L., & Srivastva, S. (2013). A contemporary commentary on appreciative inquiry in organizational life. *Organizational Generativity: The Appreciative Inquiry Summit and a Scholarship of Transformation, 4,* 3.

Cooper, C. L. (2014). Introduction. In F. A. Huppert & C. L. Cooper (Eds.). *Wellbeing: A complete reference guide, interventions and policies to enhance wellbeing* (*Vol. 6*): *Interventions and policies to enhance wellbeing.* Hoboken, NJ: Wiley.

Costa, P. L., Passos, A. M., & Bakker, A. B. (2014). Team work engagement: A model of emergence. *Journal of Occupational and Organizational Psychology, 87*(2), 414–436.

Crawford, E. R., LePine, J. A., & Rich, B. L. (2010). Linking job demands and resources to employee engagement and burnout: a theoretical extension and meta-analytic test. *Journal of Applied Psychology, 95*(5), 834.

Crawford, E. R., Rich, B. L., Buckman, B., & Bergeron, J. (2014). The antecedents and drivers of employee engagement. In C. Truss, R. Delbridge, E. Soane, K. Alfes, & A. Shantz (Eds.), *Employee engagement in theory and practice* (pp. 57–81). London: Routledge.

Croxford, B. (2014). Air quality and wellbeing. Wellbeing. 2:4:20:1–10. Hoboken: Wiley.

Csikszentmihalyi, M. (2014). The concept of flow. In *Flow and the foundations of positive psychology.* Dordrecht, The Netherlands: Springer.

Cummins, R. A. (2003). Normative life satisfaction: Measurement issues and a homeostatic model. *Social Indicators Research, 64,* 225–256.

Dawkins, S., Martin, A., Scott, J., & Sanderson, K. (2013). Building on the positives: A psychometric review and critical analysis of the construct of psychological capital. *Journal of Occupational and Organizational Psychology, 86*(3), 348–370.

Deci, E. L., & Ryan, R. M. (2012). Motivation, personality, and development within embedded social contexts: An overview of self-determination theory. In *The oxford handbook of human motivation* (pp. 85–107). Oxford, UK: Oxford University Press.

Diener, E. (1984). Subjective well-being. *Psychological Bulletin, 95*(3), 542–575.

Diener, E., & Oishi, S. (2000). Money and happiness: Income and subjective well-being across nations. In *Culture and subjective well-being* (pp. 185–218). Cambridge, MA: MIT Press.

Diener, E., & Seligman, M. E. (2004). Beyond money toward an economy of well-being. *Psychological Science in the Public Interest, 5*(1), 1–31.

Diener, E., Inglehart, R., & Tay, L. (2013). Theory and validity of life satisfaction scales. *Social Indicators Research, 112*(3), 497–527.

Diener, E., Suh, E. M., Lucas, R. E., & Smith, H. L. (1999). Subjective well-being: Three decades of progress. *Psychological Bulletin, 125,* 276–302.

Diener, E., Wirtz, D., Tov, W., Kim-Prieto, C., Choi, D. W., Oishi, S., et al. (2010). New well-being measures: Short scales to assess flourishing and positive and negative feelings. *Social Indicators Research, 97*(2), 143–156.

Di Tella, R., & MacCulloch, R. (2008). Gross national happiness as an answer to the Easterlin paradox? *Journal of Development Economics, 86*(1), 22–42.

Di Tella, R., MacCulloch, R. J., & Oswald, A. J. (2013). The macroeconomics of happiness. *Review of Economics and Statistics, 85*(4), 809–827.

Dittmar, H., Bond, R., Hurst, M., & Kasser, T. (2014). The relationship between materialism and personal well-being: A meta-analysis. *Journal of Personality and Social Psychology, 107*(5), 879.

Easterlin, R. A. (1974). Does economic growth improve the human lot? In P. A. David & M. W. Reder (Eds.), *Nations and households in economic growth: Essays in honor of Moses Abramovitz.* New York: Academic Press.

Easterlin, R. A., Angelescu, L., & Zweig, J. S. (2011). The impact of modern economic growth on urban-rural differences in subjective well-being. *World Development, 39*(12), 2187–2198.

Easterlin, R. A., Morgan, R., Switek, M., & Wang, F. (2012). China's life satisfaction, 1990–2010. *Proceedings of the National Academy of Sciences, 109*(25), 9775–9780.

Echebarria Echabe, A. (2014). System-justifying beliefs and political disaffection. *Journal of Applied Social Psychology, 44*(3), 234–240.

Eger, R. J., & Maridal, J. H. (2015). A statistical meta-analysis of the wellbeing literature. *International Journal of Wellbeing, 5*(2), 45–74.

Eschleman, K. J., Bowling, N. A., & Judge, T. A. (2015). The dispositional basis of attitudes: A replication and extension of Hepler and Albarracín (2013). *Journal of Personality and Social Psychology, 108*(5), 1–15.

Evans, G. W., Wells, N. M., Moch, A. (2003). Housing and mental health: A review of the evidence and a methodological and conceptual critique. *Journal of Social Issues, 59*(3), 475–500.

Flavin, P., Pacek, A. C., & Radcliff, B. (2011). State intervention and subjective well-being in advanced industrial democracies. *Politics and Policy, 39*(2), 251–269.

Fletcher, L., & Robinson, D. (2013). Measuring and understanding employee engagement. In *Employee engagement in theory and practice* (p. 273). London, UK: Routledge.

Flinders, M. (2014). Explaining democratic disaffection: Closing the expectations gap. *Governance, 27*(1), 1–8.

Flink, I. K., Smeets, E., Bergbom, S., & Peters, M. L. (2015). Happy despite pain: Pilot study of a positive psychology intervention for patients with chronic pain. *Scandinavian Journal of Pain, 7,* 71–79.

Foresight Mental Capital and Wellbeing Project. (2008). Mental capital and wellbeing: Making the most of ourselves in the 21st century. *Final project report—Executive summary*. London: The Government Office for Science.

Fredrickson, B. L. (2013). Positive emotions broaden and build. *Advances in Experimental Social Psychology, 47,* 1–53.

Frey, B. S., & Stutzer, A. (2005). Beyond outcomes: Measuring procedural utility. *Oxford Economic Papers, 57*(1), 90–111.

Fryer, D., & Payne, R. (1984). Proactive behaviour in unemployment: Findings and implications. *Leisure Studies, 3*(3), 273–295.

Gatenby, M., Rees, C., Soane, E., & Truss, C. (2009). *Employee engagement in context*. London: Chartered Institute of Personnel and Development.

Guest, D. (2014). Employee engagement: A sceptical analysis. *Journal of Organizational Effectiveness: People and Performance, 1*(2), 141–156.

Hackman, J. R., & Oldham, G. R. (1976). Motivation through the design of work: Test of a theory. *Organizational Behavior and Human Performance, 16*(2), 250–279.

Halbesleben, J. R. (2010). A meta-analysis of work engagement: Relationships with burnout, demands, resources, and consequences. *Work Engagement: A Handbook of Essential Theory and Research, 8,* 102–117.

Haller, M., & Hadler, M. (2006). How social relations and structures can produce happiness and unhappiness: An international comparative analysis. *Social Indicators Research, 75*(2), 169–216.

Halpern, D. (2008). An evidence-based approach to building happiness. In J. Wernick (Ed.), *Building happiness*. London: Black Dog Publishing.

Harter, J. K., Schmidt, F. L., Killham, E. A., & Agrawal, S. (2009). *Q12 meta-analysis: The relationship between engagement at work and organizational outcomes*. Washington, DC: The Gallup Organization.

Headey, B., & Wearing, A. (1989). Personality, life events, and subjective well-being: Toward a dynamic equilibrium model. *Journal of Personality and Social Psychology, 57*(4), 731.

Heger, B. K. (2007). Linking the employment value proposition (EVP) to employee engagement and business outcomes: Preliminary findings from a linkage research pilot study. *Organization Development Journal, 25*(2), 121–133.

Helliwell, J. F., & Huang, H. (2014). New measures of the costs of unemployment: Evidence from the subjective well-being of 3.3 million Americans. *Economic Inquiry, 52*(4), 1485–1502.

Hervás, G., & Vázquez, C. (2013). Construction and validation of a measure of integrative well-being in seven languages: The Pemberton happiness index. *Health Qual Life Outcomes, 11*(1), 66.

Herzberg, F., & Mausner, B. Snyderman. (1959). *The motivation to work*. New York: Wiley.

Hicks, S., Tinkler, L., & Allin, P. (2013). Measuring subjective well-being and its potential role in policy: Perspectives from the UK office for national statistics. *Social Indicators Research, 114*(1), 73–86.

Hoffman, G., Morton, A., & Renton, D. (2008). Local government: A pro-active partner in civic engagement. In *Proceedings of the 7th Global Forum on Reinventing Government*, 26–29 June 2007. Newstead, QLD, Australia: Local Government Association of Queensland.

Hone, L. C., Jarden, A., Schofield, G. M., & Duncan, S. (2014). Measuring flourishing: The impact of operational definitions on the prevalence of high levels of wellbeing. *International Journal of Wellbeing, 4*(1), 62–90.

Huppert, F. A. (2014). The state of wellbeing science. In F. A. Huppert & C. L. Cooper (Eds.). *Wellbeing: A complete reference guide, interventions and policies to enhance wellbeing (vol. 6): Interventions and policies to enhance wellbeing.* Chichester: Wiley.

Huppert, F. A., & So, T. T. (2013). Flourishing across Europe: Application of a new conceptual framework for defining well-being. *Social Indicators Research, 110*(3), 837–861.

Ichilov, O. (2013). *Citizenship and citizenship education in a changing world.* London, UK: Routledge.

Inceoglu, I., & Warr, P. (2012). Personality and job engagement. *Journal of Personnel Psychology, 10*(4), 177–181.

Inglehart, R., & Klingemann, H. D. (2000). Genes, culture, democracy, and happiness. In *Culture and subjective well-being* (pp. 165–183). Cambridge, MA: MIT Press.

Inglehart, R., Foa, R., Peterson, C., & Welzel, C. (2008). Development, freedom, and rising happiness: A global perspective (1981–2007). *Perspectives on Psychological Science, 3*(4), 264–285.

Jahoda, M. (1958). Current concepts of positive mental health. In *Joint commission on mental health and illness monograph series* (Vol. 1). New York: Basic Books.

James, O. (2009). Evaluating the expectations disconfirmation and expectations anchoring approaches to citizen satisfaction with local public services. *Journal of Public Administration Research and Theory, 19*(1), 107–123.

Jeffrey, K., Mahonay, S., Michaelson, J., & Abdullah, S. (2014). *Wellbeing at work: A review of the literature.* New Economics Foundation. http://www.neweconomics.org.

Jorm, A. F., & Ryan, S. M. (2014). Cross-national and historical differences in subjective well-being. *International Journal of Epidemiology, 43*(2), 330–340.

Karlsson, E. (2015). *Value co-creation and wellbeing in interaction-employee perspective: An empirical study on Göteborgs Färdtjänst.* Masters thesis, Service Management, Karlstad Business School.

Kahn, W. A. (1990). Psychological conditions of personal engagement and disengagement at work. *Academy of Management Journal, 33*(4), 692–724.

Kahn, W., & Heapy, E. D. (2014). Relational contexts of personal engagement at work. In C. Truss, R. Delbridge, E. Soane, K. Alfes, & A. Shantz (Eds.), *Employee engagement in theory and practice* (pp. 163–179). London: Routledge.

Kahneman, D., Krueger, A. B., Schkade, D. A., Schwarz, N., & Stone, A. A. (2004). A survey method for characterizing daily life experience: The day reconstruction method. *Science, 306*(5702), 1776–1780.

Keenoy, T. (2013). Engagement: A murmuration of objects. In C. Truss, R. Delbridge, E. Soane, K. Alfes, & A. Shantz (Eds.), *Employee engagement in theory and practice* (pp. 198–218). London: Routledge.

Keyes, C. L. (2002). The mental health continuum: From languishing to flourishing in life. *Journal of Health and Social Behavior*, 207–222.

Keyes, C. L., Myers, J. M., & Kendler, K. S. (2010). On mental well-being. *American Journal of Public Health, 100*(12), 2379–2384.

Kim, H. J., Shin, K. H., & Swanger, N. (2009). Burnout and engagement: A comparative analysis using the big five personality dimensions. *International Journal of Hospitality Management, 28*(1), 96–104.

Kok, G., Den Boer, D. J., De Vries, H., Gerards, H. J. H., & Mudde, A. N. (2014). Self-efficacy and attribution theory. In *Self-efficacy: thought control of action* (p. 245). Washington, DC: Hemisphere.

Kotakorpi, K., & Laamanen, J. P. (2010). Welfare state and life satisfaction: Evidence from public health care. *Economica, 77*(307), 565–583.

Kramer, P., & Bressan, P. (2015). Humans as superorganisms. *Perspectives on Psychological Science, 10*(4), 464–481.

Langelaan, S., Bakker, A. B., Van Doornen, L. J., & Schaufeli, W. B. (2006). Burnout and work engagement: Do individual differences make a difference? *Personality and Individual Differences, 40*(3), 521–532.

Lawrence, D., Hafekost, J., Hull, P., Mitrou, F., & Zubrick, S. R. (2013). Smoking, mental illness and socioeconomic disadvantage: Analysis of the Australian National survey of mental health and wellbeing. *BMC Public Health, 13*(1), 462.

Lavine, M. (2012). Positive deviance: A method and metaphor for learning from the uncommon. In *The Oxford handbook of positive organizational scholarship*. Oxford: Oxford University Press.

Lee, K., & Allen, N. J. (2002). Organizational citizenship behavior and workplace deviance: The role of affect and cognitions. *Journal of Applied Psychology, 87*(1), 131.

Linley, P. A., Maltby, J., Wood, A. M., Osborne, G., & Hurling, R. (2009). Measuring happiness: The higher-order factor structure of subjective and psychological well-being measures. *Personality and Individual Differences, 47*, 878–884.

Lorenc, T., Clayton, S., Neary, D., Whitehead, M., Petticrew, M., Thomson, H., et al. (2012). Crime, fear of crime, environment, and mental health and wellbeing: Mapping review of theories and causal pathways. *Health and Place, 18*(4), 757–765.

Lucas, R. E., & Donnellan, M. B. (2012). Estimating the reliability of single item life satisfaction measures: Results from four national panel studies. *Social Indicators Research, 105,* 323–331.

Luthans, F., Youssef, C. M., & Avolio, B. J. (2007). Psychological capital: Investing and developing positive organizational behavior. In *Positive organizational behavior* (pp. 9–24). Thousand Oaks, CA: Sage.

Luhmann, M., Hofmann, W., Eid, M., & Lucas, R. E. (2012). Subjective wellbeing and adaptation to life events: A meta-analysis. *Journal of Personality and Social Psychology, 102*(3), 592.

Lyubomirsky, S., Sheldon, K. M., & Schkade, D. (2005). Pursuing happiness: The architecture of sustainable change. *Review of General Psychology, 9*(2), 111–131.

Ma, Q., Jin, J., Meng, L., & Shen, Q. (2014). The dark side of monetary incentive: How does extrinsic reward crowd out intrinsic motivation. *Neuroreport, 25*(3), 194–198.

MacLeod, D., & Clarke, N. (2009). *Engaging for success: enhancing performance through employee engagement: A report to government.* Engage for Success.

MacLeod, D., & Clarke, N. (2011). *The evidence: Wellbeing and employee engagement.* Engage for Success. http://www.engageforsuccess.org/wp-content/uploads/2014/05/wellbeing-and-engagement-04June2014-Final.pdf.

Malcolm, E., Evans-Lacko, S., Little, K., Henderson, C., & Thornicroft, G. (2013). The impact of exercise projects to promote mental wellbeing. *Journal of Mental Health, 22*(6), 519–527.

Mancini, A. D., Bonanno, G. A., & Clark, A. E. (2015). Stepping off the hedonic treadmill. *Journal of Individual Differences, 32*(3), 144–152.

Maslow, A. (1955). *Deficiency motivation and growth motivation.* Lincoln, NE: University of Nebraska Press.

May, D. R., Gilson, R. L., & Harter, L. M. (2004). The psychological conditions of meaningfulness, safety and availability and the engagement of the human spirit at work. *Journal of Occupational and Organizational Psychology, 77*(1), 11–37.

McGregor, D. (1960). Theory X and theory Y. *Organization Theory,* 358–374.

Mellander, C., Florida, R., & Rentfrow, J. (2012). The creative class, post-industrialism and the happiness of nations. *Cambridge Journal of Regions, Economy and Society, 5*(1), 31–43.

Meyer, J. P., Stanley, L. J., & Parfyonova, N. M. (2012). Employee commitment in context: The nature and implication of commitment profiles. *Journal of Vocational Behavior, 80*(1), 1–16.

Michaelson, J., Mahony, S., & Schifferes, J. (2012). *Measuring well-being. A guide for practitioners.* London: New Economics Foundation.

Milner, A., Page, A., & Lamontagne, A. D. (2014). Cause and effect in studies on unemployment, mental health and suicide: A meta-analytic and conceptual review. *Psychological Medicine, 44*(05), 909–917.

Newman, D. A., Joseph, D. L., & Hulin, C. L. (2010). Job attitudes and employee engagement: Considering the attitude 'A-factor'. In *The handbook of employee engagement: Perspectives, issues, research, and practice* (pp. 43–61). Cheltenham, UK: Edward Elgar Publishing.

Newman, D. B., Tay, L., & Diener, E. (2014). Leisure and subjective well-being: A model of psychological mechanisms as mediating factors. *Journal of Happiness Studies, 15*(3), 555–578.

Oishi, S., Kesebir, S., & Diener, E. (2011). Income inequality and happiness. *Psychological Science, 22*(9), 1095–1100.

O'Neill, B. S., & Arendt, L. A. (2008). Psychological climate and work attitudes: the importance of telling the right story. *Journal of Leadership and Organizational Studies, 14*(4), 353–370.

Ouweneel, E., Le Blanc, P. M., Schaufeli, W. B., & van Wijhe, C. I. (2012). Good morning, good day: A diary study on positive emotions, hope, and work engagement. *Human Relations, 65*(9), 1129–1154.

Peterson, C., & Seligman, M. E. (2004). *Character strengths and virtues: A handbook and classification.* Oxford: Oxford University Press.

Pluess, M. (2015). Genetics of psychological well-being: Current state and future directions. In M. Pluess (Ed.), *Genetics of psychological well-being: The role of heritability and genetics in positive psychology* (pp. 266–275). Oxford: Oxford University Press.

Purcell, J. (2014). Can employee voice and participation unlock employee engagement? *Insights: Melbourne Business and Economics, 15,* 23–30.

Ratcliffe, J., Lester, L. H., Couzner, L., & Crotty, M. (2013). An assessment of the relationship between informal caring and quality of life in older community-dwelling adults-more positives than negatives? *Health and Social Care in the Community, 21*(1), 35–46.

Reio, T. G., & Sanders-Reio, J. (2011). Thinking about workplace engagement: Does supervisor and coworker incivility really matter? *Advances in Developing Human Resources, 13*(4), 462–478.

Rietveld, C. A., Cesarini, D., Benjamin, D. J., Koellinger, P. D., De Neve, J. E., Tiemeier, H., et al. (2013). Molecular genetics and subjective wellbeing. *Proceedings of the National Academy of Sciences, 110*(24), 9692–9697.

Robinson, D., Perryman, S., & Hayday, S. (2004). The drivers of employee engagement. (IES Report 408).

Rothbard, N. P., & Patil, S. V. (2012). Being there: Work engagement and positive organizational scholarship. In *The Oxford handbook of positive organizational scholarship* (pp. 56–68). Oxford: Oxford University Press.

Rothmann, S. (2014). Employee engagement in a cultural context. In C. Truss, R. Delbridge, E. Soane, K. Alfes, & A. Shantz (Eds.), *Employee engagement in theory and practice* (pp. 163–194). London: Routledge.

Ryan, R. M., & Deci, E. L. (2001). On happiness and human potentials: A review of research on hedonic and eudaimonic well-being. *Annual review of psychology, 52* (1), 141–166.

Ryff, C. D. (1989). Happiness is everything, or is it? Explorations on the meaning of psychological well-being. *Journal of Personality and Social Psychology, 57*(6), 1069.

Saks, A. M. (2006). Antecedents and consequences of employee engagement. *Journal of Managerial Psychology, 21*(7), 600–619.

Sarracino, F., & Bartolini, S. (2015). The dark side of Chinese growth: Declining social capital and well-being in times of economic boom. *World Development, 74,* 333–351.

Schaufeli, W. B. (2013). What is engagement? In C. Truss, K. Alfes, R. Delbridge, A. Shantz, & E. Soane (Eds.). *Employee engagement in theory and practice.* London: Routledge.

Schaufeli, W. B., & Bakker, A. B. (2004). Job demands, job resources, and their relationship with burnout and engagement: A multi-sample study. *Journal of Organizational Behavior, 25*(3), 293–315.

Schaufeli, W. B., Salanova, M., González-Romá, V., & Bakker, A. B. (2002). The measurement of engagement and burnout: A two sample confirmatory factor analytic approach. *Journal of Happiness studies, 3*(1), 71–92.

Schaufeli, W. B., Bakker, A. B., & Salanova, M. (2006). The measurement of work engagement with a short questionnaire a cross-national study. *Educational and psychological measurement, 66*(4), 701–716.

Schaufeli, W. B., Taris, T. W., & Van Rhenen, W. (2008). Workaholism, burnout, and work engagement: Three of a kind or three different kinds of employee well-being? *Applied Psychology, 57*(2), 173–203.

Schimmack, U. (2008). The structure of subjective well-being. In M. Eid & R. J. Larsen (Eds.), *The science of subjective well-being* (pp. 97–123). New York: Guilford Press.

Schotanus-Dijkstra, M., Pieterse, M. E., Drossaert, C. H. C., Westerhof, G. J., de Graaf, R., ten Have, M., & Bohlmeijer, E. T. (2015). What factors are associated with flourishing? Results from a large representative national sample. *Journal of Happiness Studies,* 1–20.

Scott-Jackson, W., Druck, S., Mortimer, T., & Viney, J. (2011). HR's global impact: Building strategic differentiating capabilities. *Strategic HR Review, 10*(4), 33–39.

Scott-Jackson, W. B. (2002). *Individual change competence: Development of a strategic resource.* Strategy World Congress: Oxford.

Seligman, M. E. (2012). *Flourish: A visionary new understanding of happiness and well-being.* Simon and Schuster.

Seligman, M. E., & Csikszentmihalyi, M. (2000). Positive psychology: An introduction. *American Psychological, 55*(1), 5.

Sen, A. (1993). Capability and well-being. In D. N. Hausman (Ed.). *The philosophy of economics* (pp. 30–53). Cambridge: Cambridge University Press.

Shantz, A., Schoenberg, J., & Chan, C. (2013). Relevance of employee engagement across cultures from the perspective of HR professional associations. In C. Truss,

R. Delbridge, E. Soane, K. Alfes, & A. Shantz (Eds.), *Employee engagement in theory and practice* (pp. 253–272). London: Routledge.

Shuck, B. (2011). Four emerging perspectives of employee engagement: An integrative literature review. *Human Resource Development Review, 10*(1), 1–25.

Shuck, B., & Reio, T. G. (2014). Employee engagement and well-being a moderation model and implications for practice. *Journal of Leadership and Organizational Studies, 21*(1), 43–58.

Shuck, B., & Rocco, T. S. (2014). Human resource development and employee engagement. In C. Truss, R. Delbridge, E. Soane, K. Alfes, & A. Shantz (Eds.), *Employee engagement in theory and practice* (pp. 116–130). London: Routledge.

Shuck, B., & Wollard, K. (2010). Employee engagement and HRD: A seminal review of the foundations. *Human Resource Development Review, 9*(1), 89–110.

Siedlecki, K. L., Salthouse, T. A., Oishi, S., & Jeswani, S. (2014). The Relationship between social support and subjective well-being across age. *Social Indicators Research, 117*(2), 561–576.

Simbula, S. (2010). Daily fluctuations in teachers' well-being: A diary study using the job demands-resources model. *Anxiety, Stress, and Coping, 23*(5), 563–584.

Sonnentag, S., & Fritz, C. (2015). Recovery from job stress: The stressor-detachment model as an integrative framework. *Journal of Organizational Behavior, 36*(S1), S72–S103.

Sparrow, P. (2014). Strategic HRM and employee engagement. In C. Truss, R. Delbridge, E. Soane, K. Alfes, & A. Shantz (Eds.), *Employee engagement in theory and practice* (p. 99). London: Routledge.

Sparrow, P., & Balain, S. (2010). Engaging HR strategists: Do the logics match the realities? In *Handbook of employee engagement: Perspectives, issues, research and practice* (p. 283). Cheltenham: Elgar.

Stairs, M., & Galpin, M. (2010). Positive engagement: From employee engagement to workplace happiness. In *Oxford handbook of positive psychology and work* (pp. 155–172). Oxford: Oxford University Press.

Stankiewicz, J., & Moczulska, M. (2012). Cultural conditioning of employees' engagement. *Management, 16*(2), 72.

Strom, D. L., Sears, K. L., & Kelly, K. M. (2014). Work engagement the roles of organizational justice and leadership style in predicting engagement among employees. *Journal of Leadership and Organizational Studies, 21*(1), 71–82.

Stutzer, A., & Frey, B. S. (2012). *Recent developments in the economics of happiness: A selective overview* (IZA Discussion Paper 7078).

Sweetman, D., & Luthans, F. (2010). The power of positive psychology: Psychological capital and work engagement. In *Work engagement: A handbook of essential theory and research* (pp. 54–68). New York: Psychology Press.

Tausch, A. (2011). In praise of inequality? 'Happy planet' performance and its determinants. *Australian and New Zealand Journal of Public Health, 35*(6), 572.

Taylor, T. E. (2015). The markers of wellbeing: A basis for a theory-neutral approach. *International Journal of Wellbeing, 5*(2).

Tennant, R., Hiller, L., Fishwick, R., Platt, S., Joseph, S., Weich, S., et al. (2007). The warwick-edinburgh mental wellbeing scale (WEMWBS): Development and UK validation. *Health and Quality of Life Outcomes, 5,* 63–76.

Towers Watson. (2014). *The 2014 global workforce study.* Towers Watson.

Truss, C., Delbridge, R., Soane, E., Alfes, K., & Shantz, A. (2014). Introduction. In C. Truss, R. Delbridge, E. Soane, K. Alfes, & A. Shantz (Eds.), *Employee engagement in theory and practice* (pp. 1–10). London: Routledge.

Tsai, M. C., Dwyer, R. E., & Tsay, R. M. (2014). Does financial assistance really assist? The impact of debt on wellbeing, health behavior and self-concept in Taiwan. *Social Indicators Research,* 1–21.

Tyler, N. (2014). Transport and wellbeing. *Wellbeing: A Complete Reference Guide, 2* (4), 1–34.

Ulrich, D. (1997). Measuring human resources: An overview of practice and a prescription for results. *Human Resource Management, 36*(3), 303–320.

Van Praag, B. M. S., & Ferrer-I-Carbonell, A. (2008). *Happiness quantified: A satisfaction calculus approach.* Oxford: Oxford University Press.

Varelius, J. (2004). Objective explanations of individual well-being. *Journal of Happiness Studies, 5*(1), 73–91.

Veenhoven, R. (2014). Happiness adjusted life years (HALY). In A. C. Michalos (Ed.). *Encyclopedia of quality of life and well-being research.* Dordrecht: Springer (Springer Reference Series, 2641–2643).

Veenhoven, R., & Vergunst, F. (2014). The Easterlin illusion: Economic growth does go with greater happiness. *International Journal of Happiness and Development, 1*(4), 311–343.

Wagner, R., & Harter, J. K. (2006). *12: The elements of great managing.* New York: Gallup Press.

Warkotsch, J. (2015). *Bread, freedom, human dignity: The political economy of protest mobilization in Egypt and Tunisia.* Doctoral dissertation, Department of Political and Social Sciences, European University Institute, Florence.

Watson, T. S., & Skinner, C. H. (2001). Functional behavioral assessment: Principles, procedures, and future directions. *School Psychology Review, 30*(2), 156–172.

Watson, D., Clark, L. A., & Tellegen, A. (1988). Development and validation of brief measures of positive and negative affect: The PANAS scales. *Journal of Personality and Social Psychology, 54*(6), 1063.

Weigl, M., Hornung, S., Parker, S. K., Petru, R., Glaser, J., & Angerer, P. (2010). Work engagement accumulation of task, social, personal resources: A three-wave structural equation model. *Journal of Vocational Behavior, 77*(1), 140–153.

Winefield, H. R., Boyd, C., & Winefield, A. H. (2014). Work-family conflict and well-being in university employees. *The Journal of Psychology, 148*(6), 683–697.

Winkler, S., König, C. J., & Kleinmann, M. (2012). New insights into an old debate: Investigating the temporal sequence of commitment and performance at the business unit level. *Journal of Occupational and Organizational Psychology, 85* (3), 503–522.

Wood, C. (2013). *One year on. A review of the cultural legacy of the paralympics.* London: Demos.

Wrzesniewski, A., & Dutton, J. E. (2001). Crafting a job: Revisioning employees as active crafters of their work. *Academy of Management Review, 26*(2), 179–201.

Xanthopoulou, D., Bakker, A. B., Demerouti, E., & Schaufeli, W. B. (2009). Reciprocal relationships between job resources, personal resources, and work engagement. *Journal of Vocational behavior, 74*(3), 235–244.

Youssef-Morgan, C., & Bockorny, K. (2013). *Engagement in the context of positive psychology.* C. Truss, R. Delbridge, K. Alfes, A. Shantz, & E. Soane (Eds.). London: Routledge.

World Health Organization. (1990). International Classification of Diseases Chapter V (F): Mental and Behavioural Disorders (including Disorders of Psychological Development). World Health Organization.

Zavisca, J., & Hout, M. (2005). *Does money buy happiness in unhappy Russia? Berkeley Program in Eurasian and East European Studies.* UC Berkeley: Berkeley Program in Soviet and Post-Soviet Studies.

Zhu, Y., Liu, C., Guo, B., Zhao, L., & Lou, F. (2015). The impact of emotional intelligence on work engagement of registered nurses: The mediating role of organisational justice. *Journal of Clinical Nursing., 24*(15/16), 2115–2124.

3

PACE: The Process of Active Committed Enthusiasm

3.1 PACE: What Is It?

As summarised in the previous section, there has been a substantial volume of academic research into well-being, as well as engagement, most often treated as separate phenomena. This book, however, has a practical objective to help political and organisational leaders to engender high levels of active well-being, happiness and engagement in their staff or citizens.

To that end, and building on those substantial bodies of research, we have developed the process of active committed enthusiasm (PACE), which can be used at any level of detail, from a country down to an individual, so that the reader or practitioner can decide for him or herself how to achieve the greatest impact and outcome. For instance, they could decide that when considering an outcome such as productivity, it would be appropriate to consider the impact of a company's working practices or leadership support, or alternatively, it is possible to 'drill down' into the individual context and perhaps address a specific causal factor (e.g. recognition by a leader or indeed specific personality factors that might be involved). The PACE model is versatile, in that it provides a framework not only within which one can model causes and outcomes, but also allows the measurement or estimation of the significance of a relevant causal factor.

In spite of the detail that the PACE model can highlight, because of the causal factors which can affect behaviour and outcomes, this approach represents a simplified model, although it will provide alternatives based on the

© The Author(s) 2018
W. Scott-Jackson and A. Mayo, *Transforming Engagement,
Happiness and Well-Being*, DOI 10.1007/978-3-319-56145-5_3

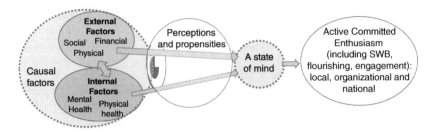

Fig. 3.1 The process of active committed enthusiasm (PACE)—high level

best available data. It enables a holistic view, whilst at the same time modelling the associations as well as the strength and interdependence of those
associations, whilst potentially considering a substantial set of variables
(Fig. 3.1).

In its simplest form, an example of the PACE model could be shown as
follows.

3.1.1   Related Constructs in the Pace Framework

We have already reviewed and considered engagement and well-being in
previous chapters, and whilst 'majoring' on defining the process of active
committed enthusiasm, we will also consider and review some closely related
concepts, such as 'flourishing' and 'citizenship behaviour'. The previous
research methodologies of all of the concepts that we consider have tended to
isolate individual constructs so that their statistical association and significance could be established and, often, causal links assumed, implied or
(rarely) demonstrated. Not only has that succeeded in exposing some key
factors but it has also helped us to understand that almost anything can have
an effect on well-being, both negative and positive. The same applies to
engagement and flourishing with all factors 'interlocking' and impacting, as
well is being impacted by, well-being.

That has always created difficulties at national and even organisational level
as far as creating coherent interventions in order to affect well-being. It is the
sheer complexity of the interdependent issues which creates that basic difficulty. Nevertheless, pragmatic solutions have been found, and some have
proved extremely successful, although inevitably there has been some criticism of such approaches. For instance, the single-item life satisfaction scale
which aims to explain such a vast complex system of subjective well-being at
national level is one example. The use of Gallup Q^{12} at organisational or
country level is another.

Much of the research has been carried out in what can only be described as relative isolation, especially when dealing with well-being, which is often focused on national and individual well-being or engagement primarily focused on an organisational context.

Well-being is a *passive* state of satisfaction, and the concept has been developed within socio-political and psychological disciplines.

Engagement on the other hand has developed primarily within the management and motivation disciplines and is an *active* state, which is considered necessary to achieve organisational objectives, such as performance.

Well-being is a key factor in many models of engagement, whereas engagement is considered a mere component in many models of well-being. Shuck and Reio (2014) found a significant correlation between high engagement and high psychological well-being and personal accomplishment. The corollary of that finding was that low engagement had an association with low well-being, emotional exhaustion and depersonalisation. As a practical example, the UK Civil Service's employee engagement programme is a combination of both performance and well-being goals having been 'established to help drive productivity and improve employee health and well-being across the Civil Service' (Civil Service UK 2015).

We suggest that the construct and approach to engagement are valid at both national and organisational level. We have found that in national and international contexts, the approach generally appears to be more suitable for the development of passive well-being, rather than an active state of engagement, which from a practical point of view is potentially more desirable. The well-being of the nation's population is not only intuitively desirable, but both the individuals and the government would benefit from the subsequent engagement of its citizens, which would then go on to be translated into enthusiastic involvement and contribution. This has become far more important, especially in recent years where, through social media, for instance, issues and problems are communicated constantly and not only a nation's views and outlook, but the 'mood' of groups or even individuals can be spread and have impact extremely rapidly.

Figure 3.2 shows described states of well-being and engagement as quadrants along two axes: Active versus Passive and Negative versus Positive.

The worst scenario for a country or an organisation is to be found in the top left corner of the diagram and it is the active/negative, which ultimately can lead to revolution or civil disobedience, whereas the opposite bottom right, which represents passive/positive, would seem equally disenfranchised, but in a passive way or, to put it another way they could be regarded as 'basking in well-being'. The ideal state is represented by the top right, which

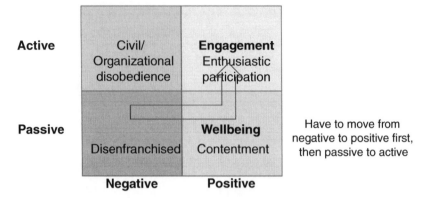

Fig. 3.2 National and organisational enthusiasm—from negative passive to positive active

is enthusiastic participation through a process of active committed enthusiasm (PACE).

From a leader's perspective, whether national or organisational, the concepts of well-being and engagement become very similar in the sense of active committed enthusiasm, and the goals of improving well-being and engagement are also similar, that is to say maximising the active participation and contribution of citizens and employees.

This approach also suggests that the most efficient path for change from a passively negative state is to increase positivism. That is because if the level of activism increases first, then the more dangerous active/negative will follow. The modern development of social media, where vast numbers of people can be 'nudged' to activism, makes it even more important that leaders maximise PACE correctly and in the right order, in order to create the environment and potential for the greater good.

PACE is a useful summarising and pragmatic framework and gives leaders of any sort a process perspective which clarifies the links between causes and outcomes, which is important because the system of process relationships, including engagement and well-being, is often conflated in what can only be referred to as a confusion between cause, process, component and outcome. PACE can also be useful in that it considers outcomes, which is useful to organisations because, whether at national or organisational level, systems tend to be goal oriented.

Seligman (2012) developed the concept of 'flourishing' within the field of positive psychology, which has become a dynamic and invaluable body of research and theory, which is only now being harnessed for enhancing the quality of life as well as individual experiences. This again is located within

PACE in the context of its primary objective and target, in which PACE is directed towards the achievement of both organisational and national objectives.

'Citizenship' is another related concept and spans all types of organisation, ranging from national to organisational. Citizenship is a more active and goal-oriented concept than well-being alone and although sometimes considered to be a relatively passive state of 'belonging' whereas national identity, is more often described as a more active state of enthusiasm.

Organisational citizenship behaviour (OCB) in a management context is again considered to be a more active and pro-social factor with organisational benefits. Pierce and Aguinis (2013) suggest that the needs of an organisation differ in some measure to the interests of society and they introduced the concept of detrimental citizenship behaviour which on occasion can be functional for an organisation, but dysfunctional for the wider society. The converse also applies, whereby every individual within an organisation acts to benefit society but to the detriment of the organisation. See Fig. 3.3:

There are many reasons for 'deviant' behaviour, ranging from self-interest to a positive intention to damage the organisation, for instance, in revenge for a sacking.

An organisation is always looking for increased productivity and other benefits for itself; therefore, any organisational engagement programme will almost certainly be aiming for active enthusiasm. With that in mind, however, it could be argued that a valid objective for national well-being, in the

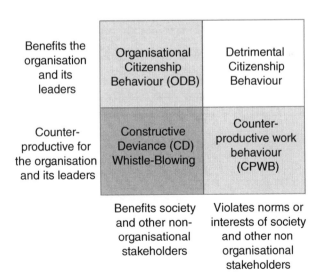

Fig. 3.3 Citizenship behaviour for the benefit of the organisation and/or society

short term, might be to have a passively satisfied population, as opposed to a passively dissatisfied population or, worse still, an actively dissatisfied population.

A country's economic and social success largely depends on the participation and effort of the population in various fields, such as employment, consumption, entrepreneurship. In addition, what is also required is the active enthusiasm of the people, for their organisation leaders, whether they are elected, appointed or inherited. Ultimately, the legitimacy of a leader, whether national or organisational, will require the active enthusiasm of the people. Therefore, a major goal for any government is exactly as it is for an organisation, active committed enthusiasm.

3.1.2 PACE and Different Cultures

If, as we have shown, an individual's personal characteristics impact on ACE through various causal factors plus their weights, it follows that cultural or national differences will also have a significant impact. The diagram (Fig. 3.4) adds cultural and identity aspects to the PACE framework, with this particular aspect of the framework becoming more and more important as more and more organisations are leading and managing businesses across several cultures, plus the concept of multi-culturalism is of increasing 'weight' as a result of immigration, leading to mixing of cultures and ethnicities within teams. In the GCC (Gulf Cooperation Countries) of the UAE, Saudi Arabia and Qatar, many people from almost every culture mix and work together in a region which has taken the pursuit of national happiness to an advanced level.

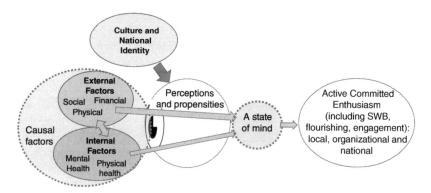

Fig. 3.4 The impact of culture and national identity on individual propensities and perceptions in the PACE framework

'Culture' in this context refers to the shared life and patterns of thinking of a group (Rothmann 2014). This concept is further complicated by the fact that there are groups within groups. For instance, one can look at a national culture, and although that will largely cascade down through the population, there are 'lower-level' identities such as families, clubs, associations and tribes as well as individuals themselves. Therefore, to appeal universally to a population, its leaders must be aware not only of the overall national culture, but an in-depth knowledge of the various variations in behaviour and thinking of any number of sub-cultures.

To date, most relevant research has been carried out in the West, within democratic political structures and privately owned companies with a strong emphasis on individualism (Rothman 2014), although more and more research is emanating from China, India and other emerging economies. Most psychological research has emanated in the same area with much of it being focused on Americans as subjects, and therefore, it is difficult to extrapolate globally, as Americans comprise less than 5% of the world's population (Arnett 2008).

3.1.2.1 Categorisations of National Culture

There have been several attempts at categorising national cultures which help to determine the impact of culture on the PACE framework: one of the most influential has been developed by Hofstede et al. (2010). However, even this study has been criticised (notably by Brewer and Venaik 2014). For instance, it can be said that because the framing culture is from a US perspective that can bias the results. Nevertheless, Hofstede's work does create a useful typology and consists of six dimensions of culture.

Hofstede

Power Distance (PDI)

This concerns the individuals' acceptance of the unequal distribution of power through a rigid hierarchy. In this context, authority is respected and considered to be legitimate, with titles and status being of paramount importance. For example, a country such as India is high on PDI, whereas Denmark and Austria are examples of low PDI countries. This variation does give an insight into the varying cultures and from that a different thinking within those cultures. For instance, in the USA, there is an often repeated phrase, which is that *anyone* can have the ambition to become the President of the USA. That concept will not be of any interest in high PDI countries such as India. The concept is completely alien to that particular culture. Nevertheless, a citizen in a high PDI country will still aspire to achieve a certain level of success and wealth, but that individual's ambitions within a PDI country will not include the same degree of hierarchic ambition.

In the context of PACE, that thought process has engagement implications, where, for instance, in a low PDI culture, individuals may find authority disengaging, whereas in a high PDI culture, authority and clear direction may be welcomed. And of course, the potential for progress up a hierarchy might be more engaging for an individual in a lower PDI culture because it is a definite possibility and therefore a legitimate cause for engagement.

Individualism Versus Collectivism (IDV)

An example of an individualistic culture may be one which consists of a loose-knit social structure in which individuals are only expected to take care of themselves and their immediate family, whereas in a collective society, the important unit is the group, whereby individuals would expect their in-group to look after them, in exchange for mutual loyalty and respect.

It is difficult to assess the degree to which individualism versus collectivism of natural culture correlates with SWB.

For instance, individualism correlates closely to other variables such as GDP, human rights and gender equality. That makes it difficult to separate out the specific impacting variable. As Triandis (2005) notes, there are cultural differences in how people evaluate life satisfaction and affect. There is evidence that individualism may correlate with SWB in high income societies (Jorm and Ryan 2014), especially in respect of life satisfaction rather than affect or emotional response.

In terms of PACE, an individual from a collective environment (whether country or organisation) will feel uncomfortable in an individualistic context and feel less psychologically safe, which is a key component of engagement. GDP per capita and individualism used to have a strong correlation, implying that individualism is either a cause or a condition for (or indeed outcome of) national wealth, as it is generally accepted that it is individual ambition, which ultimately drives success. On the other hand, the implication could be that a shift towards individualism is an inevitable consequence of increased wealth, whereas collectivism is only required where poor communities need mutual support in the absence of strong state-provided infrastructure mechanisms. However, that correlation has been challenged recently in, for instance, the resource-rich states of the GCC, where there are high GDP and huge wealth, but where collectivism is still the strong norm. That result could imply that perhaps recent and fast acquisition of wealth means that collectivism has not yet been overtaken by an unavoidable trend towards individualism, driven by inevitable changes in society as a result of that wealth. However, recent studies (Scott-Jackson and Michie 2014) indicate the retention of collectivist, relationship-focused cultures in some very wealthy states.

Masculinity Versus Femininity (MAS)

In most cultures, masculinity represents a concern for achievement, heroism, assertiveness, material rewards and competition, as opposed to a preference for cooperation, modesty and quality of life in a consensus society. This dichotomy is best represented by countries such as Japan and Austria which value assertiveness and material success plus power, whereas consensus societies such as Norway and Sweden value the quality of life, relationships, sensitivity and concern for others. This would suggest that from a PACE perspective, individual alignment with organisational values represented by MAS could be a key component of engagement and well-being.

Uncertainty Avoidance (UAI)

Uncertainty avoidance is the degree to which individual members of society are comfortable with uncertainty and ambiguity. Strong UAI suggests a rigid or controlled society with strong codes of belief and behaviour. Whereas an individual from a high UAI context might find a loosely constructed belief framework uncomfortable, an individual from a low UAI context will find a too tightly and constricting brief or task uncomfortable and will not find it engaging. Japan and Greece are examples of countries with a high UAI culture. They are characterised by not only high levels of anxiety, but low levels of tolerance of differences with deep-rooted and inflexible social norms and rules. On the other hand, countries such as Singapore, Switzerland and Denmark, which are low on UAI, are not threatened by difference and fewer social norms with more tolerance, but at the same time are more tolerant of deviant behaviour and thinking (Rothmann 2014).

PACE suggests alignment is an important factor in maximising well-being, engagement and citizenship behaviours.

Indulgence Versus restraint

Within the PACE framework, societies which are tolerant of free gratification of human drives, in other words, high indulgence cultures, will have immediate gratification as a powerful motivator, whereas the opposite would be true of a high restraint culture. Indulgence scores are higher in Latin American, parts of Africa and Europe but lower in East Asia and Eastern Europe, once again highlighting the important cultural differences when considering the PACE framework.

Long-term Versus Short-term Normative Orientation (LTO)

This dimension was subsequently devised as a result of analysis of the Chinese Values Survey (Bond 1998) and its correlations with the Hofstede findings. Long-term orientation societies are those which are essentially forward-looking and attach great value to the future whilst valuing persistence, saving and capacity for adaptation, as well as family longevity. Short-term orientation societies like to maintain strong links with the past, traditions and norms, and tend towards short-term spending, rather than saving, towards maintaining social values and seeking immediate gratification. In general terms, many Asian societies tend towards high LTO, whereas Anglo-American countries score low. Once again from a PACE point of view, any task or activity which challenges norms would be uncomfortable for an individual from a short-term orientation culture, whereas a traditional predictable role would be uncomfortable for someone from a long-term culture.

Once again from the PACE point of view, low LTO companies would tend to be focused on short-term profits, whereas high LTO would invest in the future for long-term success. As with many of Hofstede's dimensions, they can be applied individually, organisationally or nationally.

Correlations of Hofstede Dimensions with Well-Being Causal Factors

Hofstede et al. (2010) suggested that major and fast changes in wealth or organisational disruptions such as revolution or war can result in correspondingly fast changes in cultural dimensions, whereas normally these cultural dimensions are comparatively slow-changing. These dimensions correlate with other factors. For example, 'power distance' appears to correlate with income inequality and individualism with national wealth. These could both have been caused by rapid industrial development in the last century. Masculinity correlates negatively with money spent on social security. Uncertainty avoidance correlates with legal identity cards and long-term orientation. There are many other examples.

Global Leadership and Organisational Behaviour Effectiveness Survey

The GLOBE Study (House et al. 2004) specifically focused on leadership behaviours in different cultures and identified nine dimensions of culture.

Performance Orientation

An individual's active committed enthusiasm is likely to be impacted by their feelings towards the performance-based reward. This has obvious relationships with PACE and is a characteristic of a society which rewards and encourages performance. Once again one may find performance orientation individuals will consider a rewards-based approach damaging to their well-being and engagement.

Future Orientation

This as an indicator of the degree to which individuals engage in planning, investment and delayed gratification. This factor will impact the process of engagement in the same way as Hofstede's LTO dimension.

Assertiveness

Individuals within many societies (notably collective societies) respond badly to criticism and public confrontation, although some do welcome honest feedback and a robust discussion. Assertiveness, in this context, refers to the degree to which individuals are assertive, aggressive or confrontational.

Four Power Distance (PDI)

This is the degree to which individuals in a society agree and expect that power should be distributed unequally (see Hofstede's Power Distance Dimension).

Humane Orientation

Adopting a caring and humane attitude has often been shown to help an individual's own wellness. Caring for others is an intervention, highly recommended within positive psychology. Humane orientation refers to the degree to which organisations as well as individuals encourage and reward fairness, caring, kindness and helping others.

Societal Collectivism (ING)

An individual used to individualistic norms might prefer individual recognition and reward, whereas an individual with collectivist norms might prefer collective reward. Societal collectivism refers to an organisation which practices, encourages and rewards collective action.

In-Group Collectivism (INC)

This refers to the degree that individuals experience and express loyalty to families or organisations. This is slightly distinct from societal collectivism and for PACE, could be a strong influencer of well-being and engagement.

Uncertainty Avoidance (UAI)

This is all about individuals within an organisation who rely on social rituals, norms and bureaucracy in order to mitigate against the uncertainty of future events. This is very important for psychological safety.

Gender Egalitarianism (GEI)

Gender has been shown to be a factor in wellness but with variations between companies, societies and individuals. Gender egalitarianism is the extent to which an organisation or a society minimises gender differences.

Trompenaars

Trompenaars and Hampden-Turner (1998) defined four major types of culture along two dimensions: equity-hierarchy and person-task orientation.

Referring once again to PACE, it has been suggested that an alignment between national, organisational and individual cultural predispositions is a causal factor for reducing job stress, thus leading to increased well-being and increased performance/productivity. Joiner (2001) found that higher hierarchical task-oriented organisations characterised by low levels of decentralisation and high levels of formalisation (see Eiffel Tower model) could be compared to the Greek national culture of high power distance and strong uncertainty avoidance. In the PACE context, this will reduce the manager's stress levels, leading to higher productivity/performance.

The Family

This draws an analogy between a leader who is seen as a caring parent with subordinates expected to defer to him or her and carry out tasks as directed with the subordinates respecting the father figure and seeking guidance and approval. This type of organisation may not be as attractive to the individualistic person.

The Eiffel Tower

Here the emphasis is on task and hierarchy. An Eiffel Tower organisation would have numerous levels of management with role and task definitions being cascaded down the chain of command. Authority is derived from a position within the hierarchy, or rank and not necessarily on ability. This is a rank and role-oriented culture.

The Guided Missile

This type of culture places the emphasis on equality and is a task oriented. All resources are aimed at delivering tasks and goals with power and authority being based on ability rather than hierarchy or rank.

The Incubator

This is a culture which is primarily focused on the person and equality with the accent being on self-fulfilment and self-expression.

3.1.2.2   Cultural Impacts on Measurement of PACE Variables

As we have stated, cultural factors can affect the measurement of PACE variables such as engagement. For instance, Shimazu et al. (2010) found a difference when comparing the engagement levels of Japanese employees. This was low in comparison with Dutch employees. This was largely because of the Japanese suppression of positive affect and the Dutch sensitivity to positive self-relevant information.

Culturally Distinctive Antecedents of Engagement

Various models of PACE have indicated that cultural variations produce differences in variables such as well-being and engagement. There are three main models dealing with the process of employee engagement. These are the demands-resources model (Schaufeli and Bakker 2004), the personal engagement model (Kahn 1990; May et al. 2004) and self-determination theory (Deci and Ryan 2012). These three models can be considered from a cultural perspective.

Personal Engagement Model

Kahn (1990) proposed that psychological meaningfulness, psychological safety and psychological availability are the major antecedents of engagement. Various studies have been made in a range of cultures, and this work has confirmed that these relationships contribute different levels of significance, depending on the culture.

Job Demands-Resources (JD-R) Model

The JD-R model suggests that engagement is greatest when job demands are challenging but only when matched to adequate job resources. However, once again, there are cultural differences. Taipale et al. (2011) found that, in general, increases in job demands reduced engagement, but increased autonomy and support such as resources, increased engagement.

Self-Determination Theory

According to Deci and Ryan (2012), engagement is increased where certain psychological needs are met, for instance, autonomy, competence and relationships. Once again the culture and context can make a difference, and the significance of these factors varies according to nationality/culture.

3.1.2.3   Culture, Countries and Engagement

In 2006, Sanchez and McCauley found that antecedents for engagement were the same for China and the UK but not so for the USA. Whereas in China and the UK, the antecedents were the work itself, confidence in leaders and organisational communications, in the USA the primary driver appeared to be whether or not career objectives would be met, a sense of personal accomplishment, as well as confidence in the organisation's success, with opportunities for growth in support for careers. Although in China and the UK, confidence in senior management, sense of accomplishment and fair pay were important, in the USA individuals appeared to expect respect. On the other hand, in India and France the important factor was the work itself, and in Germany, an individual's co-workers appear to be important antecedents for engagement.

Lu et al. (2011) found in a study of Chinese nurses that 'family' strongly predicted work engagement, suggesting that in collective societies, satisfied family life contributes to ego strength, confidence, positive affect and SWB. Klassen et al. (2012), in a study of teachers, found that work-related benefits varied with the level of collectivism and this in turn influenced work motivations and engagement.

It is therefore very important that the improvement in well-being and engagement across cultures needs to be carefully considered in order to allow for possible differences in understanding key motivators and drivers. It is important not to simply impose 'best practice' management and human resources programmes which are derived from Western individualistic cultures. It would be wiser to use the most common shared antecedents to engagement (e.g. the work itself, development opportunities, confidence in leaders and organisational culture, Sanchez and McCauley 2006).

In 2014, Hu et al. completed a study of the levels of work engagement between East Asian countries and Western European countries. They found that people from the philosophically Christian Western culture, which tended to be more individualistic, were more engaged with work and being associated with self enhancement and personal development. On the other hand, the more collectivist and philosophically Confucian East Asians were more concerned with group enhancement and self-sacrifice. Within this type of culture, individuals subordinate personal goals to group goals and their achievement motivations are very strongly socially oriented. It could be said that they work to fulfil others' expectations, whereas within individualistic societies, the focus is on personal goals and personal achievement.

From a belief standpoint, the Protestant and Confucian work ethics both emphasise the importance of working hard, but the Protestant approach is more on individual effort, self-reliance and personal success, whereas the Confucian emphasises respect for hierarchy, family loyalty and group harmony.

The rising individual prosperity in the West has also affected the emphasis from simply working hard to the *meaning* and enjoyment of work, rather than just working to fulfil basic physical needs. This is a slight shift towards higher psychological self-actualisation rather than merely basic needs.

'Karoshi' is the Japanese term for death from overwork, and in fact, the Confucian values of diligence have led to overwork, as well as Karoshi, but it is in China where workaholism was the most prevalent but least prevalent in Japan with Western countries somewhere in the middle. The Japanese statistics could owe something to the Japanese natural reticence of completing surveys with extreme scoring, or they could be reflecting a real fallout phenomenon, or on the other hand, China's apparent workaholism could be as a result of the absence or near absence of social security and worker protection.

It is also interesting to note that the collectivist traits of eastern cultures appear very similar to the Victorian worker-traits in the UK with all trades having been deeply affected by increased trade, education and economic growth. That suggests that predispositions and traits are a dynamic and constantly evolving phenomenon which is also a function of social and economic changes.

Antecedents of engagement have been found to differ between multinational corporations (MNCs) as well as 'overriding' the local cultural tendencies. Kelliher et al. (2013) explored how the meaning and antecedents of engagement differed from culture to culture, with each MNC having its own HR practices which will also have an effect on engagement. The effects observed can be considered, not just by country, but by global sector. For instance, MNCs operating in India often transplant their own HR practices, which will be based on US and UK models with a key management decision being as to whether to 'impose' a particular company's global HR practices or whether to take note and modify HR practices based on local culture and thinking.

Björkman and Budhwar (2007) found that such an imposition of 'corporate' HR practices had a negative association with performance, whereas local adaptation of HR practices was associated with higher business performance.

Scott-Jackson and Michie (2014) identified similar issues in the context of certain collective cultures, suggesting that (1) certain HR policies, such as performance management, are likely to conflict with the leadership style preferred in collective culture, and (2) an adapted 'best practice' could be generally similar to an MNC's global operations but with purposeful design modifications for specific cultures.

The GLOBE project (House et al. 2004) found key differences in the cultural leadership dimensions between India, UK and the Netherlands. See Table 3.1:

An Egyptian study by Jones and Ghabbour in 2012 suggested that the key cultural dimensions (as defined by Hofstede et al. 2010) which impact the measurement of engagements appear to be collectivism versus individualism, power distance as well as uncertainty avoidance. In 2014, Scott-Jackson and Michie suggested that the focus on relationships, loyalty to the group and respect for authority are key factors in defining the Gulf Arab leadership style and its implications for locally appropriate HR management.

In India, in order to maximise and enhance engagement among the less mobile and less professional workers, it was found that the merging of work and community and recognising the cultural collective and in-group motivations were powerful factors (Kelliher et al. 2013). However, among the more qualified workers, the promise of self-improvement through training and development was viewed as an important antecedent for engagement. These 'professionals' adopted a more individualistic attitude.

Table 3.1 GLOBE dimensions of culture—India, England, Netherlands. From Kelliher et al. (2013: 182)

Cultural dimension	India	England	Netherlands
Power distance	High	Medium	Low
Uncertainty avoidance	Medium	Medium	Medium/high
Institutional collectivism	Medium	Medium	Medium
In-group collectivism	High	Low	Low
Gender egalitarianism	Low	High	High
Humane orientation	Medium-high	Medium-low	Medium-low
Assertiveness	Medium-low	High	High
Future orientation	Medium-high	Medium-high	High
Performance orientation	Medium	Medium	High

Kelliher et al. also established that Indian workers felt more secure than their UK and Dutch counterparts, in spite of the fact that the Western workers were actually legally more secure. This was probably as a result of their knowledge and impression of Indian growth and economic success.

This suggests that within the PACE framework, it is important for leadership to communicate effectively. That is to say that whenever there is an economic success at state level or possibly a health service which compares favourably to others, it is important for the government to communicate this, as this will enhance well-being, engagement and outcome goals.

In general terms, engagement appears to be a topic of far less interest in less developed countries where the basic and most important requirements are for paid work as well as a fully functioning labour market, as Shantz et al. suggested in 2013.

3.1.2.4   Culture, Countries and Well-Being

The considerable research into variations in well-being between countries and cultures is very important when considering the PACE process (Table 3.2).

For instance, both Singapore and Norway score very highly on the World Values Survey Question '*Taking all things together, would you say you are*':

In the above table, the difference between 'very happy' and 'rather happy' is ambiguous, and in spite of the fact that the Netherlands score appears to have shifted upwards, it is difficult to see how any meaningfully higher figures could be obtained.

The relative wealth, low income inequality, well-developed social welfare and health care, low unemployment, high social trust and ethnic homogeneity

Table 3.2 World Values Survey 2010–2014 wave. http://www.worldvaluessurvey.us/WVSOnline.jsp

	Total (%)	Country code		
		Netherlands (2010–2014) (%)	Singapore (2010–2014) (%)	Netherlands (2004–2009) (%)
Very happy	35.6	31.9	39.1	41.8
Rather happy	57.2	60.5	53.9	52.1
Not very happy	6.2	6.0	6.5	5.3
Not at all happy	0.6	0.6	0.5	0.5
Don't know	0.5	0.9	–	0.2

(Huppert and So 2013) appear to create high levels of SWB in Nordic countries with Denmark consistently producing the highest SWB, not only among Nordic countries, but in most international surveys. Denmark has low poverty, as well as high levels of individualism and civil rights, in contrast to the former European Soviet states which have less wealth, more income inequality, low welfare, more corruption and worse governance. These countries score low on SWB as does Portugal, which currently produces a low GDP in comparison with its Eurozone neighbours plus it has high income inequality, low education standards and very low levels of social trust.

Nordic countries scored highly on the various components of flourishing (Huppert and So 2013), whereas Eastern European countries rated lowest. However, in terms of vitality, there was a complete reversal with Eastern European countries showing high levels of vitality. The other surprising result was that in spite of their higher SWB scores, Nordic individuals did not score highly on *self-esteem*. In other words, they do not feel very positive about themselves. This is another one of those aspects of national propensity which could impact on well-being within the PACE framework.

France enjoys comparative wealth and scores well on the other objective factors, but it scores relatively low on measures of SWB (Huppert and So 2013), and in spite of scoring highest on engagement, France scored very low on self-esteem, optimism and positive relationships.

Variations in subjective well-being between countries have been thoroughly investigated. For example, based on the World Values Survey (WVS), Inglehart and Klingemann (2000) found that 65% of Danes were satisfied with their lives, as opposed to only 5% of Portuguese. These figures remained stable over a number of years which highlights the question of whether or not national variations may be a function of the perceptions of the individual's participating in the surveys, specifically their perceptions of the scales. For instance, whereas one individual may rate six as 'high' another may rate four as high, plus of course, there may be cultural interpretations of the words used in the survey as words don't always translate directly.

Tov and Diener (2013) found several common pan-cultural correlations with SWB: fulfilling basic needs for food, shelter and having socially supportive relationships as well as psychological needs such as mastery of important skills, autonomy and personal freedom. Income is also a factor and a function of how people evaluate their lives.

Income is a more important factor in evaluating SWB in developing countries, and this is probably because of the fact that small increments in income will have a more profound effect on those on subsistence incomes, than on those who have already met their basic needs.

Culturally specific goals are important in some regions, as are culturally valued goals. For instance, in Korea, academic achievement is more highly valued than it is, for instance, in the USA. Therefore, satisfaction with school is more strongly associated with SWB in Korea (Tov and Diener 2013).

Emotional experiences impact cognitive judgements and vice versa. In other words, cognitive judgements affect emotional experiences. In the tripartite SWB model, cognitive and emotional well-being is related but distinct.

It has been suggested by Tov and Diener (2013) that individualists perceive SWB based on their own emotional-based judgements, whereas within collective societies, not only the perceptions of SWB, but their behaviours and judgements rely more heavily on social norms. *'People in collective cultures may disregard their personal feelings to a greater degree when evaluating the overall conditions of their life'* Tov and Diener (2013: 3).

There is a cultural difference between East and West when considering negative and positive emotions. In the West, negative and positive emotions are viewed as the extremes of a bipolar scale, whereas in many Asian countries, positive and negative are viewed as engendering each other and it is stressed that there should be moderation between the two extremes.

As far as an individual is concerned, SWB tends towards a mean 'baseline' with extremes of low or high quickly returning to the mean even after major changes in life. A similar principle applies to countries. Improvements in GDP often correlate with increases in SWB, and this has been shown to be more pronounced in extreme climates where finances can make a great deal of difference to comfort. In temperate climates, the differences are less pronounced probably because they are less 'felt'.

Many societies see pride or excitement as inappropriate emotions, especially in a collective environment, because they are considered to detract from social harmony. In an individualistic society, pride or excitement may be seen as being very positive and motivating.

Comparatively speaking, SWB is very much affected by national wealth, but in comparatively poor countries such as Costa Rica, SWB is unexpectedly high (94% of people say they are able to do what they do best every day) and Laos has a lower negative emotional SWB than Nepal or Japan. This could be as a result of genetic differences with a tendency to depression under stress with the predisposition to collectivism being a construct created to minimise social stress (Way and Lieberman 2010). That may suggest that collectivism/individualism may have a genetic as well as social–historical root.

Based on The Global Leadership and Organisational Behaviour Effectiveness Survey (GLOBE), Ye et al. (2014) used WVS data on subjective well-being and data on cultural dimensions to investigate the importance of cultural versus more traditional factors in explaining differences in SWB between countries. For instance, Japan and Korea, both high on collectivism, ranked low in SWB in 2006 despite their wealth. It has been found that the individualist group of countries generally score higher on SWB than the collectivist cultures. Some have explained this as being because of individualistic societies having more freedom of choice, stronger self-identities, self-knowledge, less affected by the opinions of others and stronger self-esteem, but the causes could be affected by many other factors. For example, American/European individuals may be pursuing happiness as an end in itself, compared to the dialectic pursuit of 'balance' of East Asian people. The GLOBE study specifically focused on leadership identified nine dimensions:

- Performance orientation: the extent to which society rewards and encourages performance.
- Future orientation (FOI): the degree to which individuals engage in future planning, investment and delayed gratification.
- Assertiveness: the degree to which individuals are assertive, aggressive or confrontational.
- Power distance (PDI): the degree to which members of society agree and expect that power should be distributed unequally.
- Humane orientation: the degree to which individuals and organisations encourage and reward fairness, caring and kindness to others.
- Societal collectivism (ING): the degree to which organisational practices encourage and reward collective action and distribution of resources.
- In-group collectivism (INC): the degree to which individuals express pride, cohesiveness and loyalty to families or organisations.
- Uncertainty avoidance (UAI): the extent to which members of an organisation or society rely on social rituals, norms and bureaucracy to alleviate unpredictability of future events.
- Gender egalitarianism (GEI): the degree to which a society minimises gender differences.

PDI was the most important predicting factor.
ING was significantly negatively related.

INC was significantly positively related, being related to social networks and support.

GEI, UAI, POI and FOI were significantly positively related to SWB.

Variations in SWB between countries may be as a result of cultural differences, where PDI, for example, had more impact than the six traditional variables including income. Traditional variables account for 9.2%, whereas the cultural variables account for 91.8%. GDP accounts for only 3% of the variation.

When Americans typically report that they are happier than Asians, this could be because of cultural differences in how the question is answered rather than a fundamental truth.

In the USA, it is written into the constitution that they have an inalienable right to 'the pursuit of happiness'. That of course could mean that when an American is answering a question related to well-being or happiness, culturally, it may be unacceptable for him or her to admit to anything less than happiness, as a negative response may suggest that they are somehow 'un-American'.

In contrast, East Asian societies consider personal modesty as a key social value. In other words, one should not boast about success or perhaps declare one's high levels of well-being. Mathews (2012: 301) suggests that even to proclaim happiness in an anonymous survey is felt by some Japanese people as no less than an affront to good manners.

Some societies may see well-being as being dependent on happiness, whereas in some cultures, well-being may well be a function of a sense of achievement, with the pursuit of happiness as such, being far less powerful a 'driver'. There is little doubt that the personal pursuit of happiness is less strong in some cultures than in others. Plus, as mentioned previously, there are subtle nuances in meaning of the word 'happiness' and, of course, this would have a direct effect on any response.

It could be argued that differences in national culture are gradually diminishing as a result of the constant global inputs that individuals now enjoy. So one may suggest that instead of the idea of a national culture, it is more like a 'global cultural supermarket' (Mathews 2012: 304). So, cultural norms will now be affected by everything from social media to factors such as watching foreign television programmes. Cultural norms are also created and affected by all sorts of non-national groups such as political parties, social groups and fan groups. Mathews (2012) suggests that the only valid method to really understand the cultural influences on individuals would be through an ethnographic interview. However, bearing in mind that the purpose of studying well-being is usually to improve well-being and that either

Table 3.3 Commonly used measures of subjective well-being. After Jorm and Ryan (2014)

Measure	Example item content
Single-item, self-rated life satisfaction	All things considered, how satisfied are you with your life these days? (Response made on 10-point scale)
Single-item, self-rated happiness	Taking all things together, how would you say things are these days—would you say you're very happy, fairly happy, or not too happy these days?
Cantril's ladder	Please imagine a ladder with steps numbered from zero at the bottom to 10 at the top. The top of the ladder represents the best possible life for you and the bottom of the ladder represents the worst possible life for you. On which step of the ladder would you say you personally feel you stand at this time?
Positive affect	Respondents report whether they experienced specified feelings a lot on the previous day, including 'enjoyment', 'love' and 'smile or laugh a lot'
Negative affect	Respondents report whether they experienced specified feelings a lot on the previous day, including 'worry', 'sadness', 'depression' and 'anger'

organisational change or government policy has to address the majority of the population, then, provided the assessment is correctly sampling the population, then a survey-based measure is considered to be fit for purpose. Table 3.3 shows some commonly used measures of SWB:

Many of these measures appear simplistic, but they have proved extremely reliable (Jorm and Ryan 2014) and correlate well with independent indicators such as suicide rates, levels of depression and levels of mental ill-health. Plus similar ratings have been found to be followed across languages and cultures. For instance, they correlate with factors such as frequency of smiling, memory for good versus bad events and even momentary mood (Diener et al. 2003). Nevertheless, as noted above there is some evidence that SWB is perceived differently by people from individualistic cultures, than it is by people from collectivist cultures. That is because there is a difference in 'focus' by the individual where an individualistic culture, for instance, focuses on 'me', whereas in collectivist cultures focus is on external factors such as social norms.

Further complexity is introduced into the results because, for instance, Asians typically use less extreme scoring than Europeans. Obviously that might not affect within-country surveys and comparative studies, but will significantly affect cross-national comparisons (Jorm and Ryan 2014).

Interestingly, most people rate themselves fairly positively. For instance, in highly developed countries, the mean score is around 75 and even the lowest scores are above 50 (Cummins and Weinberg 2015). Less commonly used alternative measures include 'flourishing' (Seligman 2012), SWB inequality (Kalmijn and Veenhoven 2014) and 'happy life expectancy' (Veenhoven 2014).

Although self-reporting is not as reliable as assessing people's revealed preferences, many studies have used self-reporting or more accurately, self-reported measures of 'happiness' or life satisfaction in assessing the socio-psychological impact of various initiatives and comparing well-being across countries. Another issue is that there is a significant difference between an *experienced* utility and a *remembered* utility (Kahneman and Krueger 2006). Something remembered rather than something immediate will require some form of subconscious 'averaging' by the respondent which means that 'recency' will have an impact on any response. For instance, how I feel today will have a heavily weighted impact on a question such as '*how is your life these days?*' In other words, there will be a significant impact on the latter question by how the respondent feels today, or very recently. On a medium- to long-time continuum, mildly unpleasant or pleasant feelings are discounted, whereas the peaks and troughs are remembered more clearly by the individual.

The World Values Survey asks the question '*all things considered, how satisfied are you with your life as a whole these days?*' and most people will find no difficulty in answering that question but with a heavy short-term influence on their response.

In order to demonstrate how satisfaction can be impacted by recent events, Schwartz et al. (1987) conducted an experiment in conjunction with asking the subject to complete a questionnaire on life satisfaction. Prior to completing the questionnaire, subjects were asked to photocopy a sheet of paper. Half of the subjects found a coin placed on the photocopier, whereas the rest of the subjects did not have the coin. The ones with the coin reported a much higher satisfaction in life than the remaining subjects. Schwartz et al. consolidated this result by finding that a sample of German football players recorded higher life satisfaction after they had won a game, but significantly lower after a draw. Schwartz et al. also discovered that the same positive event could lead to an increased global satisfaction whilst leading to decreased satisfaction in the specific domain.

Another experiment consists of two sets of students being given a dummy task in varying environments. One group was placed in a pleasant room and the others in an unpleasant one. The students in the pleasant room reported higher levels of life satisfaction but lower levels of satisfaction with their environment. The students in the unpleasant room reported higher levels of satisfaction with their environment. As indicated, the pleasantness of the room impacted on global life satisfaction, whilst domain comparison (comparison between the rooms) impacted satisfaction with the housing domain.

Correlations have been found between self-reported life satisfaction and various objective criteria. For example, those with higher reported life satisfaction recovered from colds and wounds more quickly (Kahneman and Krueger 2006). Suggesting a causal effect from SWB to the objective criteria.

Visible signs of happiness such as smiling frequently and appearing happy are impacted by life satisfaction. However, some studies have demonstrated a reverse causality where smiling itself substantially improves self-reported mood (Neuhoff and Schaefer 2002), with many studies also confirming that perceived mood, for instance, through smiling is 'contagious' (Sy and Choi 2013). High income per se appears to have only a modest correlation, but rank in income within a peer group, that is to say comparative income, has much greater influence.

Kahneman and Krueger (2006: 9) indicate the following correlates of life satisfaction and happiness:

- Smiling frequency.
- Smiling with the eyes ('unfakeable smile').
- Ratings of one's happiness made by friends.
- Frequent verbal expressions of positive emotions.
- Sociability and extraversion.
- Sleep quality.
- Happiness of close relatives.
- Self-reported health.
- High income, and high income rank in a reference group.
- Active involvement in religion.
- Recent positive changes of circumstances (e.g. increased income, marriage).

The most accurate assessment of life satisfaction would be to self-report throughout the period in question in order to reduce the influence of selective memory and recall bias. There are various methods which achieve this, for instance, the Experience Sampling Method (Csikszentmihalyi and Larson 1987) and the Day Reconstruction method (Kahneman et al. 2004).

Assessments of well-being depend on an individual's self-judgement which is influenced by cultural frameworks, identities and attitudes. Typically, surveys ask people to rate their life satisfaction on the scale, for instance, one to seven, and the results are used to compare various groups on their degree of well-being. There are those who will argue that this method is flawed, as 'life satisfaction' is a concept which the respondent may only have thought about at the point of survey, whereas an informed response would require thinking about the past through a filter of current mood and memory (Krueger and Stone 2014). As mentioned before, judgements of the scale may vary where, for instance, one person's rating of four may be equivalent to someone else's six. That would automatically mean that a direct comparison would be invalid. Furthermore, as SWB is measured by self-reporting on not only the subject's life but their feelings about it, there will be differences of comprehension and understanding between countries and demographics, as well as different expectations and datum points against which perceptions of reality are compared.

Because of the different interpretations of the scale, it has been suggested that it may be useful to provide concrete examples of, for instance, what extremes of the scale actually mean because people will adopt different understandings of a scale depending on events or feelings. For instance, on winning the lottery or suffering a disability, there may be a temporary shift in an individual's perceived scale, although ultimately, this adaptation to a new base level of satisfaction will return to that individual's norm.

Kahneman and Krueger (2006) took a slightly different approach as a result of this problem and developed what is known as a 'U-index'. They introduced the concept of time by attempting to measure how long people spent in an unpleasant state (which is defined as one in which the intensity of negative emotions is greater than the intensity of positive emotions). There may be variations between individuals who might apply the scales differently, but as long as they apply them consistently within their own judgements, then the time comparison is valid.

3.2   PACE: Measurement and Analysis

We have discussed the measurement of well-being and engagement in previous sections, but it is useful to consider some key concepts and measurement issues in the context of the PACE framework.

3.2.1   Purpose of a Measure

The purpose of measurement is invariably a practical one in that it is designed so that some kind of change or improvement can be validly measured. So, from the perspective of an organisation or a nation, the ultimate purpose is to help to achieve an objective: for example, *'maximised citizenship behaviour of the population'* or *'maximise productivity of a workforce'* or perhaps *'maximise staff's mental and physical well-being*. If an organisation's ambition is to maximise productivity through maximising engagement, a good starting point would be a measure of the causal factors of engagement, as would a measure of the outcome, which, in this case is productivity.

Therefore, a measure of success would be a measure of productivity and a monitoring and modifying of the process of improvement would be achieved through a measure of engagement. The engagement measure is not a measure of success because, in this particular example, it is not an objective but an influencing variable. This is important as the measurement of causal factors may be approached differently to the measurement of goal success.

Currently, the measurement of engagement is primarily achieved through engagement surveys, which are usually carried out annually at organisation level. This may be useful as a measure of achievement if engagement itself were the primary objective. However, if what the organisation is seeking is an improvement in engagement, this is insufficient.

Engagement is never constant and is an individual experience which changes over short time periods. Therefore, ideally, a measure of engagement, which aims at improvement towards productivity outcome, would also be over a similar shorter time period with measurements, assessments, analysis and action also taking place over similarly short time periods. The iLeader tool (see Chap. 6 and www.PACEtools.org) has been developed to provide continuous feedback to the immediate leaders who are most likely to have an impact.

Causality and strength could be assessed by measuring a change in the desired outcome. Although it may not be possible to devise a precise measure, with of course many other input factors impacting on most organisational outputs, this should not stop the development of a measure which is as precise, specific and meaningful as possible. It should also be noted that nearly all variables have a causal relationship, often in both directions, with all other variables. In other words, there is an interdependency between variables. Although it is relatively straightforward to isolate relationships between specific variables, there should not be any assumption that there aren't other hidden factors impacting on both isolated variables or to assume that associations are causal and in one direction. For instance, it is generally accepted that well-being 'causes' engagement and engagement in turn 'causes' well-being.

For instance, if an organisation's goal is to reduce absenteeism, then a single measure will be appropriate as an indicator of success. However, the reasons for the phenomenon may be as a result of various factors such as individual characteristics, geography, bad management and any number of other factors which would be useful for improvement.

Academic research tends to adopt the classic scientific method of identifying hypothesised relationships between simplified and isolated variables and then carrying out rigorous statistical association tests in order to demonstrate either the falsity or significance of the hypothesised association. Attempting to demonstrate a causal association between variables is less frequently used method. For instance, imagine a situation where the national upward shift in GDP or individual income is followed by an upward shift in life satisfaction. We can easily assume that the factors shown above create the effect, but we don't really necessarily know whether there are other variables at play. For instance, it could be assumed that an upward shift in GDP is what caused an upward shift in life satisfaction, but that would be the wrong conclusion if, for instance, a simultaneous change in the country's political climate was the cause of the upward shift.

In spite of the fact that the statistical and methodological method used may appear accurate, we should not forget that they are as a result of comparatively crude models which only consider small parts of an extremely complex human socio-political system in organisations and nations. Although they do have immense value in suggesting causal relationships and strengths, they should always be used and applied with caution and in conjunction with qualitative approaches and observation-based methods.

For comparisons between countries and organisations, it may be useful to measure key aspects of PACE, for instance, life satisfaction, whereas global measures such as the OECD Better Life Index or the World Values Survey provide data to explore potential associations between various variables across countries and cultures. Similarly, the Gallup Q^{12} highlights variables which are presumed to be critical for engagement. You can see, therefore, the usefulness of not adopting a single approach but using several different methods in conjunction with each other.

We advise any country wishing to embark on such a programme to participate in these global comparative data exercises to not only help itself but to help others to understand the fundamental aspects of PACE, not forgetting that for an individual country or organisation, this sort of global comparative data has to be supplemented with its own country-/organisation-specific data in order to improve PACE.

It is evident that many aspects of government-provided services and infrastructure may affect PACE, which can be used to identify key factors and also to test which particular services/infrastructure are seen by particular groups to be the most impactful.

It is the researcher who has to decide which variables are of utmost importance, how they should be weighed, the nature of the assumed causal flow and, most importantly, define the independent and dependent variables clearly.

3.2.2 Perspectives in Measurement

Different measures encapsulate different perspectives or goals and are therefore constructed towards that perspective or goal. This does not make them invalid, but it is important to understand what is being measured and why it is being measured. For example, the calculation of the Happy Planet Index (Marks et al. 2006) includes a weighting for life expectancy because it reflects a particular view of physical well-being. It also includes ecological footprint, which reflects a socio-political view of what is important for human well-being. One could criticise both of these inclusions on the basis of the construction of an unweighted formula consisting of distinct factors with unrelated scale values.

In contrast, the Happy Planet Index uses the Cantril Ladder as a direct measure of SWB. This presumes that it is better to ask individuals to rate their own SWB rather than, as is the case in many surveys, attempting to extrapolate SWB from a whole range of *presumed* contributory factors. On the basis that the best measure of any variable is a direct measure, it is better to ask people to rate their own satisfaction with life engagement rather than attempt to extrapolate from assumed causal factors.

Marks et al. (2006): *'When asking people how they themselves feel about their lives, we allow them to decide what is important to them, to assess the issues according to their own criteria, to weight each one as they choose, and to produce an overall response. This Democratic, non-paternalistic approach does not rely on experts knowing what is 'best' for people. It also measures something which is universally considered valuable-everybody wants to feel good about their life. This applies across cultures and also across time. Another approach that could be adopted would be to create a list of things which we think are important to people's wealth-being—for, example, education, income and safety—measure them, and then bring them together into some kind of index. But how do we decide what things to include in that list, and how do we combine them? Should some things be given more weighting than others? And what does the number that comes out at the end actually mean?'*

Given that variables will have different units of measure, mathematically combining direct and indirect measures is questionable. The Happy Planet Index avoids this by allowing investigation of each variable separately as a useful measure in its own right. For instance, the index allows a country to see where it stands on longevity, which may be useful for a specific study.

Because there is such a range of definitions of well-being and engagement, the subject of any measurement must be clearly defined in order to ensure the measure actually assesses the object of interest within the appropriate policy or improvement framework. However, this suggests that cross-comparisons of measurements or indices are likely to be flawed.

3.2.3   Differing Models, Study Designs and Instruments

Even when comparing different studies in order to see common conclusions, one should be aware that various researchers may be starting from different theorised models, as well as defining variables differently. In spite of the fact that they be labelling variables in exactly the same way, they may be using different methodologies with differing degrees of control and rigour. For instance, there are very few examples of questions from national surveys. You will notice that there are subtle differences in the texts:

'*Now, thinking about your life as a whole, how satisfied are you with it?*' American National Life Survey.

'*How satisfied are you with your life overall?*' British Household Panel Survey.

'*Presently, would you describe yourself as very happy, somewhat happy...?*' Canadian General Social Survey.

Although the survey may be about well-being, the questions are not directly asking about well-being. Presumably in a question phrased '*how do you rate your well-being?*' would not be understood clearly, bearing in mind the variations in definition and understanding. The examples above therefore define well-being as 'happiness' or 'satisfaction', and are placed in different timescales, for example, 'presently' versus implied longer timescales, such as 'overall'.

That means there are several reasons why it would be incorrect to compare the Canadian and American scores, but whether we use the Canadian or American questionnaire depends very much on how we define well-being. Do we define it as 'satisfaction' or 'happiness' or something more active, such as 'enthusiasm'?

3.2.4   Individual Versus Population Measures

It is generally accepted that active committed enthusiasm, currently represented by well-being and engagement, is an individual phenomenon, even if it is measured at macro- or societal level (Allin and Hand 2014). In general terms, well-being and engagement, whether measured globally, nationally or organisationally, are no more than the well-being and engagement of participating individuals although some researchers such as Allin and Hand have proposed that certain PACE components only exist at a group level, for instance, a comparative objective factor such as 'inequality', although if we see PACE as a process, then inequality is not a component of well-being, but a causal factor.

Because it is a causal factor, and the objective level of inequality is an input to the perception of inequality and fairness, which in turn, impacts on well-being and engagement, this reinforces the view that well-being is *individual*, and that any measures at a higher level are aggregations, which illustrate the general level of well-being and from that statistical degrees of variation in the population are derived. What is being measured? It is either the well-being and degree of variation in the population, or measuring causal factors which may exist at a societal rather than individual level, but nevertheless will impact on the individual's active committed enthusiasm through their impact on the individual's experience.

3.2.5 Deviation Within Populations

In any type of comparative statistical measurement, it is important to measure the deviations within a population as it is to compare populations with each other. Veenhoven (2014) pointed out that whilst Denmark has an average life satisfaction of 8.1 compared with Zimbabwe's score of 3.3, over 14% of Zimbabwe respondents scored eight or more, and 10% of Danes scored five or less. That is an example of why it is important to measure the deviations within a population with those scoring in the extreme ranges being of crucial concern in assessing likely outcomes.

3.2.6 Association Versus Causation

Most methods describe statistical associations between variables such as, for example, inequality of income with lower life satisfaction. However, an association between two variables may not necessarily mean that there is a causal link. In other words, there may not be an association in this example, between inequality of income and life satisfaction. There may even be a reverse causality, such as low life satisfaction causing income inequality. All the variables may impact each other, creating a self-amplifying issue. In addition, both variables may be impacted by an unknown variable; for instance, poor government policy may be producing both the low income and the low life satisfaction. Causal links can be investigated through longitudinal studies where, for instance, it can be shown that a change in income inequality is followed by a change in life satisfaction and vice versa.

3.2.7 Bounded Scales

Key elements of PACE including well-being and engagement are psychological states which are a function of the individual and his or her perception (these are summarised as *subjective* well-being or SWB). Although psychological states can be improved for the individual and for the organisation or country, there is a maximum score which cannot be exceeded, even if underlying SWB improves still further. Any engagement score whether individual or on a macrolevel will eventually 'top out'. Therefore, the expectation of constant improvement year-on-year is a false hope, is futile and will lead to false analysis. However, the objective outcomes of well-being and engagement, as components of PACE, can potentially improve continuously.

The scales used in SWB research are always 'bounded', that is to say, there is always a limit and a point reached when any subsequent improvement cannot be recorded. For instance, if there is a continuing increase in GDP or personal income, which both in theory could continue indefinitely, there will be no indefinite corresponding series of increases in SWB. That in effect means that above certain rises in this type of factor there will be no discernible impact on SWB, even though it may actually be continuing to increase. In other words, there is a 'levelling-off' effect. And as far as a variable such as income is concerned in reality, it only has an effect if it changes from low to less low, whereas increasing an already high level of income has little effect on SWB. To put it simply, a billionaire's SWB will not be 1000 times greater than that of a millionaire.

We should also take into account the fact that any satisfaction score is not as a result of a rigorous self-assessment and is no more than a snapshot of feelings versus expectations.

3.2.8 Statistical Issues

Well-being is a state experienced by the individual. That in turn means a true measure of well-being will also be individual, and bearing in mind that it is a perceived state, then the measure should in fact be a measure of the *perception* of well-being. Questions such as '*overall, how satisfied are you with your life these days?* address this concept, but additional methods which do not require questions may also be useful, for instance, behavioural signals such as the study of so-called body language. In addition, the study of large-scale volumes, with individual variances, balanced out through the volume, but also demonstrates shared issues.

Another issue is that perceptual questions, such as those used for SWB, elicit a general response on a scale but could not be said to represent any absolute number, for instance, whether a response of say four is an absolute representation of satisfaction at a certain level compared to say two. Neither do they consider whether a score of four indicates a satisfaction level twice that or a 100% increase on two. These kinds of measures should not be (but are!) used for many kinds of statistical analysis, particularly comparative analyses (Schröder and Yitzaki 2015).

That in turn means that national means and standard deviations of well-being are statistically suspect, which would indicate that correlations between populations are also suspect. However, if we accept that the relative scores are approximate, then provided that statistical methods appropriate for approximate ordinal scores are used, we can accept that the primary objective is not the statistics, but the actions and then the insights they provide, and then using such question items becomes valid and useful.

However, care is still required when dealing with emotions, feelings and opinions as well as rankings about different constructs which are then turned into numbers which appear (wrongly) to be comparable.

3.2.9 Different Perceptions of Connotations and Scoring Between Cultures and Languages

International comparisons assume that there is a common understanding of scales, concepts as well as meanings. But nevertheless, there remain anomalies, for instance, Americans tend to give more positive ratings than Asians (Triandis 2005). In spite of possible translation issues, studies suggest that concepts translate similarly across cultures, so that *'the large international differences in average life evaluations are not due to different approaches to the meaning of a good life, but (truly due) to differing social, institutional, and economic life circumstances'* (Helliwell et al. 2009 abstract).

An example of backward/forward translation of the life satisfaction question from English to Arabic indicated reasonably accurate results, but obviously did not show contextual differences in connotations.

3.2.10 Weighting

Fleche et al. (2011: 2) highlighted the fact that even in some of the international best practice test methods, all factors are treated equally with no attempt to 'weight' their influence on well-being. Consequently, Fleche et al. suggested that measures are *open to criticism in that there is no clear empirical method for identifying the correct weights to attach to each outcome area. Decisions about which measures to include and the relative weights to assign them are, in these cases, necessarily subjective, and are dependent on the assumptions of the index developers about what is important.*

Once again, subjectivity is added to the equation.

One approach to minimise the subjectivity would be to weight themes and variables based on individual evaluations in order to arrive at an aggregated composite number which can then be used in international comparisons.

Some surveys, such as Gallup, have carried out analyses in order to try and determine the relative impact of sub-indices on well-being (weighting). It would be feasible to carry out PCP or correlation analysis between all the sub-indices and subjective well-being scores.

3.2.11 Return to Mean

We have already discussed the phenomenon that life satisfaction and positive affect ratings tend to return to a mean (which is primarily genetically predisposed according to Keyes et al. 2010). This 'baseline' is to be regarded as an individual's 'natural state' of life satisfaction and whether he or she experiences negative or positive changes, in time there is a tendency to return to that norm. There are difficulties in quantifying this phenomenon because if a causal factor improves SWB, which in time drops back to the individual's norm, and then another factor results in an even higher rise, the dynamic nature of the phenomenon makes it very difficult to measure. It may be useful to adopt some kind of normalising method over time, perhaps normalising against other countries in the same time or economic state or calculating degrees of change during a period to account for continuous improvement effects.

3.2.12 Chasing Ratings

Comparative ratings and rankings either between countries or organisations can lead to the phenomenon of 'target-chasing'. In such a situation, a country or organisation would target a particular ranking, irrespective of the true objectives of improving well-being and engagement. For example, the company could concentrate its efforts on 'ecological footprint' in order to maximise its ranking in the Happiness Index or if participating in Gallup Q^{12}, the company might concentrate on 'buddying' to maximise the 'I have a best friend at work' factor.

As with most measures, a focus on improvement causes a focus on the key driving components of the measure which may, or may not, be relevant for the specific organisation or country (Allin and Hand 2014: 18).

3.2.13 Validity

Measures should be valid as follows:

- Content validity: does it truly measure the concept of interest?
- Criterion validity: does it correlate with any factual measure of the concept, where, for instance, suicide rates are often cited as a good factual correlate for national SWB?
- Construct validity: does it correlate with multiple phenomena and with theoretical expectations?
- Face validity: especially in real-world situations where improvement may require persuasion and 'buy in' from stakeholders. Does it make sense to an intelligent observer?
- Any measure should also be reliable and arrive at the same result in similar circumstances.
- Any measure should also be time appropriate where, for instance, if affect varies on a daily basis then it should be measured daily.
- Any measure should be of appropriate granularity and sample size.

3.2.14 Measures of Objective Well-Being

We are certainly not suggesting that the factors often categorised as objective well-being should not be measured. These causal factors may vary in their causal impact between individuals, organisations and countries, so it is extremely valuable to assess, monitor and improve the provision and impact of various government or organisational services. However, for clarity of purpose and design, these measures should be clearly designed to measure the *effectiveness* of the service in question.

For instance, on a national level, it is crucial to understand the impact of health provision, but the impact of that health provision on the individual is indeed individual. Aggregating health measures for a collection of government ministries will provide crucial information on the performance and impact of those ministries on the health of the nation, without having to make unproven assumptions about the effects on national well-being.

3.3   Applying PACE

The PACE framework is designed to allow the modelling of causal processes and outputs together with assessments of the strength of causality so that governments and managements can devise and evaluate interventions to improve well-being and engagement to achieve organisational goals.

The PACE framework allows chosen causal factors, such as family income or attribution style, to be positioned in the process and modelled (Fig. 3.5).

Having positioned the causal factors, weightings can be applied, whether from rigorous research or best estimates in a given situation (Fig. 3.6).

Having developed a model for the specific context in the nation or organisation, interventions can be designed and evaluated by the relevant leaders (Fig. 3.7).

For example, if a policy objective for an organisation or government was to reduce time off sick, then the impact of various potential interventions could be assessed for that particular country or organisation given their specific state of development and objective levels of health (Fig. 3.8).

Seen from an engagement perspective in an organisation, a typical target might be to improve productivity.

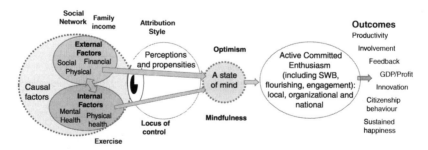

Fig. 3.5   Modelling causal factors in the PACE framework

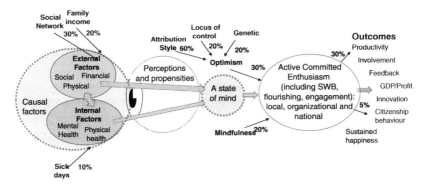

Fig. 3.6 Example weightings of factorial significance in PACE

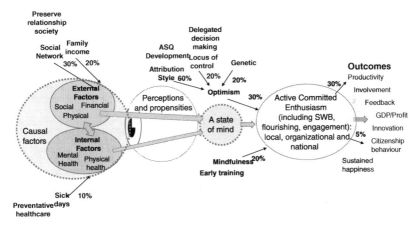

Fig. 3.7 Modelling potential interventions using PACE

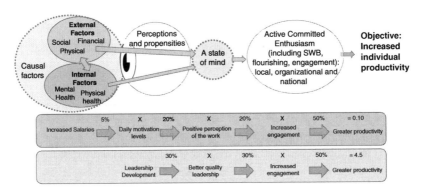

Fig. 3.8 Comparing interventions to achieve a specific objective (increased productivity)

As can be seen, by multiplying the estimated impacts of the potential interventions at each stage of PACE (in this case an advanced organisation/economy), leadership development (with an estimated impact of 4.5) would have a greater impact than simply increasing salaries (with an estimated impact of 0.10). The costs, risks and implementation issues can also be compared, and of course, it may be possible and desirable to introduce both interventions at the same time.

From a practical perspective, the percentage weights assigned to the various factors can be based on best estimates, whether from research or based on the experience of the users. The objective is to generate a view of the causal process and the relative impacts of possible interventions, not to calculate an accurate or rigorous absolute weighting which would, in any case, be impossible.

3.3.1 Government Objectives for PACE

In terms of policy and initiatives, any government has to take a national, rather than an individual view. This inevitably means that any programme introduced to meet the generalised needs of the nation will not necessarily be ideal for every individual citizen. In addition, the government has to take a long-term view, sometimes 30 years or more, and assess its policy impact on a much longer scale than the benefits often desired by the individual.

Therefore, well-being has to be viewed by government in the context of a long time frame, whereas individual well-being is not only experienced in real time, but also varies considerably. Consequently, national well-being programmes don't often appear to improve the well-being which is experienced by individuals in the present day. For instance, a government may put together a programme to improve the well-being of say, a former mining community, which, in the short term, will create individual well-being within that community, but as time passes without any measurable changes, the rise in well-being of individuals within the community will gradually erode, very often because of unrealistic or unrealised expectations.

Another example might be the building or widening of a road in an area which will initially increase the feeling of well-being because of the promise of better communication, but during the period that the road is being built with all of its associated disruption, noise, etc., there will inevitably be a negative effect on well-being.

If, in the future, it becomes possible to monitor and, more importantly, visualise these real-time individual variations, then it might also be feasible for government to utilise such measures and build rapid response mechanisms.

One of the advantages of aggregation of numbers is that the short-term vagaries of individuals and temporary swings in well-being are smoothed out by measuring large numbers of individuals over longer time periods. However, this smoothing probably obscures useful data. For instance, it has been claimed that some factors, such as inequality, are societal rather than individual (Allin and Hand 2014), but in reality, it is the perception of inequality which is crucial and that factor is individual, rather than societal.

Objective factors such as, for instance, air quality and economic indicators can be measured directly. But as far as well-being is concerned, it is not the measurement of these factors which is important to the individual, but his or her *perception* of how their well-being is being affected.

Currently, the assumption is that government or organisations can only provide generalised interventions. However, in recent years, companies have, for example, been offering 'flexi-benefits' where an individual can select a completely tailored set of benefits to suit his or her well-being needs.

This type of 'tailoring' is widely used in commerce, whereby an individual can choose a highly personalised car or pair of shoes or any number of products and it is possible that interventions by governments and organisations may be similarly tailored in the future.

Recently, the UK government has modified pension legislation, thus giving pensioners the flexibility that they demanded in how and when to use their pensions. They now have drawdown facilities, ability to choose and change what type of annuity they choose, etc. This is a very good example of a change in government policy, which on the face of it is created as a generalised change which can in fact be tailored by the individual to suit his or her needs, thus making it very specific to them.

Many companies have customised employee working arrangements which include flexible benefits in which an individual can choose, for instance, between childcare, pension, holidays, etc., and in some cases even decide the 'weighting' that they personally require between each of the benefits (Timms et al. 2014). Another example of a government or company policy is written in such a way as to make it customisable by the individual.

As has been recently shown with UK pensions, one issue which government flexibility has highlighted is whether or not the judgement of individuals is something that can be trusted. There is always a possibility that an individual will make the wrong decision and then attempt to hold the government to account.

In many individualistic societies, individuals refer to the 'nanny state' or government 'interference' which raises the issue as to whether or not national and organisational leaders should take decisions 'for the greater good' and exercise what is known as paternalistic leadership (Jackson 2013). That is the difference between a system of consensus government which allows as many people as possible to influence decisions, on the basis that government should reflect the will of the people, and on the other hand, representational government, which elects or chooses the right person or people to govern and leaves them to discharge their work without interference. Whichever system is operated by the government, it should be remembered that whether they adopt a consensus approach or a representational approach, there will always be detractors. A recent example is the UK's Brexit referendum of 2016, where the debate leading up to the referendum was based largely on perception, rather than fact. Government and opposition perceptions filtered down to individual level, and in spite of the vote result being quite definite, there remain very varied perceptions of the ultimate result of the UK leaving the European Union.

Deliberate democracy (Landemore and Moore 2014) makes the case for a non-paternalistic rule of the many, based on recent findings on collective intelligence which, however, depends on complete and accurate information mediated via the media. As described in the Brexit argument, consensus experiences its own problems as individuals tend to focus on short timescales, especially in terms of major projects such as infrastructure. The concept of 'NIMBY-ism' (not in my back yard) is a very powerful force and special interest groups can exercise a disproportionate power which can strongly affect minority interests.

At national level, well-being is often defined so widely that it includes every aspect of life and governance, from politics and employment through to infrastructure and economic climate. It then ceases to have any value as a specific construct as ultimately all that is being measured is government performance.

It could of course be argued that every aspect of government or management or leadership will contribute to well-being, but again we should avoid conflating the causal factors with the construct itself.

Through PACE, the relative weights and key factors leading to well-being can be analysed and isolated, informing leadership policy decisions at every level, from international, national to organisational.

Jorm and Ryan (2014: 9) suggest the following policy implications of well-being and engagement:

- A number of socio-economic factors are associated with a greater national well-being, including income per capita, income inequality, social welfare, individualism, democracy and freedom, social capital and physical health.
- Economic growth of poorer nations will improve global well-being.
- To achieve sustainability, wealthier nations need to focus on the determinants of subjective well-being.
- Research on cross-national well-being has lessons for psychiatric epidemiology, in terms of the types of determinants studied and the use of brief cross-culturally portable measures.

As we have mentioned before, one of the great stumbling blocks and weaknesses of current global best practice is a variation in definitions of well-being. To some extent, this is because of the underlying lack of clarity in the objectives of each specific aspect in the model of well-being. Many methods fail to clarify their objectives, or alternatively, they try to meet several conflicting objectives with a single method when, in fact, each objective should be dealt with separately.

There are any number of possible objectives for assessing well-being, so it is of paramount importance for the particular objectives to be clearly defined before defining what well-being itself means and how it should be assessed in a particular context.

Objectives could range from measuring progress against international standards through to helping individual government entities to improve their services (Table 3.4).

In general, objectives can be categorised into two main areas:

Showing progress. For example, to demonstrate progress against international comparators or to illustrate a current ranking of national well-being to citizens or to international bodies.

Driving action. For example, to help government to improve specific services or to measure the well-being impact of specific programmes.

It is, of course, quite valid to have any number of objectives, but as stated before, they might require different methodologies (see Table 3.5). For a government, the major underlying strategic objectives could include:

From a macrolevel, in other words a global or national government perspective, most well-being activities have focused on assessment and measurement rather than on improving well-being directly. However, the general motivations for government well-being programmes do include improvement, as summarised by the UK Office for National Statistics (Self et al. 2012).

Table 3.4 Potential national objectives of PACE programmes

Objective	Possible method types
Improve citizen's active committed enthusiasm	Frequent, granular, bespoke
Compare well-being internationally (ranking)	Annual, standard, sub/objective
Compare well-being internationally (progress)	Annual, standard, objective
Monitor active committed enthusiasm	Frequent, subjective, non-granular
Monitor government performance	Annual, standard, objective
Help individual government departments decide actions	Triggered, bespoke, granular
Demonstrate success to citizens and raise awareness	Annual, standard, objective
Demonstrate success to international community	Annual, standard, objective
Success of private and government initiatives	Triggered, bespoke, granular
People's opinion of government	Frequent, subjective
Demonstrate independent/objective measurement	Objective, standard
Signal unrest national, regional, local	Lead indicator, frequent, subjective
Predicting issues (leading indicator)	Lead indicator, frequent, subjective
Define government priorities	Annual, standard, sub/objective
Challenge assumptions	Frequent, bespoke
Upward feedback on issues from citizens	Frequent, bespoke, granular
For the process to inform government policies to enable significant improvement in well-being	Subjective, annual
Impact of initiatives (4 As—ASSESS, ACT, ASSESS, ACT)	Frequent, objective
Overall progress (against standards/baseline)	Annual, standard, objective
Sub-audiences (geography, demographic)	Granular
Dashboard (timing)	Frequent/sub/objective
Project management type objectives	Triggered, bespoke, granular

Clear objectives always dictate specific system requirements or causal assumptions, as shown in Table 3.4.

Currently, there is a great interest in the comparison of country rankings. Although cross-country comparisons are interesting, it is difficult to see how these comparisons can help the well-being of the country itself. Creating a single, comparable well-being index in order merely to create international rankings, bearing in mind the cultural and understanding differences discussed before, would appear to be of little practical value. Creating targets for would-be elements of different objective policy areas, such as health or the environment, is perfectly reasonable, but to create a composite index would be fallacious unless the relative weightings are carefully researched and defined, possibly with weightings not only being applied to individual responses, but also to national responses.

3.3.2 Organisational Objectives for PACE

There are several major initiatives which suggest that PACE can add value at organisational level. Many commercial enterprises have realised the benefits of helping employees to improve their physical and occasionally mental well-being. Plus there is a major interest in increasing the engagement and commitment of employees. Engagement and commitment have been shown to not only increase productivity, but also reduce staff attrition and retention of key staff. The relationship between business objectives and well-being has also been demonstrated, as well as altruistic philanthropic tendencies of commercial enterprises.

That leads to an interesting question which is whether these phenomena can also be detected in government. National leaders often have stated non-philanthropic objectives such as making a difference, staying in power and creating a legacy, and of course, this will be largely supported by a population with high well-being. In addition, a population enjoying maximum well-being is less likely to dissent or to revolt against the government.

Well-being in a workplace context is largely focused on mental and physical health and on promoting healthy lifestyles through reducing practices such as poor nutrition, physical inactivity, alcohol consumption and smoking. The outcomes of these type of programmes are usually measured in reductions in negatives, for example, unhealthy lifestyles reduce productivity and increase absenteeism and 'presentism' (the state of being at work physically but not mentally).

Such workplace programmes are important in the nation as they potentially cover a large proportion of the population, especially between the ages of 35 and 55, where statistically, life satisfaction appears to be at its lowest. Although these programs, which are primarily focused on health, will doubtless have an impact, they could be far more impactful if they focused on other causal factors for SWB and engagement, rather than just health.

Table 3.5 Objectives of well-being programmes. Data from UK office for national statistics

Policy objective	Assumptions
'Better understanding of policy impacts on well-being'	This objective assumes a direct link between a given policy and well-being, which may prove difficult given the wide range of variables which could impact well-being
'Better allocation of scarce resources via more informed policy evaluation and development'	This improvement objective requires a link back from well-being measures to policy areas, with the same difficulty as above
'Comparisons between how different sub-groups of the population are doing, across a range of topics'	The 'range of topics' implies an understanding of the impact of the various causal factors on well-being
'More informed decisions on where to live, which career to choose, based on well-being information for that area/organisation'	This improvement objective requires (a) elasticity of response by individuals, which, in labour economics, for example, has proven unfounded and (b) that the information accurately reflects causal links and is recognised as valuable by the recipients.
'Assessments of the performance of government'	This suggests a continuity of measures to allow assessment of improvement over time, when in fact these measures perhaps should evolve as more becomes known about the causes of well-being
'Comparisons between the UK and other countries'	This requires consistency of measures internationally which in turn requires a clear understanding of causal factors and/or direct measures of well-being— across cultures, political systems, economic development and societies

Activities by employers often include health risk assessments, vaccination programmes and wellness initiatives to improve healthy eating, physical activity, reduce smoking and alcohol consumption, and mental health. In addition, employers provide occupational health and programmes and initiatives which include training, appropriate working conditions and safety/protective equipment. However, employers have to balance these initiatives with issues of cost, lack of resources and time, logistical issues as well as cultural barriers (Hannon et al. 2012).

It is also evident that although employers feel a greater obligation in regard to health and safety, they are less clear in regard to subjective well-being.

A recent Australian study has shown that although most programmes focus on physical health, the area which was raised by employers as a major issue was mental health related.

Issues such as stress in the workplace were very important, as well *as 'work/life balance, mental health, and then stress... I'm dealing with a lot of people with mental health and stress issues at the moment'* from a female Australian manager quoted in Pescud et al. (2015).

The term wellbeing is mostly used by employers referring to mental health when attempting to conceptualise 'the healthy worker' with words such as *'being alert, cheerful, focused, confident, and calm. Healthy workers could also be recognised by their high productivity, their collegiality, their use of safe work practices, their healthy physical appearance, their ability to maintain a work-life life balance, and their health consciousness (e.g. maintaining a healthy diet and sleeping enough)'* Pescud et al. (2015).

As is very often the case, employers saw productivity as the key outcome of well-being programmes, but the programmes were often initiated simply as basic good practice without any specific outcomes in mind. Happiness and mood were often cited as key benefits of healthy workers:

> if someone is happy and cheerful, well they're healthy, they give better customer services, they work better with their colleagues, and you've got a happier team. If they're cheerful they will joke among each other. Having been in a position of being an unwell boss, I've known how grumpy and glum and cranky and irritable I can be (female employer quoted by Pescud et al. 2015).

Employers were wary of being accused of interfering in employees' personal lives and cited examples of unused gyms and other facilities.

Moore et al. (2010) found in their study of employer attitudes in the UK that there was a very limited understanding of workplace well-being and the employer's role. It seems therefore that the employer's objectives in respect of SWB and engagement through various programmes that are implemented are focused more on reducing physical ill-health.

A recommended approach is described as follows.

3.3.3 Improving PACE Outcomes in Organisations and Nations

The major purpose of national and organisational leaders is to achieve positive outcomes for their stakeholders. Here are some examples from varying political contacts:

Scottish Government: '*The purpose of the Scottish government is to focus government and public services on creating a more successful country, with opportunities for all of Scotland to flourish, through increasing sustainable economic growth*' http://www.scotland.gov.uk/about/performance/scotperforms/purpose.

US Government (preamble to the constitution) '*establish justice, insure domestic tranquillity, provide for the common defence, promote the general welfare, and secure the blessings of liberty to ourselves and our posterity.*' and '*we hold these truths to be self-evident, that all men are created equal, that they are endowed by their creator with certain unalienable rights, that among these are life, liberty and the pursuit of happiness. That to secure these rights, governments are instituted among men, deriving their just powers from the consent of the governed*' (Declaration of Independence) http://www.archives.gov/exhibits/charters/declaration_transcript.html.

The Chinese Government: '*the state continuously raises Labour productivity, improves economic results and develops the productive forces by enhancing the enthusiasm of the working people, raising the level of their technical skill, disseminating advanced science and technology, improving the systems of economic administration and enterprise operation and management, instituting the socialist system of responsibility in various forms and improving the organisation of work*' (Article 14, The Chinese Constitution) http://www.npc.gov.cn/englishnpc/Constituiton/2007-11/15/content_1372963.htm.

In exactly the same way that organisations have a role in enhancing the well-being of their staff, governments also have a role in creating conditions for engagement, both within organisations and the nation itself.

The UK has defined employee engagement as a key policy objective which is aimed to boost UK productivity and competitiveness.

In many fast-growth economies, the impact of multinational corporations (MNCs) attracted by foreign direct investment (FDI) incentives has imposed 'best practice' management and HR practices which can damage engagement if applied indiscriminately (Scott-Jackson and Michie 2014). In these cases, governments should advise MNCs to align their corporate management and HR practices with local culture and identity.

'Enabling the employees to have a voice' can be a major antecedent of engagement (Purcell 2014) and can be reinforced by government legislation, for instance, the 2008 UK Information and Consolidation of Employees Regulations (ICE) as well as policies which support stronger employee representation.

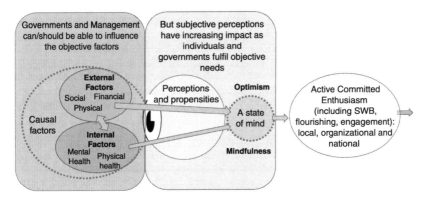

Fig. 3.9 The increasing role of individual intrinsic perceptions

If the objective quality-of-life factors improve over time then *intrinsic* factors which influence an individual's perception of his or her life become increasingly important (Fig. 3.9). These two are susceptible to intervention by governments and management.

Figure 3.10 shows how the PACE framework can suggest the application of process tools, measurement of appropriate objective and subjective factors and intervention in order to help improve the various causal factors:

Objective measures of factors such as quality of accommodation are extremely relevant for PACE, as well as for those within governments or companies who are responsible for providing them. However, as these targeted improvements raise the levels of the quality of accommodation to a perceived norm, this factor will become less impactful, although intrinsic factors such as optimism will become more relevant. This suggests that not only should measures of the quality and amount of objective factors be considered, but measures should be taken of people's *individual* perceptions of the quality and state of these factors, in addition to the *overall* assessment of people's perceptions of their lives.

The OECD Better Life Index provides an excellent example and model of these kinds of questions.

3.3.4 Applying Pace in Different Circumstances

National and organisational variations can impact many of the potential variables in the PACE framework at both national and organisational levels.

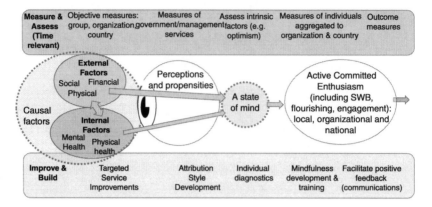

Fig. 3.10 Government and management interventions

3.3.4.1 PACE in a Resource-Based Collective Nation Versus a Diversified Individualist Nation

In a fast-growth, resource-based emerging economy within a collective society, compared to a mature diversified economy with an individualistic society, there are several distinctive factors which will impact the model (Fig. 3.11).

These distinctive factors may include the greater importance of relationships and family versus money in collective societies and therefore the relative weightings of various objective factors. For example, it might be less motivating for an individual from a relation-based society to receive a pay rise vs shorter working hours to spend with family, whereas people from more individualistic societies such as the USA, might assess their value differently.

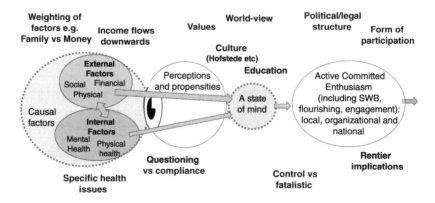

Fig. 3.11 PACE and new world economies

In emerging resource-based economies, income flows from the government to individuals, rather than from individuals to government in the form of tax as in the USA and many Western nations. This would give government a greater control over various objective levers, such as welfare, subsidies and infrastructure investment, with which to improve the quality of life of the population.

Levels of basic hygiene factors. Until basic factors such as adequate healthcare, income and housing are achieved, they will play a bigger role in the quality of life of citizens. However, once they are achieved, then personal predispositions and propensities will play a greater part. In this example of adequate healthcare, income and housing once a certain level is achieved, each incremental increase will have less impact on perceived life satisfaction.

Attitudes to government. In low power distance cultures, government actions are subject to regular questioning and criticism from the population. This can produce discussion and debate with the result that improvements can be made directly. On the other hand, in high power distance cultures, authority may remain unquestioned, but only if it is in the context of the legitimate government. Such a government has the advantage of being able to implement change quickly without discussion or debate. For example, a respected ruler or a benevolent dictator can make key decisions quickly. However, an enlightened ruler will have advisers and will consult widely in order to act in the best interest of the people.

Values. Values and identity vary greatly between nations. Many countries have a strong sense of national identity which engenders national pride, satisfaction as well as active committed enthusiasm.

Individualism versus collectivism. Individual achievement is a major driver in individualistic societies, whereas in collective societies and especially in those with strong religious values, achievement may be perceived as more of a group effort and/or fate or good fortune and maintenance of good relationships is seen as far more important than it is in an individualistic society. Opportunities to develop relationship networks, whether family or external, may be as important as opportunity for personal achievement.

If the goal is to achieve outcomes from active committed enthusiasm, it is crucial to identify or design ways in which citizens can express that enthusiasm in meaningful and goal-related ways. Changing a population from passive to active is usually unwise unless it has previously been changed from negative to positive.

3.3.4.2 PACE in a Small Charity Versus a Large Commercial Entity

Here we are comparing the factors which might differ in either a small charity or large commercial enterprise context.

Recruitment methods: A shortcut for an organisation to maximise active committed enthusiasm would be to only recruit people who are optimistic. Needless to say, this option is not available at national level for society as a whole. The difference between a large organisation and a small charity is the fact that whereas a large organisation is very likely to have a formalised selection system with formal assessment methodologies, for instance, the attribution style questionnaire (Buchanan and Seligman 2013), the smaller organisation will not only involve its leaders in the selection process but rely much more on their subjectivity (Fig. 3.12).

Meaningful roles: It is much easier for the small charity to provide meaningful roles for its employees than it is for the larger organisation. By meaningful, we are referring in terms of the scope and discretion of the work itself, plus the overall contribution to society. In the larger organisation, the need for a hierarchical structure, plus a long management line, makes it more difficult to enable empowerment. That is because the primary consideration is commercial, thus making it more difficult to promote organisation goals with *meaning*.

Income and equality: In general, reward structures within the small charity are very likely to be lower than in similar roles within a commercial organisation. In addition, a small charity is quite likely to develop an ad hoc rather than a formal reward system which can result in inequitable rewards between team members. In spite of the fact that many charities employees will have compromised on salary as a result of them having a meaningful job, they may still be impacted by perceived 'reward unfairness' within the organisation.

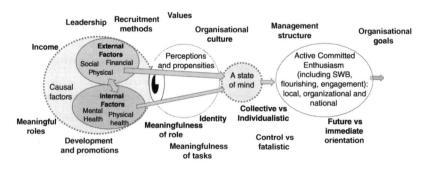

Fig. 3.12 PACE in a small charity versus a large commercial entity

Leadership: Outcomes such as retention, productivity and absenteeism are very often in direct relation to the quality of leadership, especially in the case of 'direct reports'. In a large organisation, because of the hierarchical structure and longer reporting lines, leaders will have been appointed through a formal assessment process and trained, whereas in smaller organisations, there is likely to be more informality, leading to closer personal relationships between a leader and his staff and a much flatter hierarchy.

Development and Promotion: There are obviously more paths upwards through an organisation, the larger the organisation is. A large organisation will have clear career paths with defined competency profiles and requirements plus it is likely to be providing training and development in order to help staff achieve promotion. The smaller organisation, with its flatter, informal structure, will be unable to offer promotional development in the same way, but on the other hand, will be able to offer growth in other areas such as expertise, impact and meaningfulness.

The above examples clearly demonstrate that different types of organisation will have different 'levers' with which to affect and influence active committed enthusiasm. PACE as a tool provides an outline framework within which to explore the causalities and potential impacts of various options available to either a government or organisation of any size or inclination.

3.3.5 Outcomes

The outcomes claimed as a result of well-being and engagement, and therefore valid objectives for government and organisational intervention in PACE, include the following (Table 3.6).

3.3.6 Causal Levers

When assessing or trying to identify the major levers required to achieve the above outcomes, viewing the volume of research into well-being and engagement from the PACE framework suggests that objective extrinsic factors play a major role as causal factors in SWB and engagement, and therefore also in the achievement of national and organisational objectives (Fig. 3.13).

For instance, in Oman, between 1970 and 1990, government focus was on basic provision. Between 1991 and 2010, there was a shift to economic growth and diversification followed by intensive engagement to address social and intrinsic well-being and engagement issues.

Table 3.6 Outcomes of the PACE framework from improved well-being and engagement

Organisational	National
Lower absenteeism	Reduced sickness related days lost
Higher employee retention	Improved productivity
Increased employee effort	Improved productivity
Increased productivity	Improved productivity
Improved quality and reduced error rates	Reduced customer complaints
Increased sales	Faster economic growth
Higher profitability, earnings per share and shareholder returns	Higher GDP
Enhanced customer satisfaction and loyalty	Greater well-being
Faster business growth	Faster economic growth
Higher likelihood of business success	Less business failures, less unemployment
Increased organisational citizenship	Increased citizenship behaviours (less crime, fraud and so on)
Greater organisational identity (pride, send of belonging and community)	Greater national identity (pride, send of belonging and community)
Improved individual well-being, mental and physical health	Improved individual well-being, mental and physical health, reduced health costs.
Greater innovation and intrapreneurialism	Greater national innovation and entrepreneurialism
Lower risk of sleep disorders impacting productivity and health	Lower risk of sleep disorders impacting productivity and health
Lower risks of depression and anxiety	Lower risks of depression and anxiety
	Lower risks of obesity, diabetes and hypertension and so on

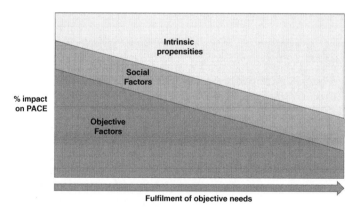

Fig. 3.13 Increasing role of intrinsic personal propensities as extrinsic needs are satisfied

Whether an organisation or country, in order to address well-being and engagement, the starting point is to ensure that the citizens or employees are not lacking basic amenities and infrastructure. If that is the case, then the focus *has* to be on these extrinsic factors. They include income, housing, job security, etc.

Eventually, these extrinsic factors begin to play a less important role in the improvement of SWB and engagement, and at this point, intrinsic propensities, such as optimism, begin to play a more prominent role. In addition, it should be mentioned that social factors (including leadership) play a key role at every stage of development of material life satisfaction. A key question is when does the point occur when extrinsic factors begin to play a less significant role than intrinsic factors. This 'perception' is comparative and so may vary between countries, organisations as well as individuals, and the best way of ascertaining that point is by asking about those perceptions. For instance, the OECD Better Life Survey demonstrates that perceptions are best captured by *asking* what people feel about various objective factors, rather than assessing the factors independently.

Asking a national or organisational population about their perceptions of the quality of extrinsic factors does not mean that objective measures of, for example, service quality should not be taken for the purposes of service improvement, management and control, but for PACE, the key would be the *perceived* service quality.

Within developed economies and in organisations where employees are reasonably paid and supported, the most important interventions within the PACE framework are most likely to be those which help individuals to improve their own SWB and engagement and those which facilitate excellent social capital. That includes effective leadership as well as social networks.

No matter what the nature or 'shape' of the organisation, whether a nation or a commercial enterprise, it is sensible for leaders to gain their citizens' enthusiastic support and commitment, although the techniques and methods of intervention would differ slightly between organisations and nations as well as between different political systems purely because of their differing natures. Even within the most participative/democratic structures, it is still desirable for leaders to set and communicate an engaging vision of the future and to demonstrate leadership by guiding their people in that direction.

Therefore, we recommend that organisations can learn from policy research at national level and vice versa. Policy makers can regulate (e.g. a smoking ban) or discourage (e.g. tax on alcohol), or encourage policies, such as ensuring cigarette cartons are not visible in shops or placing healthy foods at eye level in school canteens (collectively described as 'nudge' policies by

Thaler and Sunstein 2008; All Party Parliamentary Group on Well-Being Economics 2014; King et al. 2014).

The UK created a Behavioural Insights Team to deploy key knowledge of how people behave and apply 'nudge' theory to policy. For instance, in order to maximise organ donations, it was decided to adopt an 'opt out' choice to individuals, rather than the more proactive 'opt in'. Inevitably, people will generally take the easier route, especially if they are fairly neutral about a subject. This approach is equally valid within an organisation. For instance, if a business wanted to use the causal lever of 'caring for others', which has an association with SWB', then all the organisation has to do is provide *opportunities* for staff to help their communities or the disadvantaged. The same principle would apply if an organisation wanted to encourage networking more strong social networks. It could achieve that by supporting 'buddying' systems, mentoring, social media and generally providing facilities for informal meetings and events.

Although the purpose of this book is not to review the many ways in which governments and management can improve objective factors, the final chapter introduces a 'toolkit' which will certainly be a very valuable aid both governments and management to consider their individual strategies.

As we have stated earlier, active management of communications and management of expectations is a very important element in both government and organisational intervention, including, of course, effective use of social media. For instance, engagement levels would doubtless be enhanced by the government communicating the nation's economic security. This can of course be done by announcement or edict, but it is far more effective if citizens are involved in the development of effective communications by consultation. This includes working closely with other key stakeholders such as the private sector or any other specific demographic. For example, the Dubai and Omani governments, which are at the forefront of actively creating well-being and engagement, created initiatives to better understand what well-being meant to a specific slice of the population, for instance, young people, and they not only engaged that particular demographic but received input from them so as to better understand what that particular group understood about well-being.

External circumstances have been shown to account for only 10% of the variation in well-being between individuals (Sheldon and Lyubomirsky 2006), and changes in external circumstances result in only short-term effects on hedonistic well-being.

However, long-lasting effects on SWB, life satisfaction and psychological well-being have resulted from changes in *individual* responses and activities such as resolving to 'count one's blessings', 'commit random acts of kindness' or 'pursue meaningful personal goals' (Sheldon and Lyubomirsky 2004: 128).

It is therefore perfectly legitimate to help individuals improve their own well-being and engagement. There are enabling methods to achieve this, many of which stem from the discipline of positive psychology and with which government and organisations can intervene for the benefit of their citizens or staff. This was illustrated by Huppert (2014), when he showed that this could result in a shift of the population distribution so that a greater proportion of individuals experience positive SWB and flourishing.

3.3.7 Individual Perception: A Key Node in PACE

Objective factors which are often confused with objective well-being, for instance, income, are perceived by the individual through a filter of his or her own propensities (this is often confused with subjective well-being). Such a propensity might be optimism, which will create a state of mind (engagement) either facilitating (or not), active committed enthusiasm, which in turn generates outcomes. Also, there are an enormous number of objective inputs, material/socio-psychological and external/internal.

In PACE, however, it is the perceptual filter of the individual created by factors such as optimism. In fact, other factors are also mitigated or affected through this process filter of perception. This is reflected in the increasing academic focus on 'subjective well-being', 'flourishing' and 'flow', all of which deal with these intrinsic causes of perception.

Unsurprisingly, the question from a government or organisational leaders is: *'Which are the most impactful levers to focus on within the PACE framework?'*, bearing in mind that this changes constantly as countries as well as individuals achieve certain basic levels of objective satisfaction. Veenhoven (2014) suggested that overall happiness is tending to improve in line with improvements in social equality. This phenomenon is driven mainly by improvements in what were low scoring countries, whereas the high scoring nations tend to flatten off.

As far as the individual is concerned, this reflects the findings of Maslow (1943) and Hertzberg et al. (1959), in which they both concluded that individual motivations are arranged in a hierarchy of needs with basic needs for food and safety at the bottom and self-actualisation at the pinnacle. Or, to put it another way, individuals have to satisfy their physical needs before they can even think about satisfying their psychological needs.

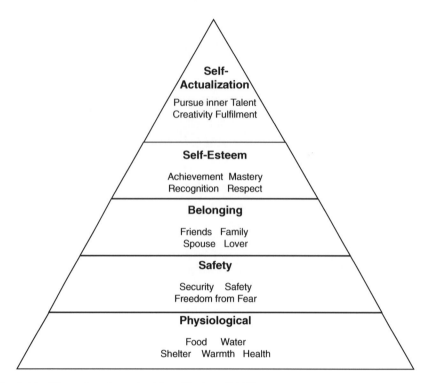

Fig. 3.14 Hierarchy of needs. After Maslow (1943)

Maslow (1943) suggested that people's motivations start at the bottom of this pyramid (see Fig. 3.14) and then change towards self-actualisation as other lower-order needs are fulfilled. Maslow also suggested that the model is dynamic in that individuals can 'climb the pyramid' and also 'slide down the pyramid'. That means, for instance, that if a government ensures that its citizens have achieved basic physical needs by having taken care of, for instance, health, food, shelter, etc., but the work is not completed, because it is very easy for some individuals who have achieved all their physical needs and as a result experience an element of self-esteem, well-being and engagement, to experience an event which takes them right back to the bottom of the pyramid.

Hertzberg et al. (1959) identified similar needs such as pay and conditions which were very important to the individual although below a certain level, if he or she are not satisfied, this would cause dissatisfaction. However, beyond a certain level only higher-order 'motivators' such as recognition and social feedback would act as positive motivators.

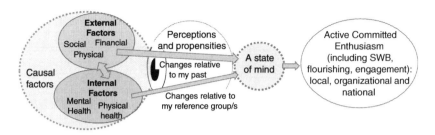

Fig. 3.15 Individual perceptions and propensities in the PACE process model

The same principle applies at national level where studies of well-being show that above a certain 'norm', income increases have decreasing impact on SWB. It can legitimately be extrapolated that the same might apply to other objective factors. So, as a country or an individual achieves a certain level of extrinsic satisfaction, the importance of intrinsic propensities has an increasingly stronger influence on PACE and its goals (Fig. 3.15).

Therefore, for a government or organisation whose citizens are located, in terms of quality of life, towards the left-hand side of this model, the focus should be on improvement of basic objective factors. Conversely, for a government or organisation whose citizens/staff are towards the right-hand side of the model, and whose objective needs are satisfied, then far more impact will be gained by focusing on the intrinsic propensities of citizens/staff.

It may be considered inappropriate to help modify an individual's innate balance of, for example, extraversion, neuroticism and conscientiousness (all of which are implicated in optimism and propensity for well-being) if they are within a 'normal' range. It is considered legitimate for today's populations to be advised to take exercise and various other interventions to help our hunter-gatherer bodies to deal with a twenty-first-century lifestyle. It should therefore also be useful and valid to adapt personality factors to deal with a very different lifestyle to that of our ancestors. Our biologically determined norms are not necessarily the most functional or even appropriate for the current time. Purely on that basis, it could be seen as not just legitimate but an obligation for organisational and government leaders to facilitate interventions.

Objective factors are not only more visible and tangible, but easy to modify. Therefore, from a government/management perspective, they represent a more legitimate target for intervention than, say, psychological propensities. But it does seem, from the evidence of these material/tangible factors, that objective factors may indeed act as hygiene factors, that is to say

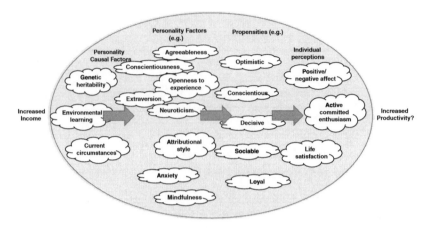

Fig. 3.16 Detail of the PACE perceptions and propensities node

highly impactful up to a certain level but then becoming less significant as basic needs are addressed and satisfied.

It also appears that 'basic' is a relative perception which shifts upward over time, so it would still be necessary to keep up with the norms of a 'developed' world. See Fig. 3.15:

Any of the nodes shown in the above diagram can be described in far more detail. For instance, the perceptions and propensities node can be viewed as a system in itself. See its description in Fig. 3.16.

The granularity within the PACE perceptions and propensities node allows detailed analysis and illustration of the causal flow system in many ways, such as genetic heritability through personal factors such as neuroticism, as well as learned responses such as attribution style through to propensities such as optimism and to perceptual factors such as positive affect.

When this nodal sub-system is included in the overall PACE, it allows an analysis of the impact of these various elements on the individual's perception rather than on an objective stimulus, such as an increase in income, and the subsequent resulting outcome, such as increased productivity. Such an analysis enables management or government to estimate that a key enabling lever would be to help individuals to enhance their levels of optimism and that a modifiable causal factor could be to enhance and facilitate early positive experiences or to provide focused mindfulness training at an early stage.

Following on from that and research studies cited in early chapters, it should be possible to calculate a very approximate estimate of the *relative* impact of various interventions.

For example, one might estimate that an increase in income above basic needs would have less impact than modifications to optimism. From a negative impact perspective, it would be possible to model, roughly, the potential impact on citizenship behaviours of a reduction in, for example, welfare payments.

References

All Party Parliamentary Group on Well-being Economics. (2014). *Wellbeing in four policy areas.* UK Houses of Parliament.

Allin, P. & Hand, D. J. (2014). *The wellbeing of nations: Meaning, motive and measurement.* John Wiley and Sons.

Arnett, J. J. (2008). The neglected 95%: Why American psychology needs to become less American. *American Psychologist, 63*(7), 602.

Björkman, I., & Budhwar, P. (2007). When in Rome…?: Human resource management and the performance of foreign firms operating in India. *Employee Relations, 29*(6), 595–610.

Bond, M. H. (1988). Finding universal dimensions of individual variation in multicultural studies of values: The Rokeach and Chinese value surveys. *Journal of Personality and Social Psychology, 55*(6), 1009–1015.

Brewer, P., & Venaik, S. (2014). The ecological fallacy in national culture research. *Organization Studies, 35*(7), 1063–1086.

Buchanan, G. M., & Seligman, M. (2013). *Explanatory style.* Routledge.

Civil Service UK. (2015). *Employee engagement in the civil service.* Retrieved from http://www.civilservice.gov.uk/about/improving/employee-engagement-in-the-civilservice.

Csikszentmihalyi, M., & Larson, R. (1987). Validity and reliability of the Experience-Sampling Method. *The Journal of nervous and mental disease, 175*(9), 526–536.

Cummins, R. A., & Weinberg, M. K. (2015). Multi-item measurement of subjective wellbeing: Subjective approaches. In W. Glatzer et al. (Eds.), *Global handbook of quality of life* (pp. 239–268). Netherlands: Springer.

Deci, E. L. & Ryan, R. M. (2012). Motivation, personality, and development within embedded social contexts: An overview of self-determination theory. *The Oxford handbook of human motivation* (pp. 85–107).

Diener, E., Oishi, S. & Lucas, R. E. (2003). Personality, culture, and subjective well-being: Emotional and cognitive evaluations of life. *Annual Review of Psychology, 54*(1), 403–425.

Fleche, S., Smith, C. & Sorsa, P. (2011). *Exploring determinants of subjective wellbeing in OECD countries.* OECD.

Hofstede, G., Hofstede, G. J. & Minkov, M. (2010). *Cultures and organizations: Software of the mind: Intercultural cooperation and its importance for survival.* McGraw-Hill: London.

Hannon, P. A., Hammerback, K., Garson, G., Harris, J. R., & Sopher, C. J. (2012). Stakeholder perspectives on workplace health promotion: A qualitative study of midsized employers in low-wage industries. *American Journal of Health Promotion, 27,* 103–110.

Helliwell, J. F., Barrington-Leigh, C. P., Harris, A. & Huang, H. (2009). *International evidence on the social context of well-being* (No. w14720). National Bureau of Economic Research.

Herzberg, F., & Mausner, B. Snyderman. (1959). *The motivation to work.* New York: Wiley.

House, R. J., Hanges, P. J., Javidan, M., Dorfman, P. W., & Gupta, V. (Eds.). (2004). *Culture, leadership, and organizations: The GLOBE study of 62 societies.* Newcastle upon Tyne: Sage publications.

Hu, Q., Schaufeli, W., Taris, T., Hessen, D., Hakanen, J. J., Salanova, M., et al. (2014). East is east and west is west and never the twain shall meet: Work engagement and workaholism across eastern and western cultures. *Journal of Behavioral and Social Sciences, 1*(1), 6–24.

Huppert, F. A., & So, T. T. (2013). Flourishing across Europe: Application of a new conceptual framework for defining well-being. *Social Indicators Research, 110*(3), 837–861.

Huppert, F.A. (2014). The State of Wellbeing Science. In Huppert, F. A., & Cooper, C. L. (Eds.). (2014). *Wellbeing: A Complete Reference Guide, Interventions and Policies to Enhance Wellbeing (Vol. 6): Interventions and Policies to Enhance Wellbeing.* John Wiley & Sons.

Inglehart, R. & Klingemann, H. D. (2000). Genes, culture, democracy, and happiness. *Culture and subjective well-being* (pp. 165–183).

Jackson, T. (2013). Seeing the middle east through different inflections implications for cross-cultural management research. *International Journal of Cross Cultural Management, 13*(2), 133–136.

Joiner, T. A. (2001). The influence of national culture and organizational culture alignment on job stress and performance: Evidence from greece. *Journal of Managerial Psychology, 16*(3), 229–242.

Jones, S., & Ghabbour, A. G. (2012). Cultural barriers to employee engagement in the not-for-profit healthcare sector in egypt. *Effective Executive, 15*(4), 28.

Jorm, A. F., & Ryan, S. M. (2014). Cross-national and historical differences in subjective well-being. *International Journal of Epidemiology, 43*(2), 330–340.

Kalmijn, W., & Veenhoven, R. (2014). Index of inequality-adjusted happiness (IAH) improved: A research note. *Journal of Happiness Studies, 15*(6), 1259–1265.

Kahn, W. A. (1990). Psychological conditions of personal engagement and disengagement at work. *Academy of Management Journal, 33*(4), 692–724.

Kahneman, D., Krueger, A. B., Schkade, D. A., Schwarz, N., & Stone, A. A. (2004). A survey method for characterizing daily life experience: The day reconstruction method. *Science, 306*(5702), 1776–1780.

Kahneman, D., & Krueger, A. B. (2006). Developments in the measurement of subjective well-being. *The Journal of Economic Perspectives, 20*(1), 3–24.

Kelliher, C., Hailey, V. H. & Farndale, E. (2013). Employee engagement in multinational organizations. In C. Truss, R. Delbridge, E. Soane, K. Alfes & Shantz (Eds.), *Employee engagement in theory and practice* (pp. 180–194). London: Routledge.

Keyes, C. L., Myers, J. M., & Kendler, K. S. (2010). On mental well-being. *American Journal of Public Health, 100*(12), 2379–2384.

King, D., Thompson, P., & Darzi, A. (2014). Enhancing health and wellbeing through 'behavioural design'. *Journal of the Royal Society of Medicine, 107*(9), 336–337.

Klassen, R. M., Perry, N. E., & Frenzel, A. C. (2012). Teachers' relatedness with students: An underemphasized component of teachers' basic psychological needs. *Journal of Educational Psychology, 104*(1), 150.

Krueger, A. B., & Stone, A. A. (2014). Progress in measuring subjective wellbeing. *Science, 346*(6205), 42–43.

Landemore, H. & Moore, A. (2014). Democratic reason: Politics, collective intelligence and the rule of the many. *Contemporary Political Theory, 13.*

Lu, C. Q., Siu, O. L., Chen, W. Q., & Wang, H. J. (2011). Family mastery enhances work engagement in Chinese nurses: A cross lagged analysis. *Journal of Vocational Behavior, 78*(1), 100–109.

Marks, N., Abdallah, S., Simms, A., & Thompson, S. (2006). *The happy planet index*. London: New Economics Foundation.

Maslow, A. H. (1943). A theory of human motivation. *Psychological Review, 50*(4), 370.

Mathews, G. (2012). Happiness, culture, and context. *International Journal of Wellbeing, 2*(4).

May, D. R., Gilson, R. L., & Harter, L. M. (2004). The psychological conditions of meaningfulness, safety and availability and the engagement of the human spirit at work. *Journal of Occupational and Organizational Psychology, 77*(1), 11–37.

Moore, A., Parahoo, K., & Fleming, P. (2010). Managers' understanding of workplace health promotion within small and medium-sized enterprises: A phenomenological study. *Health Education Journal, 70*(1), 92–101.

Neuhoff, C. C., & Schaefer, C. (2002). Effects of laughing, smiling, and howling on mood. *Psychological Reports, 91*(3f), 1079–1080.

Pescud, M., Teal, R., Shilton, T., Slevin, T., Ledger, M., Waterworth, P., et al. (2015). Employers' views on the promotion of workplace health and wellbeing: A qualitative study. *BMC Public Health, 15*(1), 642.

Pierce, J. R. & Aguinis, H. (2013). Detrimental citizenship behaviour: A multilevel framework of antecedents and consequences. *Management and Organization Review,* 1740–8784.

Purcell, J. (2014). Can employee voice and participation unlock employee engagement? *Insights: Melbourne Business and Economics, 15*, 23–30.

Rothmann, S. (2014). Employee engagement in a cultural context. In C. Truss, R. Delbridge, E. Soane, K. Alfes, & A. Shantz (Eds.), *Employee engagement in theory and practice* (pp. 163–194). London: Routledge.

Sanchez, P., & McCauley, D. (2006). Measuring and managing engagement in a cross-cultural workforce: New insights for global companies. *Global Business and Organizational Excellence, 26*(1), 41–50.

Shuck, B., & Reio, T. G. (2014). Employee engagement and well-being a moderation model and implications for practice. *Journal of Leadership and Organizational Studies, 21*(1), 43–58.

Sheldon, K. M., & Lyubomirsky, S. (2004). Achieving sustainable new happiness: Prospects, practices, and prescriptions. *Positive psychology in practice*, 127–145.

Sheldon, K. M., & Lyubomirsky, S. (2006). Achieving sustainable gains in happiness: Change your actions, not your circumstances*. *Journal of Happiness Studies, 7*(1), 55–86.

Schaufeli, W. B., & Bakker, A. B. (2004). Job demands, job resources, and their relationship with burnout and engagement: A multi-sample study. *Journal of organizational Behavior, 25*(3), 293–315.

Schwarz, N., Strack, F., Kommer, D., & Wagner, D. (1987). Soccer, rooms, and the quality of your life: Mood effects on judgments of satisfaction with life in general and with specific domains. *European Journal of Social Psychology, 17*(1), 69–79.

Schröder, C. & Yitzhaki, S. (2015). *Revisiting the evidence for a cardinal treatment of ordinal variables* (No. 772). DIW Berlin. The German Socio-Economic Panel (SOEP).

Scott-Jackson, W. & Michie, J. (2014). Universal HRM and the gulf leadership style: The perils of best practice. *Cases on Management and Organizational Behavior in an Arab Context, 1.*

Self, A., Thomas, J. & Randall, C. (2012). *Measuring national well-being: Life in the UK.* UK Office for National Statistics.

Seligman, M. E. (2012). *Flourish: A visionary new understanding of happiness and Well-Being.* Simon and Schuster.

Shantz, A., Alfes, K., Truss, C., & Soane, E. (2013). The role of employee engagement in the relationship between job design and task performance, citizenship and deviant behaviours. *The International Journal of Human Resource Management, 24*(13), 2608–2627.

Shimazu, A., Schaufeli, W. B., Miyanaka, D., & Iwata, N. (2010). Why Japanese workers show low work engagement: An item response theory analysis of the utrecht work engagement scale. *BioPsychoSocial Medicine, 4,* 17.

Sy, T., & Choi, J. N. (2013). Contagious leaders and followers: Exploring multi-stage mood contagion in a leader activation and member propagation (LAMP) model. *Organizational Behavior and Human Decision Processes, 122*(2), 127–140.

Taipale, S., Selander, K., Anttila, T., & Nätti, J. (2011). Work engagement in eight European countries: The role of job demands, autonomy, and social support. *International Journal of Sociology and Social policy, 31*(7/8), 486–504.

Thaler, R., & Sunstein, C. (2008). *Nudge: The gentle power of choice architecture.* New Haven: Yale.

Timms, C., Brough, P., O'Driscoll, M., Kalliath, T., Siu, O. L., Sit, C., et al. (2014). Flexible work arrangements, work engagement, turnover intentions and psychological health. *Asia Pacific Journal of Human Resources, 53*(1), 83–103.

Tov, W., & Diener, E. (2013). *Subjective well-being* (p. 1395). Paper: Research Collection School of Social Sciences.

Triandis, H. C. (2005, March). Issues in individualism and collectivism research. In R. M. Sorrentino, D. Cohen, J. M. Olson & M. P. Zanna (Eds.), *Culture and social behavior: The ontario symposium, 10*, 207–225.

Trompenaars, F., & Hampden-Turner, C. (1998). *Riding the waves of culture.* New York: McGraw-Hill.

Veenhoven, R. (2014). Happiness adjusted life years (HALY). In A. C. Michalos (Ed.), *Encyclopedia of quality of life and Well-Being research* (pp. 2641–2643). Dordrecht: Springer.

Way, B. M., & Lieberman, M. D. (2010). Is there a genetic contribution to cultural differences? Collectivism, individualism and genetic markers of social sensitivity. *Social Cognitive and Affective Neuroscience, 5*(2–3), 203–211.

Ye, D., Ng, Y. K. & Lian, Y. (2014). Culture and happiness. *Social Indicators Research*, 1–29.

4

How to Maximise Individual Propensity for Active Committed Enthusiasm

One of the main stages defined within the process for active committed enthusiasm (PACE) is that engagement and well-being are in reality determined by the perceptions of the individual of their lives, work and so on. This perception is the main determinant of active committed enthusiasm (ACE) and is itself determined, to a large extent (especially when a certain level of material satisfaction is reached) by the individual's own propensity for optimism. With demonstrable success over many years, the field of positive psychology and, in particular, training in attribution style and mindfulness, provide straightforward tools to help people improve their own optimism and propensity for ACE (see Chap. 6 and www.PACEtools.org for practical tools).

We have described the process of active committed enthusiasm above, and this section focuses on the conditions which need to be in place in order to create and maintain active committed enthusiasm (ACE). The book has, so far, discussed various aspects of well-being and engagement, but it is useful to briefly review the concept of commitment and how it might be achieved.

4.1 Commitment

Whereas enthusiasm is a feeling of intense and eager emotion towards something, in this context, commitment is best described as a dedication to a particular country, organisation, group or even person, and a willingness to become enthused. An individual will become enthused, but only if he or she believes that their effort is important and appreciated. If those conditions are met, then enthusiasm will be sustained and that can only be achieved by

© The Author(s) 2018
W. Scott-Jackson and A. Mayo, *Transforming Engagement,
Happiness and Well-Being*, DOI 10.1007/978-3-319-56145-5_4

ensuring that the individual remains committed. It also follows that if a country or organisation manages to create commitment, thus engendering enthusiasm, the more momentum can be generated in order for commitment as well as enthusiasm to grow. This combination results in active committed enthusiasm (ACE).

Commitment is one of the most important aspects of belonging to a country or organisation and is what gives the country or organisation not only its identity, but its strength. 'Belonging' is another one of those aspects of creating engagement which is important. And it is creating commitment which creates that belonging, which in turn delivers ACE.

Commitment is one factor which gives ACE its momentum and it is for the following reasons:

- Committed people, whether they are leaders or not, will influence those around them. This not only engenders team thinking and team spirit, but a totally committed group will influence other groups and individuals thus creating a committed and engaged atmosphere.
- Committed people will not be discouraged as easily as those that are less committed, and they will transmit that commitment to others, not only through what they say, but through their work practices.
- Committed people tend to cooperate with other committed people and through that cooperation will create trust.
- Committed people have a willingness to learn, both as individuals and as a group and through these relationships, say learn.

National and organisational leaders should also remember that commitment is not a phenomenon which can be simply switched on. It is a process which grows within individuals and, as we have seen, how long that commitment 'grows' is very much a function of leadership as well as that of the individual. The leader cannot demand commitment.

As John W Gardner said, commitment grows when people:

- Work together.
- Feel successful at what they do.
- Make decisions together.
- Work through conflicts.
- Support one another's leadership.
- Have fun and play together.
- Overcome obstacles.
- Hold each other to high principles.
- Appreciate and respect one another.

- Challenge one another and take the next step.
- Build relationships.
- Experience a victory together.
- Learn from mistakes and setbacks.
- See the leaders model commitment and example.

At a national level, individuals need to see their leaders, not only demonstrating commitment to them, but also to the cause or the state. At an organisational level, directors and managers should also demonstrate commitment to their staff, as well as their organisation. When we talk about leaders demonstrating commitment to their people, it has to be a constant process rather than an occasional slide in a presentation.

Many of us have seen the type of high-level presentation, normally delivered by a CEO or chairman at, say, an annual general meeting. As you might expect, most of the time such a meeting is concerned with numbers, predicted profits, returns on investment, sales figures, etc. Then, at the end of the presentation almost as an afterthought, the CEO says something along the lines of '*and of course our most important asset is our people!*' That is not necessarily demonstrating senior management's commitment to the people. Active commitment is a continuous process and it does not just refer to the commitment of the individual to the company. Active commitment is something which leaders should not only feel, but also demonstrate towards their people on a continuous basis.

If the individual is not convinced that those senior to him are committed to him, not only can commitment decrease but it can disappear altogether. So how do leaders demonstrate their commitment?

If you are the leader of a group of people, whether large or small, their commitment to you will grow naturally, but only if your commitment to them is not only clearly communicated, but clearly demonstrated.

A leader needs to communicate to his/her people that s/he is willing to listen to them. You need to let them know that they can criticise him to his/her face, without expecting sanctions. Whenever there is any type of change envisaged either countrywide, organisation wide or even within departments, there is one very simple rule and that is a leader *cannot* over-communicate. Only then will the individual feel part of the organisation and gradually build his commitment to it via the leader.

Commitment is something that can be very easily built into the culture of a country or an organisation. But although at first glance it does appear to be a nebulous concept, it is important to know *how* commitment can be not only mobilised but also sustained in the long term.

4.1.1 Why Do People Commit?

Individuals will commit to an organisation or country for a variety of reasons, but ultimately it is to achieve some sort of gain, primarily for themselves. For instance:

- They may feel that they're accomplishing something significant.
- They may be given the opportunity to either work on or develop an issue which is important to them.
- They may wish to expand their skills.
- They may enjoy being part of the team.
- The may admire the leader to the extent that they themselves want to lead one day.
- They may enjoy a challenge.
- They may be team players who enjoy working with like-minded people.
- They may be convinced that they are helping the company or the community.

If the leader is looking for engagement from his or her people, he needs their commitment and, in order to gain a common commitment, the people need to be told and believe that they are being offered something of value. By implication, it may be an increase in salary, it may be career progression, it may be a spiritual 'home' or any number of things which are important to that individual.

Not every individual's needs are the same.

What is important to the individual?

When asked the question 'why are you committed to your project, organisation or country?' and 'why have you become involved or 'engaged'?' The reasons will vary. For example:

- My role within the organisation or group is important.
- I am hoping to learn.
- I derive satisfaction from belonging to this organisation/group.
- I have invested a lot of time in this organisation and I want to succeed.
- The goals of the group are important to me.
- I admire the leader and agree with a lot of what s/he says.
- I admire and like the people that I work or associate with.

There will of course be other reasons, but it is important for the leader of the group or organisation to understand that the basic building block of engendering engagement is to foster commitment from the individual and from that will come commitment from others.

If you look at, for instance, the RSPB, they have a just cause which attracts many volunteers, people are learning and people enjoy the team aspect of belonging. The goals of the RSPB seem very important and its leaders are people to be admired both personally and intellectually, and each individual within the organisation feels that they are making an important contribution in an area of significance.

Consequently, the organisation has grown exponentially and became a very effective campaigning group with a large number of fully committed and engaged volunteers.

Inclusion creates commitment.

An organisation such as RSPB genuinely welcomes members and volunteers, and many organisations nowadays, from the National Trust to the RSPCA, still (very successfully) welcome members into their organisations by stressing the importance of the individual, whether it's through planting a tree somewhere or even adopting a snow leopard somewhere in the Himalayas; it is important that in order to gain commitment, the individual is made to feel important and able to contribute.

It is very often the case that if an individual is made to feel genuinely welcome into a group, they will give commitment both to the leader and to the group.

A good leader will personally welcome every new member of staff, ask some questions and show genuine interest in them. Even if that leader is extremely senior and the likelihood of that individual ever speaking to their leader again is slim, he or she will feel included and welcome, and the process of commitment will have started because from day one that individual will feel included.

Many organisations have included this principle of welcoming into their culture, whereby, for is an inducinstance, if there tion course, somebody very senior will turn up and spend time informally chatting to new delegates. Other organisations have Welcoming Committees and others have what is known as a 'buddy' system which immediately makes people feel part the team.

Reasons for Commitment and Engagement

Leaders should be aware of the fact that commitment and engagement are all about creating an atmosphere where the individual shares the same goals and principles as the leader and the company. Individuals need to be told what it is that they are committing too. Therefore, whether a country or organisation, every individual, in order to become committed and engaged, needs to be familiar with the organisation's mission, its principles and its goals and ambitions. In other words, some sort of basis for engagement.

Individuals need to be told by their leaders of the goals and principles under which the organisation operates and they need to be convinced that the leader believes in those goals and principles.

4.1.2   Demonstrating Commitment

As far as commitment is concerned, it is the commitment of the leadership of the government or company which is of paramount importance. Not only is it their ability to *voice* that commitment but to *demonstrate* it. This is not through what the leadership *says* but is demonstrated to the individuals by attitudes and more importantly *actions*. 'Our most important asset is our people' is a very fine statement, but if it is not clearly demonstrated by leaders and management actions, then it is all but useless. The same applies at government level, where the government may say *'we are going to look after the little people'* and if then nothing happens, there will be absolutely no commitment to that government from 'the little people'. The individual will always look to the leader in order to see whether he or she is truly committed.

At an organisational level, commitment to the company is demonstrated very easily, and because commitment is contagious, it can be created very simply and very quickly. For instance, if people see that the chief executive is willing to work hard, they are far more likely to be willing to do the same. The converse is also true. A word of caution though: if the leader works very hard and looks as if he's about to burn out and the staff can see that work is making him or her unhappy, then it is very unlikely that individuals will commit. Commitment to anything must never appear to be a burden.

Commitment Through Work or Being Given Something to Do

A group or an individual, when given something to do, will show a certain level of commitment, but the important thing to remember here is that whatever they are given to do it needs to be meaningful, important to them as well as to the organisation.

It is not enough for an individual to feel that he is making a contribution, although that in itself is very useful. He or she must feel that they are making an important or significant contribution at local or organisational level. For instance, a leader can find out what specifically interests a group or an individual and create projects on that information. That too is a great shortcut to obtaining commitment and engagement.

Commitment Through Challenge

Most people are motivated and committed to a task when their abilities are stretched. That can be a difficult management skill, but it is important that any tasks given to individuals are such that they are not too easy for them to complete, but when completed, will give the individual a sense of achievement and a feeling of success. We are going to look at the concept of happiness a little bit later in this chapter, but it is important that in order to gain commitment and engagement, the individual needs to feel good about him or herself. And by being given challenging tasks, they will remain excited and motivated about their work and they can be developed by being given more and more challenging tasks and concepts.

This type of approach not only develops the individual, but at the same time also makes him or her feel that the organisation is interested in them and the work they do, thus creating more and more commitment and engagement.

Mutual Respect

In order to help people become committed to a cause and thus create engagement, they must not only be appreciated, but respected. That will help them to remain connected, committed and engaged. This is one of those aspects of management which does not particularly require any management models or specialist knowledge and is a time when leaders' human skills need to come to the fore as follows:

- *Vocalise* your appreciation. In other words, tell either the individual or the group that you appreciate their work.

- *Include* people not only when you talk to them individually, but also in meetings by asking them to talk about their progress and achievements. If you are a leader, this is a very powerful technique for making people feel part of *your* team.

- *Conflict management* Whenever there are disagreements or conflicts, as long as they remain positive and constructive, they will do little harm to retaining people's commitment and engagement, but it is always important to ensure that the conflict is not destructive and without any personal attack. However, whenever there *are* personal conflicts between individuals, it is important that this is dealt with immediately, either by the leader mediating in a positive way, possibly inviting an outsider without any preconceived ideas to help in the process.

Active Listening

Continuing the theme of making people feel valued, it is important that they are not only listened to but that it is shown that they are being listened to and that the organisation has confidence in them as individuals. If it is not clearly demonstrated by an organisation that it is listening to its people, disillusionment and disaffection soon lead to disengagement, so listening is a very important aspect of maintaining engagement. One of the most motivating and commitment-creating things to do to any individual is to ask their opinion.

Knowledge Leadership

For the last 10 years or so, we have witnessed the gradual erosion of hierarchical, rank-based leadership, leading to much flatter management structures or in many cases a total lack of structure. This has taken place primarily because different individuals within a team can lead at different times because of their specific knowledge. You may have noticed that even at national level, governments are acquiring the services of non-elected experts to advise and sometimes to lead when a certain amount of innovation is required. For instance, we may have a Bioethics Czar, Economics Czar, Pandemic Czar, etc. This approach can be replicated at micro- or local level and once again be a great 'cementer' of commitment and engagement.

Commitment—A Summary

There is no 'magic bullet' for creating commitment and engagement. It is a gradually developing process, and therefore, some people will take longer to commit and become engaged than others. Nevertheless, whatever level of engagement or commitment is achieved by an individual, it should be appreciated by a leader and then developed. Commitment and engagement are not something that can be demanded either by an organisation or by a country state, and it is also worth mentioning that if an individual feels that he or she is a disappointment to his or her leader, then they will not maintain commitment or engagement.

4.1.3   Interventions to Improve Personal Propensities

We have already established that although both SWB and life satisfaction may be measured and compared at national level, they are functions of the individual. In other words, they are felt by individuals uniquely. PACE confirms this by showing that well-being and engagement are defined 'as experienced by the individual'. Therefore, major causal factors are the innate propensities of the individual, for example, their propensity to optimism. These affect the perceptual filter through which the other objective and subjective causal factors are viewed. Therefore, interventions targeting individuals are likely to have the greatest effect even if they are delivered 'en masse' because personality is established at an early age and has a major causal role in SWB, engagement and flourishing. A key focus for government intervention would be early education (Huppert 2014).

This could include positive psychology learning and practice for 'normal' children (which also be of benefit to parents and teachers). There are existing school-based programs designed to improve well-being through mindfulness training and these are already proving highly effective (Schonert-Reichl et al. 2015), to such an extent that a UK parliamentary subcommittee has recommended mindfulness training for educators (All Party Parliamentary Group on Well-Being Economics 2014). Positive psychology suggests many approaches for the assessment and improvement of individual propensities, some of which are reviewed below.

4.2 Happiness and Positive Psychology

Positive psychology is a term first coined by Abraham Maslow, and his ideas have been developed in recent years by Martin Seligman (and many others), who encapsulated the concept of commitment and enthusiasm in 2002 as follows:

'Use your signature strengths and virtues in the service of something much larger than you are'.

4.2.1 Positive Psychology Interventions

Positive psychology focuses on the improvement of individual factors such as hope, optimism, resilience and self-efficacy to enhance SWB and engagement (Meyers et al. 2013). Meyers also summarised numerous studies which have confirmed the benefits of various positive psychology interventions for SWB and the avoidance of depression.

Interventions tend to employ techniques for remembering positive subjective experiences such as broadening, strengthening, using positive traits and identifying and utilising valued characteristics of groups. These include increasing optimism, which is a relatively stable trait but can be enhanced through:

- Three weeks of daily 5 min sessions imagining one's best possible self (Seligman 1991).
- Systematically making more optimistic explanations for events (Meevissen et al. 2011).
- Cognitive behavioural therapies (see below), more often used in clinical settings (Buchalter 2014).
- Gratitude interventions—where individuals are encouraged to experience their lives in a state of gratitude, which forces a positive evaluation. An example would be to list things the individual feels grateful for. It is suggested that gratitude prolongs positive affect and counteracts the hedonistic adaptation to return to a 'happiness norm' after a positive experience.
- PsyCap intervention—this has been designed to be effective, but brief, with minimum disruption. It involves a series of exercises, for example, identifying a meaningful goal and optimistic pathways to achieve it. Dawkins and Martin (2014) report improvements in the four components of hope, resilience, self-efficacy and optimism, both via an online version and in-house delivery. A particularly interesting observation is that the psychological capital of leaders has a direct effect on the well-being and engagement of followers (Haar et al. 2014) and to an extent, vice versa.
- Best-self exercise—where individuals are asked to provide examples of when they were at their best and thereby recall and relive those moments (Roberts et al. 2005).
- Loving-kindness meditation—where individuals utilise altruism and empathy by directing their attention towards helping others (starting with those closest and ending with everyone). This has been proved effective, even via an Internet intervention (Galante 2014). This demonstrated a significant increase in well-being, with much less anxiety than a control group.
- Solution-focused coaching—where participants first identify their strengths and past success, visualise a desired condition of a chosen life area and describe small specific actions that could lead to that desired future. Second, the participants keep track of positive changes over 10 days including relevant events, positive changes, their own actions, feelings and possible actions for the next day. Pakrosnis and Cepukiene (2014) report increases in SWB even from a self-help version of solution focus.
- Cognitive behavioural therapy (CBT) is designed to help participants evaluate and modify their own thoughts, attitudes and behaviours through a guided process based on professional guidelines (the British Association for Behavioural and Cognitive Psychotherapies (BABC P), for example). CBT has been shown to improve well-being, job satisfaction and productivity through modification to attribution style, Proudfoot et al. (2009).

In a meta-review, Meyers et al. (2013) found that all the interventions improved well-being and, where measured, various aspects of performance and productivity as well as the underlying characteristics of hope, optimism, self- efficacy, resilience and assertiveness.

Through research over many years, Seligman et al. (2005) found that the most happy people were those who had either discovered or had been helped to discover their own strengths. His conclusion was that happiness has three dimensions, which can be cultivated:

- The pleasant life.
- The good life.
- The meaningful life.

4.2.2 The Pleasant Life

Seligman's concept of the Pleasant Life was based more or less on Maslow's basic or physiological needs, such as food, shelter, bodily needs and companionship. For many people, the Pleasant Life is enough, and for much of the world's population, satisfying these basic needs is all that individuals strive for and if, for instance, a government is able to provide what is termed a reasonable 'standard of living' (i.e. the provision and protection of people's basic needs), then they may well become and remain committed to that government. To put it in simple terms, if a government is able to provide healthcare, ensure that the population is reasonably fed and has water and shelter, then the basic building block is in place in order for that government to obtain and maintain commitment and engagement from its people. As in Maslow's model, unless an individual's physiological needs are satisfied, his or her psychological needs are unlikely to be triggered. The Dubai government has described this as the basic needs in their ABCD happiness model (see case study).

4.2.3 The Good Life

This is roughly equivalent to what Maslow suggested as the psychological or 'brain' needs of an individual. Once the physiological needs have been satisfied, a life can be enhanced by the individual discovering his or her strengths and virtues in using them to improve their lives. This is an aspect which comes from within the individual, but can be noted and encouraged by good governance or leadership. Seligman et al. (2005) suggests that one of the best ways of discovering this is by 'nourishing' our unique strengths in contributing to the happiness of our fellow humans'. The Dubai government equivalent is the cognitive element of the ABCDE model.

4.2.4 The Meaningful Life

This is about the individual looking 'outwards'—outside his or her immediate sphere—and it is at the heart of commitment and engagement through finding a sense of fulfilment by engaging in a meaningful quest, idea or purpose greater than the individual.

It is through the simple model above that Seligman's theory reconciles two opposing views of human happiness. The first is the individualistic approach which is that we should take care of ourselves, and the second is the altruistic approach, which is the nucleus of engagement.

Seligman (2002, p. xiv): 'The very good news is there is quite a number of internal circumstances (…) under your voluntary control. If you decide to change them (and be warned that none of these changes come without real effort), your level of happiness is likely to increase lastingly'.

Seligman's research has been in the area of positive emotion and not just in the areas of pleasure or gratification, but he seeks to help individuals acquire skills to be able to deal with their lives in much more meaningful ways.

In 1998, he pointed out during his inauguration as president of the American Psychological Association that psychology is needed to study what makes people happy. He went on to suggest that, so far, psychology had been concerned primarily with curing mental illness rather than building psychological *strengths* (Seligman 1999).

It was Abraham Maslow in fact, who initially called attention to the type of humanistic psychology, which focused on strength and potential rather than neuroses and pathologies.

Following Seligman, a whole field of scientific study of positive emotions has developed and how they affect health, performance and life satisfaction.

Most importantly, however, research is showing that happiness can be taught, and in the context of this book, this can be achieved either at individual or at global (macro) level. That is to say an organisation or government can teach individuals and groups to be actively happy and through that they will become committed and engaged.

4.2.5 A Mental Toolkit

Seligman created a mental 'toolkit' which enables people to think constructively about the past, create optimism and hope for the future and as a result achieve greater happiness in the present. This is important because unhappy people will not commit or engage.

4.2.5.1 Dealing with the Past

Gratitude and forgiveness are two strategies which Seligman recommends for combating unhappiness in the past. This view is diametrically opposed to what we in the West are usually taught as far as dealing with issues is concerned, in that we are what is known as a 'ventilationist society' and that it is viewed as honest and healthy to express our anger in order to deal with issues which have made us unhappy. Seligman recommends the approach used in Eastern Asian culture which is to deal with difficult situations *quietly* without expressing any negative emotions. Seligman suggests that people who internalise and refrain from expressing negative emotions and use passive strategies with which to deal with stress tend to be happier (Seligman 2002).

4.2.5.2 Dealing with the Future

The majority of stress is about the future, that is to say perceived or imagined consequences of past and present action. Seligman recommends an effort to generate a positive outlook, which is full of hope for the future. If you consider this approach at national level, you will notice that most, if not all governments adopt this approach by very often spending an inordinate amount of time telling its citizens how positive and hopeful they feel about the future.

The approach is in three stages, which are (1) dealing with negative emotions of the past; (2) building optimism for the future and then creating some sort of change in the present; and (3) enjoying and saving experiences and using mindfulness in ways to increase happiness in the present.

4.2.5.3 Positive Emotion

Positive emotion is something which all leaders, whether national or corporate, should attempt to engender in their people. There has been a lot of research into the power of positive emotion on life and outcomes. Positive emotions are often accompanied by what can be termed fortunate circumstances such as a long life and better health.

However, as Seligman wondered and as the old saying goes *'Do we sing because we're happy or are we happy because we sing?'* whether positive emotions create happiness, or whether happiness causes positive emotions.

Nevertheless, there does appear to be a definite relationship in individuals who are inherently happy and go on to experience positive lives.

4.2.5.4   Shortcuts to Happiness

Seligman suggests that there are no shortcuts to happiness although an individual's positive emotion can indeed create happiness. In order to create an enduring happiness, it is important to explore the realm of *meaning*. He suggests that happiness without context and without the application of an individual's strengths, plus being a part of something, and becoming involved in a more creative existence, will give a more permanent and greater sense of happiness.

'[Positive psychology] takes you through the countryside of pleasure and gratification, up into the high country of strength and virtue, and finally to the peaks and lasting fulfilment: meaning and purpose' (Seligman 2002, p. 61).

4.3   Mindfulness

It has been confirmed by numerous studies that there is a causal link between well-being and mindfulness (e.g. All Party Parliamentary Group on Well-Being 2014, Schutte and Malouff 2011).

Mindfulness is a set of simple practices, developed through many years of clinical research into stress, anxiety and depression which help people to develop a more balanced view of their lives and feelings. It also prevents normal feelings of stress, sadness and anxiety spiralling downward into long periods of unhappiness and exhaustion or even clinical depression.

Dealing with severe depression is known as mindfulness-based cognitive therapy (MBCT) and is recognised as an effective treatment by the UK National Institute for Health and Clinical Excellence (NICE). It has also recently been proposed as one of the four main policy interventions on wellness by the UK All Party Parliamentary Group on Well-Being Economics (2014).

Mindfulness suppresses the natural propensity, when faced with problems, to seek solutions 'by analogy'. That is to say that an individual searches through his or her memory for similar situations which then act as triggers to reinforce negative feelings of sadness or anxiety. The triggering of negative feelings can be very non-specific with a relatively minor negative event 'snowballing' to create much stronger nations. Mindfulness creates mental clarity by suppressing the unconscious trigger and allowing time for the conscious to intervene to relate relatively simple meditation techniques.

The benefits of mindfulness practices, suggested in numerous research studies, include:

- Increased happiness and contentment (e.g. Shapiro et al. 2006).
- Increased mental resilience (e.g. Garland et al. 2011).
- Decreased anxiety, depression and irritability (e.g. Hofmann et al. 2010).
- Improved memory, reaction times and stamina (e.g. Jha et al. 2010).
- Better relationships (e.g. Schutte et al. 2011).
- Reduced stress and hypertension (e.g.Blom et al. 2014) Abbey, S.
- Increased pain resistance and immune response (e.g. Salomons and Kucyi 2011). Structural changes in the relevant brain regions following an 8 week mindfulness-based stress reduction (MBSR) course (e.g. Hölzel et al. 2011).

It is an obligation of both governmental and organisational leaders to help their populations to maximise well-being. Interventions such as mindfulness training clearly contribute to well-being. Perfectly legitimate interventions could include mindfulness training in schools (Huppert and Johnson 2010) as well as training for teachers and medical practitioners (All Party Parliamentary Group on Well-being Economics 2014).

At an organisational level (Chapman 2011), interventions would mainly focus on training (Feicht et al. 2013), education/information and, perhaps, guides and tools.

Finally, here is a quote from All Party Parliamentary Group on Well-being Economics (2014), which is an example, which emphasises the importance of both organisations and governments being aware of the concept of mindfulness and its potential benefits when considering well-being and engagement:

Mental health problems cost the UK economy an estimated £70 billion annually. Training new medical and teaching staff in mindfulness techniques would embed a culture of well-being in health and education, and reduce a later burden on the NHS by improving the availability of mindfulness-based therapies.

4.4 Attribution Style

Attribution theory is concerned with the ways in which individuals interpret external stimuli, ranging from interpreting events to the actions of other people. Individuals assess the causes of positive and negative events, not just on factual evidence but also on the basis of a 'style' of interpretation, hence attribution *style*.

It is believed that in 1958, Fritz Heider was the first to consider the implications of attribution styles. Following on from his research, the ideas of Beck (2002), Ellis (1987), Seligman et al. (1973) and others were concerned with how individuals make sense of the world around them and how these perceptions guide their feelings and actions. Attribution theory was developed in clinical psychology and has gained significance in occupational settings through a number of applications. These include achievement motivation, the relationship between satisfaction and performance, staff retention and increased sales performance. The theory has also been applied to selection tests for sales people (Silvester et al. 2003) to interview success (Scott-Jackson 1998) and to resilience in change situations (Scott-Jackson 1998).

Attribution style refers to a person's internal explanations for the causes of positive and negative events in their lives. These are internal explanations which appear to form a common pattern, known as the attribution style, and it affects their general outlook on life as either optimistic or pessimistic. Every individual develops their own attribution style through their experiences and environmental influences which added to 'rational data' governs how they view any positive or negative event.

The nature of their response is a precursor to the process by which people perceive their own well-being, especially in response to events or change. If they perceive a change as potentially positive, they will act accordingly and research has shown that this will maximise the benefits of the change for them as well as the organisation. Even in a negative situation, if a person sees change as positive, they will achieve more and benefit more than a person who sees the change as negative. Therefore, a slightly inaccurate optimistic attribution style is the most functional.

Individuals who adopt a positive exclamatory style are likely to achieve greater SWB and success. Individuals are constantly involved in the comparative appraisal of personal performance versus other causes. For instance, they may ask themselves a question as to, for instance, whether their success at a job interview was a result of their presentation skills or luck. This type of evaluation is the core to the way individuals evaluate their abilities and achieve perceptions of self-worth.

Seligman et al. (2005) suggest that attribution style forms a founding theoretical basis for the development of 'positive psychology'. Attribution style is also evident in analysis, within the context of well-being, including Smith et al. (2013), Sin and Lyubomirsky (2009) and Gordeeva et al. (2011).

Although some argue that personal control is less relevant than other factors, attribution style is normally described as comprising four main dimensions (see Table 4.1).

For SWB and effective function, the most important aspect of attribution style is how the individual interprets negative events. A productive attribution style for negative events has been identified as shown in Table 4.2.

There is substantial evidence to support the claim that a pessimistic style predisposes individuals to poor performance and to interpreting objective factors negatively. Fortunately, however, attribution style is a largely learned behaviour, so it can be modified, either through training or cognitive behavioural techniques which have been used successfully to enhance motivation and attainment (Newland et al. 1997). Attribution style has also predicted effective leadership behaviours (Martinko et al. 2007) and is also been shown to predict higher levels of engagement and well-being (Carver and Scheier 2914).

Table 4.1 Dimensions of attribution style

Internal	Attributing events to something the individual has done or had an influence upon but not necessarily within their control
Stable	Viewing factors surrounding events as being permanent and fixed
Global	Viewing factors surrounding events as being widespread
Personal control	Belief that one's actions determine the outcome of the situation

Table 4.2 Functional attribution style for negative events

External	Attributing events to something that was done by, or under the influence of, others
Non-stable	Viewing factors surrounding events as open to change
Specific	Viewing factors surrounding events as being specific to the current situation
Personal control	Realistic belief that one's actions determine the outcome of the situation

Government and organisational leaders would be advised to consider the integration of attribution style interventions or training in childhood and on organisations' induction courses.

4.5   Individual Propensity for Enthusiasm

As previously discussed, it has been found that a major component of optimism, and therefore active committed enthusiasm, is the individual's own propensity for enthusiasm which varies significantly between individuals. Anyone thinking of a group of friends or colleagues will recognise that some seem to be 'naturally' more or less enthusiastic than others. These differences depend, to a certain extent, on fairly fixed traits, but a much larger component of this propensity is due to learned behaviour over the person's life. Because it is a learned behaviour, it can be modified through an intensive, but relatively simple process based on attribution style, which is fully described in Chap. 6, with tools available at www.PACEtools.org.

References

All Party Parliamentary Group on Well-being Economics. (2014). *Wellbeing in four policy areas*. UK Houses of Parliament.

Beck, A. T. (2002). Cognitive models of depression. *Clinical Advances in Cognitive Psychotherapy: Theory and Application, 14*, 29–61.

Blom, K., Baker, B., How, M., Dai, M., Irvine, J., Abbey, S., et al. (2014). Hypertension analysis of stress reduction using mindfulness meditation and yoga: Results from the harmony randomized controlled trial. *American Journal of Hypertension, 27*(1), 122–129.

Buchalter, S. (2014). *Raising self-esteem in adults: An eclectic approach with art therapy, CBT and DBT based techniques*. London: Jessica Kingsley Publishers.

Chapman, M. (2011). Mindfulness in the workplace: What is all the fuss about? *Counselling at Work*, 20–24.

Dawkins, S., & Martin, A. (2014). Enhancing the psychological capital of teams: Adapting an individual-level intervention for multi-level delivery and evaluation. In *Corporate wellness programs: Linking employee and organizational health* (p. 79).

Ellis, A. (1987). A sadly neglected cognitive element in depression. *Cognitive Therapy and Research, 11*(1), 121–145.

Feicht, T., Wittmann, M., Jose, G., Mock, A., von Hirschhausen, E., & Esch, T. (2013). Evaluation of a seven-week web-based happiness training to improve psychological well-being, reduce stress, and enhance mindfulness and flourishing: A randomized controlled occupational health study. *Evidence-Based Complementary and Alternative Medicine, 2013.*

Galante, M. J. (2014). Internet-based randomised controlled trial of the effect of loving-kindness meditation on wellbeing and helping behaviour. Doctoral dissertation, Cardiff University.

Gardner, J. (1990). *On leadership.* New York: The Free Press.

Garland, E. L., Gaylord, S. A., & Fredrickson, B. L. (2011). Positive reappraisal mediates the stress-reductive effects of mindfulness: An upward spiral process. *Mindfulness, 2*(1), 59–67.

Gordeeva, T. O., & Osin, E. N. (2011). Optimistic Attributional Style as a Predictor of Well-Being and Performance in Different Academic Settings. In *The human pursuit of well-being.* Netherlands: Springer.

Haar, J. M., Roche, M., & Luthans, F. (2014). Do leaders' psychological capital and engagement influence follower teams or vice versa? *Academy of Management Proceedings, 2014*(1), 11058.

Heider, F. (1958). *Interpersonal relations.* New York: Wiley.

Hofmann, S. G., Sawyer, A. T., Witt, A. A., & Oh, D. (2010). The effect of mindfulness-based therapy on anxiety and depression: A meta-analytic review. *Journal of Consulting and Clinical Psychology, 78*(2), 169.

Hölzel, B. K., Carmody, J., Vangel, M., Congleton, C., Yerramsetti, S. M., Gard, T., et al. (2011). Mindfulness practice leads to increases in regional brain gray matter density. *Psychiatry Research: Neuroimaging, 191*(1), 36–43.

Huppert, F. A. (2014). The state of wellbeing science. In F. A. Huppert & C. L. Cooper (Eds.), *Wellbeing: A Complete Reference Guide, Volume 6, Interventions and Policies to Enhance Wellbeing.* Chichester: Wiley.

Huppert, F. A., & Johnson, D. M. (2010). A controlled trial of mindfulness training in schools: The importance of practice for an impact on well-being. *The Journal of Positive Psychology, 5*(4), 264–274.

Jha, A. P., Stanley, E. A., Kiyonaga, A., Wong, L., & Gelfand, L. (2010). Examining the protective effects of mindfulness training on working memory capacity and affective experience. *Emotion, 10*(1), 54.

Martinko, M. J., Harvey, P., & Douglas, S. C. (2007). The role, function, and contribution of attribution theory to leadership: A review. *The Leadership Quarterly, 18*(6), 561–585.

Maslow, A. H. (1954). *Motivation and personality. (Under the editorship of Gardner Murphy).* New York: Harper & Bros.

Meevissen, Y. M., Peters, M. L., & Alberts, H. J. (2011). Become more optimistic by imagining a best possible self: Effects of a two week intervention. *Journal of Behavior Therapy and Experimental Psychiatry, 42*(3), 371–378.

Meyers, M. C., van Woerkom, M., & Bakker, A. B. (2013). The added value of the positive: A literature review of positive psychology interventions in organizations. *European Journal of Work and Organizational Psychology, 22*(5), 618–632.

Newland, J., Boul, L., & Scott-Jackson, W. B. (1997). *Attributional training manual.* Oxford: CSA.

Pakrosnis, R., & Cepukiene, V. (2014). Solution-focused self-help for improving university students' well-being. *Innovations in Education and Teaching International, 52*(4), 1–11.

Proudfoot, J. G., Corr, P. J., Guest, D. E., & Dunn, G. (2009). Cognitive behavioural training to change attributional style improves employee wellbeing, job satisfaction, productivity, and turnover. *Personality and Individual Differences, 46*(2), 147–153.

Roberts, L. M., Dutton, J. E., Spreitzer, G. M., Heaphy, E. D., & Quinn, R. E. (2005). Composing the reflected best self-portrait: Building pathways for becoming extraordinary in work organizations. *Academy of Management Review, 30*(4), 712–736.

Salomons, T. V., & Kucyi, A. (2011). Does meditation reduce pain through a unique neural mechanism? *The Journal of Neuroscience, 31*(36), 12705–12707.

Schonert-Reichl, K. A., Oberle, E., Lawlor, M. S., Abbott, D., Thomson, K., Oberlander, T. F., et al. (2015). Enhancing cognitive and social–emotional development through a simple-to-administer mindfulness-based school program for elementary school children: A randomized controlled trial. *Developmental Psychology, 51*(1), 52.

Schutte, N. S., & Malouff, J. M. (2011). Emotional intelligence mediates the relationship between mindfulness and subjective well-being. *Personality and Individual Differences, 50*(7), 1116–1119.

Scott-Jackson, W. B. (1998). *Individual change competence: The development of a strategic human resource.* Ph.D. thesis, Oxford Brookes University.

Seligman, M. E. (1991). *Learned optimism.* New York: AA Knopf.

Seligman, M. E. P. (1999). *Transcript of a speech given by Dr. Martin EP Seligman at the Lincoln Summit in September of 1999.*

Seligman, M. E. (2002). Positive psychology, positive prevention, and positive therapy. *Handbook of positive psychology, 2,* 3–12.

Seligman, C., Paschall, N., & Takata, G. (1973). Attribution of responsibility for a chance event as a function of physical attractiveness of target person: Outcome and likelihood of event. In *Proceedings of the Annual Convention of the American Psychological Association.* American Psychological Association.

Seligman, M. E., Steen, T. A., Park, N., & Peterson, C. (2005). Positive psychology progress: Empirical validation of interventions. *American Psychologist, 60*(5), 410.

Shapiro, S. L., Carlson, L. E., Astin, J. A., & Freedman, B. (2006). Mechanisms of mindfulness. *Journal of Clinical Psychology, 62*(3), 373–386.

Silvester, J., Patterson, F., & Ferguson, E. (2003). Comparing two attributional models of job performance in retail sales: A field study. *Journal of Occupational and Organizational Psychology, 76*(1), 115–132.

Sin, N. L., & Lyubomirsky, S. (2009). Enhancing well-being and alleviating depressive symptoms with positive psychology interventions: A practice friendly meta-analysis. *Journal of Clinical Psychology, 65*(5), 467–487.

Smith, T. W., Ruiz, J. M., Cundiff, J. M., Baron, K. G., & Nealey-Moore, J. B. (2013). Optimism and pessimism in social context: An interpersonal perspective on resilience and risk. *Journal of Research in Personality, 47*(5), 553–562.

5

The Effect of Leaders on Engagement and Well-Being

As the previous sections have shown, our findings are that, alongside the individual's own 'propensity for engagement' and optimism, the behaviour of the immediate leader is the major causal factor in achieving engagement or active committed enthusiasm. Others have reached similar conclusions, for example, McLeod (2009), in a major review of employee engagement, concludes that 'In our view the joint and consequential failure of leadership and management is the main cause of poor employee engagement'.

5.1 Leadership or Management?

The popular word today for being responsible for other people is leadership. Day-to-day management has become a poor relation in terms of attention, training and monitoring. Yet most things that go wrong in organisations operationally are in fact due to bad management, the *processes* of planning, organising, directing and monitoring the use of resources. The iLeader toolkit mentioned in Chap. 6 mostly addresses these management failings but also, in doing so, instils some key facets of effective leadership. 'Leadership' has a multitude of definitions—Google returns 359 million results to the request for one. However, it generally adds up to something more personal, having and communicating a vision, inspiring others, taking them with you and so on.

John Adair, whilst teaching at the UK's military training college Sandhurst, was one of the first to use the term leadership (instead of 'management') in his 1979 book *Action Centred Leadership*. He deftly combined both leadership and management aspects of a person who is responsible for the work of others in his

© The Author(s) 2018
W. Scott-Jackson and A. Mayo, *Transforming Engagement,
Happiness and Well-Being*, DOI 10.1007/978-3-319-56145-5_5

three-circle model. These interlocking circles combined meeting the needs of (a) the task to be achieved, (b) the individuals in the group and (c) the team as a team. Adding the third circle was an innovation at the time, when most management models in existence worked on the two dimensions of task and people. The day-to-day interaction of an employee with their 'boss' demands a range of skills in what we might call their leader–manager. The way they are applied has a significant impact on engagement and enthusiasm.

This is true at any level in an organisation. But as we move upwards to divisional or corporate executives, it is the leadership aspect that has the greater influence, especially in the position of the CEO or equivalent. Without effective leadership at the top, organisations will drift aimlessly and reactively, and lack innovation and change. Employees are quick to sense a lack of direction, and top level decisions that will affect them personally inevitably have an effect on how they feel about their employment.

So for the purposes of this chapter, we need to look at the balance of influence between the effects of senior leadership decisions and behaviours in an organisation and those of an employee's immediate manager. Building a *sustainable* PACE is a combination of both.

5.2   Engaging Senior Management Themselves

We often think of engagement or ACE in the context of an individual, but in an organisation the individual is not an island. ACE can be infectious. It can travel both down an organisation and across a team. John Adair recognised that creating 'team spirit' is a powerful part of effective leadership. Teams— i.e. a group of people sharing the same purpose—are much more likely to be found at the bottom of an organisation. As we go upwards, we frequently find groups of individuals sharing the same boss but with quite different roles and therefore not really a team.

Until we reach the top. The CEO often struggles with building the shared team spirit of those in the C suite—each with their own portfolio and pre-occupying objectives. But he or she knows how vital it is to their own personal success, and finds it a tough leadership challenge to achieve. The effective executive wears two hats comfortably, taking cabinet responsibility as well as personal. If the CEO can build ACE in each person sitting round the top table, there will be a doubly positive effect. The collective enthusiasm of the team will be visible to all, and the individual enthusiasm will be transmitted downwards.

It is a big mistake to dump the engagement programme onto the HR function. They can certainly facilitate it in many ways, but it must be owned by, and very much alive, with the senior team. How does a chief executive create ACE in the team?

There are many arguments against the common practice of the new CEO firing the existing team and bringing in his or her own people that they know they can trust. But Jim Collins, author of the classic *From Good to Great* (2001), would argue that making sure the *right* people were in the right place in the team is the first task. He puts it this way:

You are a bus driver. The bus, your company, is at a standstill, and it's your job to get it going. You have to decide where you're going, how you're going to get there, and who's going with you.

Most people assume that great bus drivers (read: business leaders) immediately start the journey by announcing to the people on the bus where they're going—by setting a new direction or by articulating a fresh corporate vision.

In fact, leaders of companies that go from good to great start not with 'where' but with 'who'. They start by getting the right people on the bus, the wrong people off the bus, and the right people in the right seats. And they stick with that discipline—first the people, then the direction—no matter how dire the circumstances.

What is meant by 'the right people'? It does not of course mean 'clones of the boss', but it does mean that each is able to align themselves with a shared set of values and priorities. To immediately clear out the executive suite of yesterday's men and women is a great error, since there needs to be time to discuss those values and priorities. Those that must get off the bus are those who do not line up with the agreed way forward. Most CEOs today will listen to others before defining the way forward; some of course come to the role with a strong personal vision, particularly if they are internal appointments.

What is it that will bind people together around the executive table and create collective ACE? We can start with shared focus. This comes in two ways. The first is what we want to be known for; what will be distinctive about us. Our number one goal may be building shareholder value, but so it is for nearly everyone else in the private sector. We can only do that by being excellent at something. For American Express, it is great customer service. For Virgin and South West Airlines, it is the customer experience. For Disney, it is to 'make people happy'. Sony's focus was miniaturisation; Walmart's is the best price. Organisations cannot be good at everything, although many try and fail.

The second kind of focus is to do with achievement. Collins (2001) found that 'great' leaders always found a 'big idea' to become the driving force for the organisation. He called it 'the Hedgehog Concept' and defines it as follows:

Picture two animals: a fox and a hedgehog. Which are you? An ancient Greek parable distinguishes between foxes, which know many small things, and hedgehogs, which know one big thing. All good-to-great leaders, it turns out, are hedgehogs. They know how to simplify a complex world into a single, organizing idea—the kind of basic principle that unifies, organizes, and guides all decisions. That's not to say hedgehogs are simplistic. Like great thinkers, who take complexities and boil them down into simple, yet profound, ideas (Adam Smith and the invisible hand, Darwin and evolution), leaders of good-to-great companies develop a Hedgehog Concept that is simple but that reflects penetrating insight and deep understanding.

There are many examples of where this has worked powerfully and where the 'big idea' has spread amoeba-like throughout the organisation so that everyone shares it. Komatsu famously coined the slogan 'Karu-C' ('Encircle C'), referring to their much larger competitor Caterpillar. Everyone in the company knew it, employees walked over doormats every morning emblazoned with this mission.

Hamel and Pralahad in (1989) gave the term 'strategic intent' to this concept of the focused goal. Some mission and vision statements are similarly engaging, capturing employees with what the company is there for. Sadly, however, many such statements are uninspiring, unmemorable and indistinctive—such will never lead to any engagement in themselves.

Here is a real-life example of a statement that is distinctly uninspiring, even if well meaning. (The company has now changed it so it would be unfair to mention the name.)

ABC Global Statement of Purpose: '*The purpose of ABC Global is to honorably serve the community by producing products and services of superior quality at a fair price to our customers; to do this so as to earn an adequate profit which is required for the enterprise to grow, and by so doing provide the opportunity for our employees and shareholders to achieve their reasonable personal objectives*'.

The classic example, often quoted, of feeling part of a clear and inspiring mission is the story of the janitor at Cape Canaveral. President Kennedy visited a few days before a launch and asked him what his job entailed, he answered without hesitation: 'I'm helping to get a man to the moon'.

Open Arms, a charity that runs an orphanage in Kenya, has its slogan '*Transforming lives, one at a time*'. This is a platform not only for inspiring those who work with it but also for the individual stories of those that are 'transformed'. So one test of the way a purpose is expressed is 'how easy is it for employees to tell people what you do with pride?'

It is admittedly easier for some organisations than others to come up with inspiring missions. Cancer Research UK has its slogan 'Lets beat cancer sooner'. Microsoft's early days were driven by 'a computer on every desk and in every home'—a vision that the large manufacturers at the time laughed at. Many organisations are much less glamorous but every senior team needs to find a clear purpose and it can be done. When a new director took over the Department of Civil Status and Passports of the Kingdom of Jordan in 1992, he found a chaotic, corrupt department where citizens suffered an intensely bureaucratic process that took at least 2 days to get a passport, once one had arrived at one of the very few offices. He set a target that people would get their passport on the same day of application, and they would be known as service providers rather than 'favour providers'. He galvanised all employees to this goal, even taking some people 'off the bus', unheard of in a government department previously. He published a personal phoneline for citizens to call him with any complaints. Three years later, the average time to obtain a document was two hours and employees' pride in their department was an all-time high (Assaf 1998).

However, mundane the product or service, it has a purpose and benefits some customers (or the public) in some way. The question is how do we make that feel worthwhile and even exciting for all our people? It has to be made a part of the life and language of the organisation. The way it is communicated will vary culturally, from the company song in Japan to the emblazoned overalls in the USA.

We may conclude therefore that the first task of the senior leadership team is to find a focus for everyone in the organisation that will inspire them and give them a sense of purpose and pride.

5.3 Values and Culture

The second task of this team is to define *how* the organisation will operate in pursuit of its goals. This is creating an environment with values, principles and behaviours that make up the culture or 'the way things are done around here'. *'Culture eats strategy for breakfast'* is attributed to Peter Drucker and reflects the very strong cultures at the heart of many great companies. Collins and Porras (1992) in their study of long-lasting successful companies (*Built to Last*) found the consistency of culture to be one of the key elements of sustainable success.

It should be the task of all C suite teams to set and review the culture and the values that underpin it, and to decide if it is 'fit for purpose'. Culture always starts with the founders of an organisation and have many elements built up through history. Founders are often charismatic and powerful personalities, with strong views of what they want their organisation to be like *and not like*, and their imprint can pervade an organisation. It is often a legacy and lives on after they have gone. Such bosses are ruthless about 'the right people' and the behaviours expected of them.

One example is Ove Arup Partners, an international firm of consulting engineers. The firm has been involved in many famous constructions, such as the Sydney Opera House, the Channel Tunnel Link, the new Hong Kong airport and London's Swiss Re building. OAP has the unmistakable stamp of its founder, Sir Ove Nyquist Arup, who in 1970 gave *The Key Speech* to a group gathered in Winchester, UK. This defined what Arup would be about, and to this day is a foundational reference. Arup would in no way be characterised by greed either as an organisation or as an individual. It would take pride in engineering excellence first and foremost, followed by the integrity of dealings with customers and a 'humane' environment for its 'members'. The *Key Speech* lists six 'main aims of the firm' which constitute its values:

- Quality of work
- Total architecture
- Humane organisation
- Straight and honourable dealings
- Social usefulness
- Reasonable prosperity of members.

These should result in:

- Satisfied members
- Satisfied clients
- Good reputation and influence.

And this will require:

- A membership of quality
- Efficient organisation
- Solvency
- Unity and enthusiasm.

The year 2013 marked the 70th anniversary of Johnson and Johnson's 'Our Credo', the business philosophy of the company that stands in the reception of every office around the world. Written by General Robert Wood Johnson and presented to the Board of Directors in December 1943, it was one of the earliest statements of corporate social responsibility (www. kilmerhouse.com/2013/12/the-writing-of-our-credo/).

It is not just the older organisations that can demonstrate a consistency of culture and values. There are many modern examples. One such is JetBlue, the US airline. David Neeleman, the CEO and founder, developed his business philosophy working in the slums of Brazil. He developed the airline based on the principles of equity in service (no first class, more legroom for people in the back of the plane) and same services for all. This equity applied to employees regardless of position. He also set up a crisis fund for JetBlue employees that goes beyond standard corporate health benefits. Every worker can donate voluntarily from their pay cheque to the JetBlue Crewmember Crisis Fund. 'Employees know they're coming to a great job where they get full benefits', Neeleman says. 'And if something terrible happens to them, the other employees will help them out'.

The most famous modern example in this field is probably Google. The founders had been in business for a few years before they decided to write down what they were about. Their corporate slogan is 'Do No Evil' and they listed ten beliefs or guiding principles. These are more helpful than values, being more explicit about the 'way we will do things' (www.google.com/about/company/philosophy/).

- Focus on the user and all else will follow.
- It's best to do one thing really, really well.
- Fast is better than slow.
- Democracy on the web works.
- You don't need to be at your desk to need an answer.
- You can make money without doing evil.
- There's always more information out there.
- The need for information crosses all borders.
- You can be serious without a suit.
- Great just isn't good enough.

The influence that such strong cultures have on engagement and ACE is immense. Employees know what they are signing up to. They can find trust and integrity in the consistency of a clearly defined culture, and they have a choice whether they sign up to it or not. The majority of organisations, however, do not have such legacies or foundations to work with. It is very rare (though not impossible) for public sector organisations to develop and sustain an engaging culture. Many private organisations have been subject to restructuring, frequent changes of leadership or dominance by financial requirements. Establishing a consistent culture takes some years.

And we never start from a clean sheet. Edgar Schein (1992) one of the world's leading authorities on organisational culture, uses the analogy of personality. 'You do not just change personality because you think it would be a good idea'. You cannot in fact do it at all; you can only manage it differently. Likewise with 'cultural change" an existing culture is the product of many influences over time and they are our starting point. We first need to understand what we have and where it came from and then decide how we would like to develop or reshape it.

If, however, we understand the benefits to all stakeholders of creating ACE in as many people as possible, it will be time well spent for the executive team to collectively define the character of the organisation they want to build and then to role model it as individuals. Culture in practice is a set of processes and behaviours that are consistent with an agreed set of values. Most organisations like to create a set of values. However, only few embed them in every aspect of the organisation. They have no credibility unless:

- Every employee and manager knows how they apply to their own role and can say 'this means that I *will* do these things and it means I will *not* do those things'.
- Deviations from accepted behaviours are 'disciplined'.

By 'discipline' we do not mean this in an HR sense, but that a trespassing individual is spoken to and counselled that 'this is not the way we do things around here'.

When we define values, care is needed to make sure they can be realistically modelled. A middle eastern bank went through an awayday exercise to come up with a set of values and was proud of the result, which also formed a nice memorable acronym. The problem was that every one of them, except perhaps for 'integrity' was completely counter to the way they had operated to date. In the conservative environment of this bank, there was no hope of changing 2000 people to think and operate so differently. Any exercise in articulating values must reflect the reality of the organisation as it is, and any that are aspirational must be realistic to achieve.

The visible signs of a culture are in (a) the processes that make an organisation work, (b) in the behaviours of employees at every level and (c) the decisions that are taken, especially under pressure. Most of the processes that impact on customers or employees are created by central departments such as HR, Finance, IT and Marketing. Every process has to be put through the filter of the values to check for conflict. Classic areas of conflict occur with values such as 'Empowerment'; 'Respect'; 'Humility'; 'Excellence'; and 'Customers First'. Clashes between reality and the avowed values will only cause cynicism and reduce ACE.

5.4 The Multiplier Effect

Consultants Aon Hewitt did some interesting research (2012) on engagement at different levels in organisations. It is no surprise that successful organisations show a high level of engagement at the senior level. In highly engaged organisations, leaders were significantly more effective (by roughly 1.7 times) than their counterparts at low engagement organisations. The more engaged they are, and the more they understand what engages them, the more likely it is for them to transmit that enthusiasm downwards. Firstly, they will care about the levels of engagement in their part of the organisation, taking personal interest in survey results and the resulting actions. Secondly, they will show 'engaging' behaviours in their own leadership style.

Aon Hewitt concluded there were three key elements needed to engage senior leaders:

Strategy Connect: Leaders are passionate about what the organisation is aiming to achieve and driving this should give them a sense of accomplishment.

Culture Connect: They have an alignment of personal and organisational values and ways of operating.

Top Team Connect: They connect with other senior leaders in the organisation and take collective accountability for the organisation as a whole.

The CEO's job is to create and sustain these 'connections' and to work with the HR people to ensure they become universal through the organisation.

5.5 How Senior Leadership Influences the Degree of ACE

One secret of success in relations to others is that of managing expectations. Just as an organisation's brand value—built up over many years—can be heavily reduced by one incident, even one proven not to be their fault, so engagement can be hit by a senior management decision that is unexpected, unwelcomed and inconsistent with the stated values and beliefs.

No leadership team can protect against bad things happening. They are wise to prepare for scenarios through intelligent risk analysis and planning, and manage staff levels through strategic workforce planning. They can prepare everyone in the organisation for future possibilities, through honest involvement and communications. Organisations with the highest engagement levels are characterised by openness, transparency and trust in their relations with their staff. These require positive and deliberate actions on behalf of management, providing opportunities for discussion and listening.

It is inevitable that the level of ACE will oscillate with time and circumstances, and it is in fact difficult to measure reliably in the first place. However, an aim would be to keep the amplitude of oscillation low and on average steadily increasing. Some of the activities of senior leadership that can have an influence are summarised as follows:

5.5.1 Communicating an Inspiring Sense of Purpose for the Organisation

We have discussed the importance of this above. It is more than the stage management or the initial fanfare of announcing the purpose. It needs to become an ongoing backdrop, featuring regularly in communications and celebrating successes. One test will be that at least every employee knows what it is; better still if they are proud of it.

5.5.2 Maintaining Trust

Trust is like brand reputation, taking a long time to build and minutes to destroy. It is the failure to meet expectations—of behaviour, of promises, of decisions, of integrity. Sometimes, especially in the private sector, decisions have to be taken which senior management would much rather not take. They are nervous about the reactions to them and often hide behind minimal or 'spun' communication.

JormaOllila led Nokia from 1992 to 2006 and not only put Finland on the world map but established a world leading global company. Its cultural core was the 'Nokia Way', a clear and well-publicised statement of the way the company would operate, a role model of such documents. Ollila passed over the reins at a time when the company began to face challenges in a fast developing market. They had not faced laying off people and closing facilities for many years, but in January 2008 they decided to close a factory in Bochum, Germany, and concentrate production of that product group in

Romania. About 2300 employees were affected and another 2000 or so dependent on the factory in various ways in this small town. Nokia had no idea of how integrated industry, politics and labour unions are in Germany, and their sudden decision was met with outrage, such that the executive delivering the news fled to the airport in fear for his safety. The state government authorised an investigation, and shortly afterwards, 69% of an online poll of 56,000 people said they would never buy a Nokia product again. The final settlement cost Nokia some €80,000 per workers, one of the biggest such settlements ever made in Germany (Sucher and Winterburg 2015).

Nokia never forgot this humiliation. Conditions continued to worsen for the company, and in 2011, they decided they must restructure and lose some 18,000 employees over a number of countries between mid-2011 and mid-2012. The 'Bridge' programme that was developed to manage this is an exemplar of downsizing management and is written up in an excellent Harvard case study. In the guiding team was the ex Prime Minister of Finland Esko Aho. In addition to redundancy money, Nokia invested some €50 m (on top of the €1.6bn main restructuring cost) in the management and benefits of the programme, which offered five pathways to a new future. Some two-thirds of those affected across the world reported satisfaction with the programme. Engagement levels of remaining employees and trust in leadership *increased* over the period 2011–2013.

This is an example of how trust can be quickly lost—and the cost and effort required for its restoration. A key platform of Bridge was the CEO's 'burning platform' letter to all employees explaining why it had to be done, the beginning of a very comprehensive communications exercise.

5.5.3 Systematic Communication of What, How and Why

Failures in communication are normally the first complaint of employees, although for some, however much management does it is never enough. Leaders need to communicate the reality of the business frequently, honestly and truthfully, giving people the chance to ask questions and answering them. Even if the response is 'we don't know', employees appreciate that their concerns are being heard. This is especially important in difficult times.

Times have moved on since the practice of cascading messages verbally down through the management chain. Intranets and social media provide immediate and universal opportunities for information and for feedback.

5.5.4 Costs Have to Be Reduced Sometimes, but Changes that Affect People Need Careful Management

Employees are well aware that costs matter. However, when they themselves are clearly treated as 'costs walking around on legs', disposable at the whim of short-term market or political forces, their commitment to an organisation inevitably suffers. The US consultancy Masterworks describes on their website the story of one of their colleagues as follows:

As a recovering HR person, I have felt and experienced 'engagement' and watched as it was methodically stripped out of company cultures. 'Being engaged' USED to mean: my values were in synch with this organization; I knew why the organization existed and what it wanted to be … and I supported that larger picture … it's congruent with my own goals and wishes; I see top people walking their talk … they make decisions that are values-based and support the long term viability of the enterprise. They don't just drive share price.

Starting in the 80's, we systematically outplaced and early-retired the keepers of our cultures; the mentors and story tellers who taught us newbies how to get ahead and how to do it right behaviour. As the various 'loyalty/employment contracts' were broken it became clear that engagement shifted from feeling fully involved in my work … to doing whatever it took to keep a job that provided a means to have a life after work. Engagement used to mean going the extra mile for the good of the other; now I will do what is expected, so long as I am sufficiently compensated.

I experienced systemic disengagement as each of my employers focused on cost reduction. The message was clear. We are all expendable … and worse, any horrible counter-cultural behaviour was tolerated and even rewarded, as long as 'the numbers' were made.

It is always best to involve employees in seeking cost reduction opportunities than imposing policies such as 'no more free coffee'. What may be a small saving may have a large effect on the ACE of employees. If there is a need to reduce the number of employees, there are many great case studies to learn from such as Nokia described above. And yet stories abound on sites such as YouTube of harsh and impersonal layoff programmes. It is not only those that depart that have negative reactions, but maintaining ACE with those who remain—the 'survivor syndrome'—is a challenge and needs to be part of the planning.

5.5.5 Ensuring Processes Are Symbiotic with the Stated Values and Principles

It is processes and procedures that employees interact with every day. This is probably the prime area where they can see whether the 'espoused values and culture' are a reality or not. Often process changes are instituted by 'middle managers' in HQ departments, who may be so task focused that consistency with values does not occur to them as a priority. It is the job of senior leaders —in approving such things—to run that check and ask the appropriate questions.

5.5.6 Ensuring Behaviours Are Consistent with the Stated Values and Principles

Jack Welch at General Electric instituted many distinctive management practices. One of them was the annual performance assessment of managers. He used a two-by-two matrix which balanced on the one axis the achievement of financial results and on the other the exhibition of required leadership behaviours. Each had equal value. Achieving the numbers was not enough in itself.

Senior leaders who have not thought through the practical meaning of the values and culture they have espoused, and continue to permit inconsistent behaviours, will inevitably cause negative reactions and cynicism, punching holes in the engagement of people. Jack Welch did not fire people immediately, they were always given a year to change or improve.

An essential part of building a desired culture is holding workshops where every employee can understand how their own role and tasks are impacted by the values and/or principles.

5.5.7 Ensuring Decisions Are Consistent with the Stated Values and Principles

Short-term pressures and dilemmas easily create temptations to make expedient cost-based decisions. As we have noted, it is when leaders are under pressure that their true colours come through. People notice. They quickly conclude they cannot trust their leaders when they see them ready to compromise in such circumstances.

5.5.8   Investing in the Talent (s) of Employees

The worst thing to do in so-called talent management is to leave it to the HR department. They may well be very professional about understanding talent processes, but their role is supportive. It is the leaders' job to:

- Identify people with talent
- Nurture them
- Invest in them
- Provide opportunities for them
- Challenge them
- Ensure they get coaching and mentoring as needed
- Put internal people first when vacancies occur.

For most people, career opportunities are important. Organisations that have a record of offering career development to their people not only correlate with business success but also are more likely to engage their people in the PACE.

5.6   Motivation in the Workplace

Whereas the level of ACE can be destroyed very quickly by senior management decisions, or lack of them, an employee interacts with his or her immediate manager on a regular basis. If that interaction is consistently negative, whatever the senior management does positively is unlikely to affect that person's ACE. However, the reverse can be true. Military memoirs give us many examples of where an officer in profound disagreement with decisions made above still motivates his or her group towards their own objectives. However, as we noted in 5.4 above, there is a cascade of engagement. If an immediate manager has disengaged themselves, then the challenge of engaging their people is made much greater.

The starting point as always is the level of conviction of the individual manager that engagement or ACE matters. Study after study shows the causal links between engagement and results, so it would appear to be a no brainer that every manager should put maximum effort into creating PACE. The reality is clearly not so. What John Adair called 'the needs of the task' dominates many managers in their day-to-day actions. If people just seem to get on with the job, managers easily make assumptions that they are 'OK'.

In Chap. 3, we mentioned Gallup's Q12 questionnaire, probably the most widely used measurement instrument for engagement. It does not measure engagement itself as an outcome, but defines 12 'drivers' most likely to influence it. Standard Chartered Bank was one of the early enthusiasts for using this and quickly realised that at least 11 of the 12 questions are within the remit of an immediate manager to influence, regardless of culture or other external factors. This led to a massive investment in people skills for first-line managers and team leaders.

Without the mindset that the level of ACE matters, and matters to my success as a manager, no amount of measurement and discussion with HR about the results is going to have an effect. If there is no action on a survey, people become disillusioned and reluctant to participate in the future. Driving that mindset through the reward system by basing part of a bonus on the results is of questionable benefit. Managers should not be paid extra money just for doing their job as a manager-leader. Such incentives can also induce hypocritical behaviours and even corruption as employees are encouraged to score highly.

5.6.1 ACE Cannot Be Cloned

One of the weaknesses of most measurement approaches is that they are based on the 'averages'. Firstly, the instrument that is used will have inbuilt assumptions about 'these are the factors that motivate people'. The Gallup Q12, for example, was based on a statistical analysis of 'one million' pieces of data from staff opinion surveys. Secondly, the administration of such surveys is usually anonymous, and the individual results subsumed into the team results. There are serious objections to both of these approaches.

Regarding the first point, it is self-evident that the factors that influence engagement are not going to be the same for, e.g. middle managers as they are for van drivers. So, a one-size-fits-all measuring instrument administered to all is questionable if we seek the truth. If for practical reasons we do need to use the same measurement instrument for all, then it is important to build in the 'second column'. When we ask how someone feels about a factor, we should ask also 'how important is this to you?' It is the combination of the two questions that lead towards the truth.

In addition to this, the level of ACE for an individual has its own unique causal route. It is a combination of 'subjective well-being' and 'objective well-being' as discussed in some detail in Chap. 1. A person comes into a working environment. That person brings with them their unique personality and approach to life, to work, to setbacks, to other people. They bring their interests, values and sometimes passions for particular kinds of work. The working environment then provides them with a mix of encouragement or otherwise the various 'drivers' of engagement that many studies have identified. The assumption is that all employees react in the same way to those drivers. They do not. What motivates one person does not necessarily do so for the next. Take 'recognition' as one example: some people do not notice whether it happens or not nor does it bother them; others are acutely sensitive to it or the lack of it.

The second objection is about anonymity. There is an accepted HR myth that anonymity is needed to guarantee honesty. This is based on the assumption that an atmosphere of openness does not exist. There are certainly situations where that is true and employees are in fear of being honest. But it depends on the climate that the individual manager has created. The reality is that if the measurement instrument can be discussed face to face with a manager all the difficulties about individualism discussed above will be neutralised, and a personalised engagement action plan can be made. However, a manager does need to take feedback constructively and that remains a challenge for many.

5.6.2   Employee Expectations—the Psychological Contract

One of the very important activities for a manager to do at any level is to understand the 'engagement/motivation' mix of each person they manage. The 'subjective' side is a matter of recruitment and selection; it is going to come with the person. Virgin Atlantic, the airline, has always recruited its cabin crew primarily on personality believing all the needed 'technical' skills can be added. Google is well known for the thoroughness of its recruitment process to make sure recruits are going to fit their culture and values. Perhaps the most important factor, however, is the level of passion people can have for the work they are going to do.

Individuals exchange their services and skills for a mix of financial and non-financial benefits. The latter is often called the 'psychological contract' and it sums up the expectations given at recruitment time of the benefits to be expected. The financial benefits include salary, bonus and contractual benefit packages. The non-financial element embraces benefits such as:

- challenging and interesting work
- equipment and resources that would not otherwise be accessible to them

- being associated with an organisation of high repute
- status and self-esteem
- recognition by the person's managers, or by peers, or even publicly
- opportunities for personal growth and career development
- interesting colleagues to work with
- a satisfying and stimulating environment
- social interaction and events
- opportunities for travel and perhaps high standards of accommodation.

Figure 5.1 shows a simple format to help individuals evaluate what is important to them. An individual takes 100 'motivational points' and first decides the proportion to allocate to financial and to non-financial benefits. They then look at the latter and decide how to distribute between the items listed above based on what matters to them most.

This exercise has been conducted with hundreds of individuals, and so far, there has been no duplication of 'motivation profiles'. It is also very rare, even with young people, to find the allocation to financial benefits more than 70%.

A typical example might be where an individual allocates say 45% to financial and 55% to non-financial. Then, of the non-financial, they might split the profile between Opportunities for Promotion 20%; Reputation and Status 10%; Challenging work 10%; Job Security 8%; and Opportunities for Travel 7%, and of the Financial, they might split between Basic Salary 15%; Benefits 20%; and Bonus 10%.

Distribute 100 points, firstly between the two columns and then broken down into specific aspects of each

Financial	Non-financial
Total	

Fig. 5.1 Understanding an individual's motivational profile

A manager can request each employee to complete one of these exercises which only takes a short time as a basis for a 1:1 discussion. He or she then has an indication of what is likely to *most* motivate or demotivate each person if their expectations are frustrated. Depending on their degrees of freedom, they can take action appropriately, and if they cannot, then they can assess the risk of losing an individual.

5.6.3   Hygiene Factors and Well-Being

Herzberg (1968), the famous industrial psychologist, in his study of what caused motivation or otherwise at work, found a distinction between what he called 'hygiene factors' and those that were motivators. A hygiene factor had a threshold below which a person would experience dissatisfaction, or we might say 'negative well-being'. An example would be relations with one's supervisor or working conditions. If any such dissatisfaction existed, it would counter the motivators and in extreme cases could destroy them completely. So a first step towards engagement is to ensure that no dissatisfaction with such factors exists.

His list of these hygiene factors was as follows:

- Company policies (far the greatest source of dissatisfaction)
- The nature of supervision
- Relations with supervisor
- Working conditions
- Salary
- Relationship with peers
- Personal life issues
- Relationship with subordinates
- Status
- Security.

Four of Gallup's Q12 questions relate to such factors.

5.6.4   Drivers of Engagement

Hertzberg's list of 'motivators' directly stimulates what we are calling ACE and might be considered the first list of the 'drivers of engagement'. They are:

- Personal growth
- Advancement
- Responsibility

- The Challenge of Work Itself
- Recognition
- Achievement.

Six of Gallup's Q12 questions are covered by the above. Interestingly, Q12 does not feature the challenge and satisfaction from work itself. Herzberg felt this to be so important he devoted his later work to the design of more meaningful jobs.

A large number of surveys are available for testing how people are feeling, and some organisations use the annual survey which covers many issues. The general consensus is that surveys specifically aimed at engagement should be shorter (10–15 questions) and more frequent (every 3 or 4 months) than the traditional annual survey. It is important that they also clearly separate the *evidence* of engagement from the *drivers*.

5.7 Individual Leadership Style

Theories and models about leadership abound, and this is not the place for a summary of them. Certain 'styles', however, can have a significant influence on the PACE.

5.7.1 Charismatic Leadership

Perhaps the type of leadership that comes first to mind is that of charismatic leadership. If leadership is about building willing followers, then charismatic leadership is doing so 'by force of personality, persuasion and eloquent communication'. This ability may sometimes override many other deficiencies in the kind of qualities defined by corporate competency frameworks, for example, integrity, collaboration or professionalism. And yet such leaders can certainly create ACE in their followers. We will mention some in para 5.11 on the political scene, and they are to be found in all walks of life.

Shamir, House and Arthur (1993) set out to study the motivational effects of charismatic leaders. The effect of such a leader, they postulated, has significant psychological and behavioural effects on their followers:

- It increases the value of effort in the eyes of the followers: their work is seen as a meaningful contribution to the greater purpose.
- Effort and work increase the follower's self-esteem and self-worth.

- Being part of a group dedicated collectively to the same mission provides support and resilience even when times are difficult.
- Such leaders inspire by giving faith in a better future.
- A willingness to make sacrifices by followers.

All this generates an internal and personal commitment which reflects the passion of the leader.

Since this type of leadership is built around personality, charm and persuasion, it does not depend on formal authority or position. It can emerge at any level. It is, however rare, especially in the everyday life of organisations.

They are, however, a rare species, and charisma is not something that can be learned. Many would say this is a good thing, as history shows in many walks of life that there is a dark side to charisma. It can lead to narcissism, dilution of rational judgement, addiction to admiration and to psychopathic tendencies.

Goffee and Jones looked at how any leader could nevertheless generate followers whether having charisma or not (*Why Should Anyone Be Led By You?* 2000). They concluded the following four qualities were fundamental:

- They are prepared to reveal their weaknesses, selectively. This is about acknowledging their humanity, lack of perfection and being honest.
- At the same time, they discover what is distinctive about themselves that makes them different and capitalise on it,
- They are excellent sensors, skilled in emotional intelligence and picking up signals from people and situations.
- They learn to practice 'tough empathy'. That is, they manage skilfully the balance between care for people and doing what has to be done for the organisation.

5.7.2   Situational Leadership

We discussed above the uniqueness of an individual employee's 'motivational profile'. One theory of leadership that takes account of this is known as 'contingency theory' and this is illustrated in the example of Hersey and Blanchard's 'situational leadership' model (1977). Fig. 5.2 illustrates their concept:

This model illustrates four styles on a continuum, and its foundation is that the mature and effective leader is able to choose the most appropriate style for the situation and the individuals involved. The 'situation' is a function of:

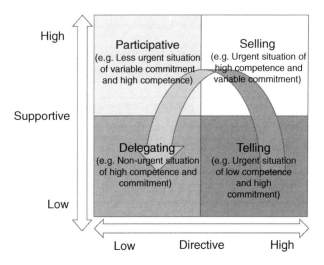

Fig. 5.2 Simplified situational leadership model

- *the situation itself* or task to be addressed. Considerations here are the level of urgency or time pressure, the organisational culture and the nature of the problem to be solved;
- *the current needs of the individual or group involved.* Here the leader takes into account their knowledge, experience and confidence; their involvement in and commitment to the problem; their tolerance for ambiguity and uncertainty; their readiness to assume responsibility; and their own needs for independence and influence.

These considerations may lead to a rational conclusion as to the most appropriate style to be used. But overlaying this is the personal ability and inclination of the leader. It is critical to be authentic, and the leader needs to be aware of his or her own ability to tolerate ambiguity, their willingness to trust and delegate to subordinates, and their own values and philosophy of management.

The mature leader is able to adopt any of these styles adapting to the needs in order to maximise ACE with each individual and the team.

5.7.3 Leadership Competencies

Many organisations put their faith in (variably) researched compendia of leadership competencies, against which leaders are judged. These are attempts to characterise what makes a leader successful and are a blend of personality and personal skills. Some such lists have nothing at all (amazingly) about motivating and engaging people. Here are some relevant examples, however:

- Inspiring others: Positively affects the behaviour of others, motivating them to achieve personal satisfaction and high performance through a sense of purpose and spirit of cooperation. Leads by example (3M).
- Vision and strategy: Creates and communicates a customer-focused vision, corporately aligned and engaging all employees in pursuit of a common goal (3M).
- Lead by example: Be consistent—act with integrity—create trust (Ericsson).
- Personal energy: Engages others through uplifting personal energy (Kingfisher).

Here is an example from a generic set from a consultancy firm:

INSPIRE TRUST AND MOTIVATION

Definition:
Foster motivation and trust by consistently acting with honesty and integrity.
Descriptive Behaviours:

- Demonstrate consistent support and alignment with the mission, vision and values of the organisation.
- Trust others' judgment, recognising that the best decisions are not always made at the top.
- Inspire others to stretch beyond what they thought they could do.
- Inspire action without relying solely on authority.
- Foster a culture that makes people feel valued and respected.
- Create an environment in which performance excellence is rewarded.

These competencies may be used in various ways. They can be used for selection or for in-job development. They may be turned into a 360-degree assessment model and the results used in feedback and coaching.

5.8   What the Immediate Manager Can Do (at Any Level)

5.8.1   Finger on the Pulse

The problem with an annual survey for testing how people feel is that they complete it on one day only of the year and they do not feel the same every day. Hence the argument for more frequent surveys. The recently developed tool called 'iLeader' is described in the toolkit of Chap. 6. This tool utilises mobile phone devices and covers various management/leadership skills. Included in it is a *daily* rating by each team member of how they feel the day has been in terms of both their engagement and their productivity. The tool collates the data from all the team members and gives the leader a picture day by day, which may lead speedily to a problem-solving meeting if needed.

5.8.2 Responding to Survey Data

The response to a survey is a key part of the process and no more so than in this field. As indicated above, there is much to support the open individual discussion with each employee; failing that a useful approach is to hold a meeting and discuss together the results of the survey. This may be a form of group feedback to the manager and require considerable maturity on the manager's part to take on board changes in the way he or she manages the group.

5.8.3 Meeting Individual Needs

At the beginning of this chapter, we noted the work of John Adair and his three sets of needs to be met by the leader–manager. His list for meeting the needs of individuals stands the test of time and is as good a guide as can be found:

- understand the team members as individuals: personality, skills, strengths, needs, aims and fears
- assist and support individuals: plans, problems, challenges, highs and lows
- identify and agree appropriate individual responsibilities and objectives
- give recognition and praise to individuals: acknowledge effort and good work
- where appropriate reward individuals with extra responsibility, advancement and status
- identify, develop and utilise each individual's capabilities and strengths
- train and develop individual team members
- develop individual freedom and authority.

To this list, we might add:

- ensuring individuals have an opportunity to voice their opinions and ideas;
- ensuring their personal 'hygiene factors' (as described previously) are satisfied.

5.8.4 Engaging the Team as a Team

Adair recognised the fact that a team has its own needs as a team. He listed the following needs that a team has from their leader. His first two points relate to the issues of values and culture discussed in para 5.3.

- establish, agree and communicate standards of performance and behaviour
- establish style, culture, approach of the group, soft skill elements
- monitor and maintain discipline, ethics, integrity and focus on objectives
- anticipate and resolve group conflict, struggles or disagreements
- assess and change as necessary the balance and composition of the group
- develop team working, cooperation, morale and team spirit
- develop the collective maturity and capability of the group, progressively increase group freedom and authority
- encourage the team towards objectives and aims, motivate the group and provide a collective sense of purpose
- identify, develop and agree team and project leadership roles within group
- enable, facilitate and ensure effective internal and external group communications
- identify and meet group training needs
- give feedback to the group on overall progress, consult with, and seek feedback and input from the group.

The sixth point is about morale and team spirit, the 'well-being' of the team. 'Team building' events are popular in today's world, usually involving elements of fun and supporting this point.

5.8.5 Leading a Virtual and/or Global Team

Today, we have teams of employees who never meet physically and who operate in their own time and space. How do we stimulate the level of ACE for such people?

Often such teams will be a mix of contractors and employees, with quite different motivational profiles. Aon Consulting (2009) found that productivity of such teams is usually higher, up to 40%, than location-based teams. Telecommunications and Internet technology have made worldwide teams possible, including visual interaction. Without the latter one of the risks is that people are multitasking whilst on team calls. The levels of ACE and well-being will not be as accessible as when people interact face to face regularly, and there is a need for some disciplines which ensure a manager keeps close to individuals. The normal leadership skills are still needed but some additional ones are:

- the need to schedule on 24/7 accessibility
- the clarity of what has to be delivered
- ensuring individual contributors see how their work fits into the big picture
- maintaining trust in diverse cultures, where national cultures and norms interact with organisational ones.

5.9   The Challenges of Engaging Volunteers

On the face of it, this should be no problem, nobody volunteers for something they don't want to do, so are they not engaged by definition? Anyone who has led or managed volunteers knows for certain that it has real challenges.

The reality is that people volunteer for activities and organisations for many different reasons. Understanding the answer to 'what's in it for me' is critical. Here are some reasons:

- Something to add to the CV to demonstrate an interest in the wider community. Examples are being a school governor or playing a part in a professional network or association. These are usually busy people with other priorities in their life and the most difficult to energise into productive contributions.
- People who have no further need to work (or no available work) and are looking for 'something to do'. One of the guidelines for volunteer organisations is that volunteer skills need to match a real need. 'Finding work' for willing people is not a route to engagement. Such people, especially those temporarily out of paid work, are unlikely to have a long-term commitment.
- People who have a real passion for what the organisation is doing and really want to help make a difference. These people are already engaged with the mission. However, they may have very personal views about what should and should not be done and follow their own individual path. The leadership challenge is to ensure there is no conflict with others and such people can share in a common approach.

It is often the mission of the organisation that is the inspiration rather than any individual leader, although there are of course many charismatic leaders particularly in the charity and religious sectors. Key priorities of a leader–manager are particularly in communication—both keeping people informed and listening to ideas; in building a team spirit where everyone's contribution is valued; in recognising and celebrating successes; and in the allocation and coordination of tasks. Often much patience is demanded to accommodate different views, knowing that the thread that holds people to the organisation is much thinner than if their livelihood depends on it.

5.10   A Note on National Leadership and Well-Being

The relationship between national leadership and citizens varies enormously between the different political models that are followed. Any traveller to developing countries is always struck by the apparent contentment of small village communities who have very little materially and who elect their own chief and elders to look after them.

Western style democracies choose their leaders and have the opportunity to change them if their 'well-being' is felt to be threatened. One could take the position that 'well-being' drives leadership rather than the other way around. Changes happen relatively frequently, and few leadership groups last as long as 10 years. However, levels of dissatisfaction with political leadership probably exceed levels of comfort most of the time.

Leaders of course have their own ideas of a better society and always campaign on something that will appeal to the well-being of their citizens, or so they hope. In Britain, the incoming Prime Minister in 2010, David Cameron and his Coalition deputy Nick Clegg introduced the concept of 'The Big Society'. In a government paper dated 18 May (12 days after the election), they announced their intention to:

'put more power and opportunity into people's hands. We want to give citizens, communities and local government the power and information they need to come together, solve the problems they face and build the Britain they want'. (Cabinet Office 2010). Their promises included:

- Give Communities more power
- Encourage people to take an active role in their communities
- Transfer power from central to local government

- Support co-ops, mutual, charities and social enterprises
- Publish government data transparently.

It contained several new initiatives such as the National Citizen Service for young people and was innovative in many ways. However, by 2013 it was clear that it had failed to achieve much support in the country and the government ceased to talk about it. The Guardian Newspaper reported in January 2014 that a former aide to the Prime Minister said that it had run out of steam 'due to lack of leadership'.

Examples of true multiparty democracies in the developing world are few, at least where leaders change at the ballot box. One outstanding example is Ghana. But at the opposite end of the spectrum are single leader autocracies, some of whom can claim to be initially 'elected' by the people but in practice end up as one party states. Here we can look at distressing examples of creating negative well-being, the regime of Pol Pot in Cambodia, of Idi Amin in Uganda and of Robert Mugabe in Zimbabwe. Examples of positive well-being in autocracies are scarce in the modern world (although history has many examples over the centuries). The Khama dynasty in Botswana is often cited as an example and it does indeed shine on many fronts; however, it has big issues with AIDS/HIV, rural drunkenness and poverty.

The outstanding example of a semi-democracy is Singapore.

Singapore is by most counts one of the most successful societies since human history began and has probably improved the living standards of its people faster and more comprehensively than any other society. It leads Asia in the 'Human Development Index' and is ranked 11th globally.

When Singapore was expelled from Malaysia in 1965 and thrust into an unwanted independence, it was a typical 'developing' country. Its per capita income of $500 was about the same as Ghana at that time. It is now $62,000. In May 2016, the IMD World Competitiveness Survey ranked Singapore 4th in the world. Infant mortality reduced from 35/1000 live births to 2, ranking with the best in the world.

In education, the OECD ranked 15-year-old Singaporean children number one in the world in a recent global ranking of 'Universal Basic Skills' in mathematics and science. Singapore students also topped the OECD PISA problem-solving test in 2012.

In housing, from the many slums of 1965, Singapore now has the highest home ownership of any country in the world, with 90% of residents living in homes they own. Even among households in the lowest 20% of incomes, over 80% own their own homes.

Singapore has been consistently rated among the least corrupt countries in the world by Transparency International. In 2011, the World Justice Project's *Rule of Law Index* ranked Singapore among the top countries surveyed with regard to 'order and security', 'absence of corruption' and 'effective criminal justice'. However, the country received a much lower ranking for 'freedom of speech' and 'freedom of assembly'.

This has all been brought about by the firm and enlightened hand of the late Lee Kuan Yew, who became the first Prime Minister, together with the lesser-known architect of the economic miracle that ensued, Dr. Goh Keng Swee. Mr Lee implemented three key policies:

- Meritocracy: neither 'connections' nor race would overrule the best and most able citizens for key positions'
- Pragmatism: willing to copy best practices from anywhere. Also a willingness to foster and keep good relations with all other nations, including China whose political system was so radically different.
- Honesty with zero corruption, even to the extent of making 'tipping' illegal.

There is no doubt these initial principles were turned into practical reality and became core capabilities of the country and contributors to its success. Throughout the 50 years, the country has been led by one party, the People's Action Party. Lee Kuan Yew was not only a visionary but was able to build leadership below and around him, which over the years established a continually developing culture throughout the nation of both hard work and conformism. They achieved continuity by passing on batons whilst retaining the predecessor in the cabinet with a special portfolio.

The Middle East provides us with examples of dynastic sultanates and monarchies who owe their continuity, partly at least, to their concern for the well-being of their citizens. Fortunately, the wealth of natural resources has allowed the elimination of poverty. The Sultanate of Oman is an outstanding case. This case is written up in detail in Jawal and Scott Jackson (2016) and describes the progress of the country under the leadership of HM Sultan Qaboos and his advisers in three phases. In 1970, the Sultanate was a desert backwater, with only three schools. The first phase (1970–1990) was aimed at the delivery of basic provisions for a modern world. Phase 2 (1990–2010) focused on economic growth and diversification. Phase 3 (2010-) specifically targets social well-being. The authors conclude:

Oman's example provides a strong illustration of how the components of the PACE model can enhance and drive policy making—every time a 'norm' is attained, policymakers need to adapt in order to focus on new priorities and challenges. Leadership can engage with citizens, but in doing so, there are specific requirements: the need to establish a vision, demonstrating intent to fulfil objectives, articulating a compelling story and maintaining positive relationships with citizens.

The populations of Botswana, Singapore and Oman are approximately 3 m, 6 m and 3.5 m. They are small enough for national leaders to keep closely in touch with what is happening in their countries. Most (not all) leaders know that their legitimacy and continuity to some extent depend on steadily improving citizen well-being and will look for policies and programmes that give that message. They may not, however, always deliver on them.

References

Adair, J. (1979). *Action centred leadership*. London: Gower.

Aon Hewitt Consulting. (2012). The multiplier effect. Insights into how senior leaders drive employee engagement higher. Retrieved January 25, 2017, from http://www.aon.com/attachments/thought-leadership/Aon-Hewitt-White-paper_Engagement.pdf.

Assaf, M. (1998). Business process Re–engineering in the public sector: The case of the department of civil status and passports in Jordan (DOCSAP). Granada, Euro Arab Management School.

Cabinet Office UK. (2010). *Building the big society, UK Government paper*.

Collins, J. C. (2001). *From good to great*. New York: William Collins.

Collins, J. C., & Porras, J. I. (1994). *Built to Last*. New York: Harper Business.

Ferrazzi, K. (2014). Getting virtual teams right. *Harvard Business Review*.

Goffee, R., & Jones, G. (2000). Why should anyone be led by you? *Harvard Business Review* OnPoint. September-October. Product 5890.

Google Inc. Retrieved January 25, 2017, from https://www.google.com/about/company/philosophy/.

Hersey, P., & Blanchard, K. H. (1977). Management of organizational behavior: Utilizing human resources (3rd ed.). New Jersey: Prentice Hall.

Herzberg, F. (2003, [1968]). One more time—how do you motivate employees? *Harvard Business Review* OnPoint. Product 388X.

Jawad, A. Q., & Scott-Jackson, W. B. (2016). *Redefining well-being in nations and organizations—A process of active committed enthusiasm*. London: Palgrave.

Johnson and Johnson Inc. Retrieved January 25, 2017, from http://www.kilmerhouse.com/2013/12/the-writing-of-our-credo/.

Mcleod, D., & Clarke, N. (2009). *Department of business, innovation and skills, UK Government*.

Pralahad, C. K., & Hamel, G. (1989). Strategic intent. *Harvard Business Review*.

Shamir, B., House, R. J., & Arthur M. B. (1993). The motivational effects of charismatic leadership: A self-concept based theory. *Organization Science*, 4(2).

Schein, E. (1992). *Organisational culture and leadership*. San Francisco: Jossey Bass.

Sucher. S. J., & Winterberg, S. J. (2015). Nokia's bridge program: Redesigning layoffs. *Harvard Business Review Case Study*. 9-315-002.

6

Transforming Well-Being and Engagement: A Toolkit

The toolkit is an evolving set of tools within the overarching PACE framework to help organisational and national leaders to maximise the happiness, well-being and active committed enthusiasm (ACE) of their people. This toolkit will be added to and improved as new techniques and tools become available. To keep up to date, to access and use the various tools and to contribute, please sign in at www.PACEtools.org.

As well as these specific tools, the preceding chapters also include many recommendations, examples of instruments and so on. The tools currently included in the toolkit are those which have been developed specifically in the process of the research and development involved in this book. There are obviously lots of other checklists, processes and systems to help with engagement, happiness and well-being, but we have focused on a specific and limited set which match the findings of our research and support the maximisation of ACE.

As shown previously, much of the confusion and lack of success in improving happiness, well-being and engagement worldwide stem from the fact that several similar concepts are treated separately and there is a confusion between causes, outcomes and the concepts themselves. The toolkit therefore commences with a process framework to allow these elements to be properly identified, especially in terms of their impacts on desired outcomes such as productivity, citizenship or indeed happiness itself. This framework will allow any specific set of causes/inputs and outcomes to be modelled and more clearly understood, especially as each potential input, for example, 'health', could have a myriad of inputs of its own, for example, 'exercise' and each of those could have a range of inputs such as 'gym provision'.

© The Author(s) 2018
W. Scott-Jackson and A. Mayo, *Transforming Engagement,
Happiness and Well-Being*, DOI 10.1007/978-3-319-56145-5_6

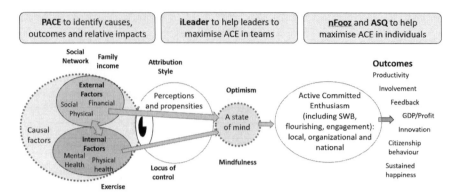

Fig. 6.1 The PACE toolkit

In the previous chapters, we have also identified two major common causes of ACE that seem to apply widely. These are the individual's own individual propensity for enthusiasm and the behaviour of immediate leaders (especially in a work context). The following tools provide specific help with these two primary causes:

- The Active Committed Enthusiasm Questionnaire (ACQq) and nFooz app to help individuals to maximise their own optimism and enthusiasm.
- The iLeader tool for leaders to maximise their impact on well-being and active committed enthusiasm and to monitor and act on continuous changes in enthusiasm and productivity in their teams.

The toolkit therefore currently comprises (Fig. 6.1):

- PACE model for analysing the specific process of engagement and well-being in the leader's context, especially the primary causal factors, and to help determine which initiatives will have the most impact for the least effort/cost.
- iLeader tool to help maximise the active committed enthusiasm of teams
- ACEq and nFooz tools to help maximise individual propensity for active committed enthusiasm.

6.1   The Process for Active Committed Enthusiasm (PACE)

PACE, as described in Chap. 3, enables national and organisational leaders (or their designates such as strategy or HR departments) to model the flows of causes and outcomes related to active committed enthusiasm (ACE). It can be completed for a specific country, organisation or even team, and for specific situations (such as a change management programme) or to achieve specific outcomes (such as reduced absenteeism).

The evidence of these causal relationships, relative weights of causality, costs and benefits can be based simply on the collected opinions of experts or on data such as the results of surveys, experiments, independent research or 'big data' extracted from cloud-based sources. The opinions of those involved or other experts can be as illustrative as independent data for the purposes of the model, which simply tries help organise and visualise, and thereby stimulate thinking and insights, on the causal flow leading to ACE and its relevant outcomes.

The following highly simplified model illustrates the main stages in building a PACE model. The content and weightings are illustrative examples. A specific model would of course be built within the specific context and purpose.

Stage 1: The first stage in building a PACE model is to define the relevant outcomes (Fig. 6.2).

For an organisation, these could include increased productivity or reduced absenteeism, for example. For a nation, these could include overall levels of happiness (however measured), economic performance or decreased popular dissent or tax avoidance. Of course, a model is always a highly simplified view of the world but allows the causal logic of a process to be visualised and

Outcomes

Fig. 6.2 Example outcomes of the PACE model

modified as well as the ability to apply weights, costs and benefits to compare initiatives.

Stage 2: is to begin to identify the potential candidate causes of ACE and, most importantly, their impact on the individuals' propensities, perceptions and state of mind which act as subjective filters to any objective causes such as income or health (Fig. 6.3). As before, these causes can have been identified by specific research or experimentation, generalised research or data gathering or the ideas and opinions of those involved or other experts.

Stage 3: Having identified a set of candidate causes, it is now possible to populate the model with actions/initiatives that might impact these causal areas (Fig. 6.4). Some of these may act on the objective causes, such as health, but some might act directly on the state of mind (e.g. actions to increase optimism). These actions can, again, be based on research or (sometimes more productively) brainstorming ideas among those involved and/or experts.

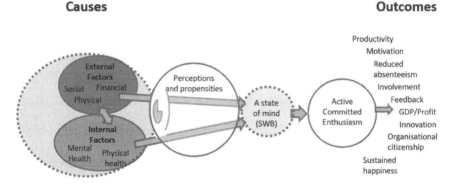

Fig. 6.3 Identify the candidate causes

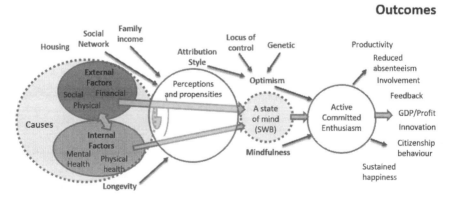

Fig. 6.4 Identify actions to impact the causal flow

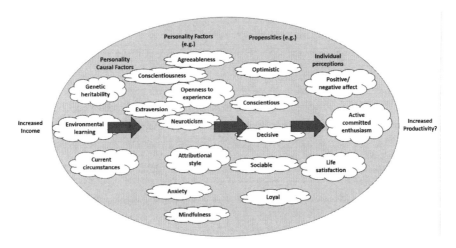

Fig. 6.5 Example personality factors which might impact propensity for ACE

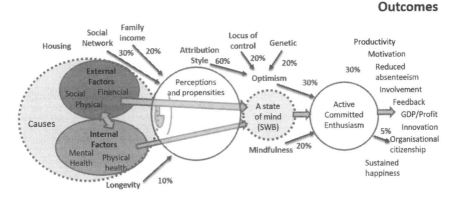

Fig. 6.6 Weight the various candidate causes

As noted above, this analysis can be carried out to a high level of detail. For example, it would be possible to examine the following factors and many more, as part of the analysis of the causal flow impacting perceptions (Fig. 6.5).

Stage 4: Now, the relative causal weightings of the various initiative areas can be estimated by the team involved (Fig. 6.6). For example (working from the right hand 'outcomes'), how much does ACE impact reduced absenteeism compared to, say, having paid sick leave. Similarly, how much impact does family income have on my perception of well-being?

Stage 6: For those initiative areas that appear to have the highest relative weightings (i.e. potential impact) what actions could be taken to modify that factor (Fig. 6.7). For example, if ACE is impacted at a level of 30% by optimism and optimism is impacted at 20% by the individual's locus of control (a psychological term to describe the sense of how much control a person has over their own decisions, work and life), then what specific actions could impact locus of control. A programme or training to introduce delegated decision-making, for example, might improve locus of control and therefore optimism and thereby ACE itself. Similarly, for a nation or organisation, if my social network and relationships have a positive impact on my perception of well-being, then what actions could improve my capability to create positive social networks? In the UAE, for example, there are various initiatives to preserve the beneficial aspects of the high-relationship society so that it is not eroded through rapid development.

Stage 7: Having built the model and populated the flow with the various causes, initiatives and weightings, it is possible to use the model to compare initiatives. For example, suppose our goal was to reduce time off sick. We have enough funding to either provide increased health facilities or introduce mindfulness training in schools. Working through the model, we can estimate that the increased provision of health facilities we can afford might have a 10% impact on the health of our workforce (all figures are simply examples), this might impact my perceptions of my health by 20% and this might increase my sense of well-being by 20%, which in turn might impact absence

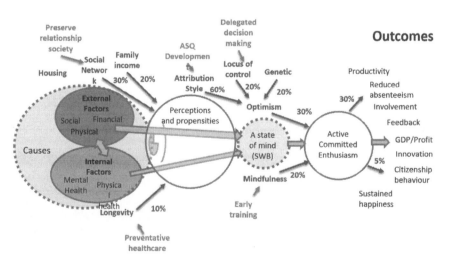

Fig. 6.7 Identifying causal factors and impact

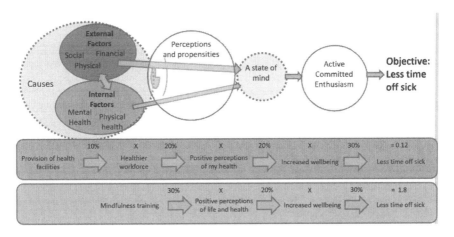

Fig. 6.8 Using PACE to compare the ROI of initiatives

time by say 30%. By simply multiplying the weightings together, we arrive at an impact rating of 0.12 (Fig. 6.8).

Carrying out a similar exercise for mindfulness training suggests a rating of 1.8. If the two initiatives were similar in cost, then this would predict that mindfulness training would be more effective. Mathematically, this method also reflects the fact that the more directly an initiative impacts perceptions and state of mind, then the less steps in the PACE process and the more direct the impact.

6.2 The Active Committed Enthusiasm Questionnaire (ACEq)

As previously identified, governments and organisational leaders worldwide have recognised that the economic success, as measured by GDP, is simply a component of a much wider goal, the engagement, well-being and happiness of their people. Recent research (Jawad and Scott-Jackson 2016) has identified that most current interventions at national level actually facilitate, and measure, the more passive variant of happiness, loosely described as contentment, whereas efforts in organisations have tended to focus on engagement with a goal of increasing productivity commitment and so on. These two different approaches have developed distinct tools, methods and measures, whereas recent research has suggested that an active variant of happiness, described as active committed enthusiasm, is a proper goal of any organised body of people, from a team to a nation.

At the same time, work by the Smart Dubai Office (see Chap. 7) has similarly identified that many current interventions focus on maximising affective and cognitive happiness but do not focus on the deeper, eudaimonic needs or indeed the basic factors involved in objective well-being.

The Questionnaire for Active Committed Enthusiasm (ACEq) has been developed as a measure of active committed enthusiasm (ACE) in organisations and nations and to reflect the balance of affect, cognitive, basic and eudaimonic needs. It is based on an analysis of many of the existing robust measures from the fields of happiness (subjective well-being) and engagement.

The criteria for the questions in the instrument were:

- That each question should be diagnostically useful for the organisation, i.e. the results help to drive actions for improvement.
- That they should allow the analysis of affective, genitive, basic and eudaimonic needs.
- That they should measure ACE (as opposed to just contentment or affect).
- That they should be based on well-proven questions from an analysis of the relevant robust academic instruments in the fields of well-being, happiness and engagement.

To accomplish this, a database was produced of all the questions from the major academically developed instruments:

- World Values Survey Single Item: Cheung, F., & Lucas, R. E. (2014). Assessing the validity of single-item life satisfaction measures: Results from three large samples. Quality of Life research, 23(10), 2809–2818).
- Cantril's Ladder as used in the UN World Happiness Index: Cantril, Hadley. PATTERN OF HUMAN CONCERNS DATA, 1957–1963. ICPSR ed. Ann Arbor, MI: Inter-university Consortium for Political and Social Research [producer and distributor], 1977.
- iLeader: Jawad, A. Q., & Scott-Jackson, W. (2016). Redefining Well-being and Engagement: Why Bother? In *Redefining Well-Being in Nations and Organizations* (pp. 1–12). Palgrave Macmillan UK.
- DRM: Kahneman, D., Krueger, A. B., Schkade, D. A., Schwarz, N., & Stone, A. A. (2004). A survey method for characterizing daily life experience: The day reconstruction method. *Science*, 306(5702), 1776–1780.
- Attribution Style Questionnaire: Jawad, A. Q., & Scott-Jackson, W. (2016). Redefining Well-being and Engagement: Why Bother? In

Redefining Well-Being in Nations and Organizations (pp. 1–12). Palgrave Macmillan UK.

- PERMA: Butler, J., & Kern, M. L. (2016). The PERMA-Profiler: A brief multidimensional measure of flourishing. *International Journal of Well-being*, 6(3), 1–48.
- TLQ: Alimo-Metcalfe, B., & Alban-Metcalfe, J. (2005). Leadership: time for a new direction? *Leadership*, 1(1), 51–71.
- Utrecht Work Engagement Scale: Schaufeli, W. B., Bakker, A. B., & Salanova, M. (2006). The measurement of work engagement with a short questionnaire: A cross-national study. *Educational and psychological measurement*, 66(4), 701–716.
- Pemberton Happiness Index (PHI) Hervás, G., & Vázquez, C. (2013). Construction and validation of a measure of integrative well-being in seven languages: The Pemberton Happiness Index. *Health and quality of life outcomes*, 11(1), 66
- Gallup Q12: Wagner & Harter (2006). *12: the elements of great managing.* Gallup.
- IES Engagement Statements: Robinson, D., Perryman, S., & Hayday, S. (2004). *The drivers of employee engagement.* Report. Institute for Employment Studies.

From this review, 28 questions were developed to meet the criteria above. The questionnaire and completion instructions are available at www. PACEtools.org.

6.2.1 Attribution Style as Part of ACEq to Maximise Individual Active Committed Enthusiasm

As we have seen, active committed enthusiasm is highly impacted by the individual's own propensity for enthusiasm, driven by underlying traits or tendencies such as optimism. In any group of people, one can often identify individuals who seem more positive and optimistic than others, and similarly those who seem more pessimistic. Fortunately, and contrary to popular belief, this particular psychological characteristic is not fixed or genetically predetermined but is, to a large extent, 'learned' through experiences. It can, therefore, be modified and, as we have seen, a specific methodology known as attribution style (or explanatory style) has been successfully deployed and demonstrated as effective in a wide range of contexts, including treatment for depression (in combination with cognitive behavioural therapy) and numerous non-clinical contexts such as increasing the optimism and capability of sales people. Three attribution questions are included in ACEq, and the rationale and methodology are given as follows.

In brief, attribution style refers to a person's internal explanations for the causes of positive and negative events in their lives. These explanations form a common pattern, the attribution style, and this has a direct influence on whether their outlook on life is optimistic or pessimistic. Everyone has developed their own attribution style through life experiences which, together with 'rational data', drives how they will view any negative or positive event. This is a key precursor to the process by which people perceive their own well-being and how they see the future. In the context of change management, for example, if they see a change as potentially positive, they will act accordingly and our research has shown that this will maximise the benefits of the change for them and the organisation. Surprisingly, this is true even if the objectively assessed implications of the change were potentially slightly negative. Even in a negative situation, a person who sees change as positive will achieve more and benefit more than a person who sees the change as negative. So a slightly inaccurate optimistic style is the most functional.

The reason for this is that a person's attribution style affects how they behave so that, for example, if I believe I failed an interview because I am terrible at interviews, then I am likely to perform badly in future interviews. This feedback loop (Fig. 6.9) can only be broken by a different interpretation of the event, either based on factual information (e.g. you find out you actually failed because the job had been cancelled) or, more likely (as facts about causes are rarely available), by a change in your attribution style.

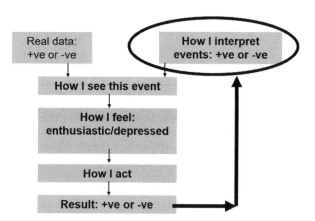

Fig. 6.9 Attribution style feedback loop

Generally, it has been found that people with a more functional attribution style tend to be more engaged and positive about their work and are more likely to display active committed enthusiasm.

Individuals who display an optimistic explanatory style for both positive and negative events are likely to achieve greater satisfaction and success. Individuals are constantly involved in the comparative appraisal of personal performance versus other causes, e.g. "was a success at a job interview due to presentation skills or luck?". These explanations are core to the way individuals evaluate their abilities and achieve feelings of self-worth.

The following is a brief description of the three dimensions of attribution styles which have been shown to have the most impact. These are then mapped against some explanations for an unsuccessful interview (Fig. 6.10). These dimensions can be reliably measured through the Attribution Style Questionnaire.

Internal	Attributing events to something the individual has done or had an influence upon but not necessarily within their control
Stable	Viewing factors surrounding events as being permanent and fixed
Global	Viewing factors surrounding events as being widespread

A productive attribution style, for negative events, has been identified as:

External	Attributing events to something that was done by, or under the influence of, others
Non-stable	Viewing factors surrounding events as open to change
Specific	Viewing factors surrounding events as being specific to the current situation

The most functional attribution style would be D, and the least functional would be B. In occupational settings, the importance of attribution styles cannot be underestimated. It is based on clear research and well-documented theoretical findings. There is evidence to support claims that dysfunctional explanatory or pessimistic styles negatively impact well-being and enthusiasm—and thus job satisfaction and performance. A dysfunctional attribution style can lead to feelings of lack of control in one's life. Therefore, selecting on attribution styles has important implications for organisations. In addition, as attribution is a learned behaviour, training programmes have been successfully used to enhance motivation and attainment. Of course, factual analysis of causes of events is a

	Stable/ unstable	Internal/ External	Global/ Specific
A. I wasn't 100% that day	U	I	S
B. I'm not bright enough	S	I	G
C. I didn't try, as I didn't really want it	U	I	S
D. The process wasn't very good	U	E	S
E. I'm not good at interviews	S	I	S

Fig. 6.10 Dimensions of attribution style mapped against explanations of an unsuccessful interview

vital capability for learning and an 'over-positive' attribution style could blind the individual to useful experiences. But, as noted, a slightly inaccurately positive attribution style is generally the most functional.

6.2.2 Attribution Style Questionnaire

The ASQ is a single, self-completion questionnaire, which can be administered on paper, electronically (via an Intranet/Internet) or during an interview. We have found that the dimensions of 'internal', 'global' and 'stable' are the most differentiating and useful. Our version of the attribution style questionnaire (Fig. 6.11) also includes three of the most common 'well-being' type questions to check correlation with ASQ. These are now included in the ACEq provided at www.PACEtools.org. An example of one of the questions is given below:

Questions from the OSC ASQ include:

- You do some work that is highly praised.
- A work colleague doesn't follow your instruction.

4. You can't finish a project on time.

Now rate this on the following scales (tick the appropriate box)

A. In similar situations, will this cause again influence what happens?

Will never again influence what happens ☐ ☐ ☐ ☐ ☐ ☐ Will always influence what happens

B. Is the cause something that just affects this situation or does it influence other areas of your life?

Influences just this situation ☐ ☐ ☐ ☐ ☐ ☐ Influences all areas of my life

C. How much are you responsible for causing this situation?

Not at all responsible ☐ ☐ ☐ ☐ ☐ ☐ Completely responsible

Fig. 6.11 Example question from attribution style questionnaire (© Oxford strategic consulting 2014)

- You are given a promotion.
- You can't finish a project on time.
- You are asked to be leader of a team.
- You apply unsuccessfully for a position.
- You achieve the best results of anyone in your team.
- A co-worker criticises you.

We also include single-item questions on subjective well-being, mood and resilience/coping. The questionnaire takes approximately 10–20 min to complete and, based on numerous studies of the basic form of the ASQ, has a reliability comparable with other personality profiling tests. The various 'situations' that prompt responses can be changed to reflect organisational or other situations, if required. The negative and positive events could be changed to reflect married life, for example, provided that they require the respondee to imagine the situation.

The questionnaire is particularly well suited to repeat testing, as participants do not tend to 'learn' the correct answers. Therefore, this approach can be used to measure improvements in attribution over time.

6.2.3 Feedback Report

The results of the assessment can be presented and discussed during a one-to-one meeting, where the outcomes can be explained and development options considered (Fig. 6.12).

As can be seen, this person has scored much more highly in regard to positive events (Pos) than negative (Neg) and this is very typical. In fact, causes of positive events seem to have much less impact on attribution style and resulting positivism and optimism than how we respond to negative events. This may be because, from an evolutionary perspective, we learn from negative events far more than from positive. This respondee's mood, coping and well-being are similarly above the mid-range. The most interesting scores are for the first three lines where the scores for negative events have a low score for internal (i.e. causes of negative events are something to do with me), lower for global (i.e. this cause will impact other types of event) and even lower for stable (i.e. this cause will impact similar events in future). So this person, in response to a failed interview, for example, would tend to think the cause was something to do with them (e.g. I am stupid) that it would impact future interviews (my stupidity means I am likely to fail) and other types of events (if I were asked to do a report my stupidity would cause failure). In this

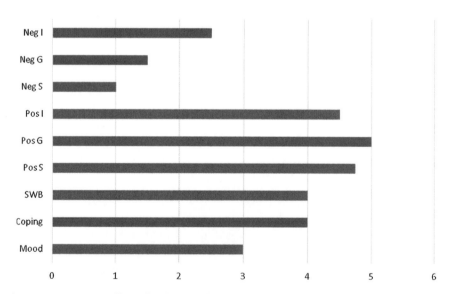

Fig. 6.12 Your overall attribution results

case, it is important to remember that the respondee had no facts or evidence from the assessment to suggest that kind of cause. However, this kind of response would undoubtedly impact optimism, well-being, engagement and future behaviour adversely.

Interventions to improve attribution style range from simply understanding that many judgements about causes of events are actually based on a 'style', through to practicing (often in a formal setting) different candidate causes (i.e. perhaps I failed the interview because the interviewer wasn't very good?) and, in clinical settings, cognitive behavioural therapy or similar interventions. In a business non-clinical context, we have found that a 1-day workshop can have good results, especially if followed up at two subsequent sessions 3 months apart.

6.2.4 Group-Level Feedback

Individual results can be aggregated at group level (Fig. 6.13) and compared with various norm scores from other academic studies. Presentation of results can include the following, which are used to promote group discussion and learning.

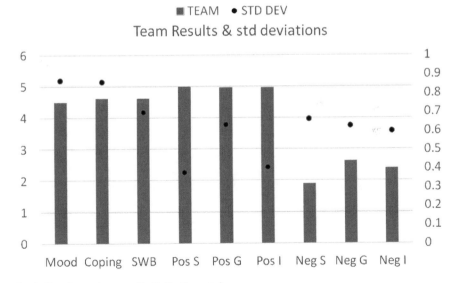

Fig. 6.13 Group's overall attribution style scores

6.3 ILeader Tool for Leaders to Maximise Their Impact on Well-Being and Active Committed Enthusiasm

As we have identified, a major causal factor in engagement and well-being is the behaviour of the immediate line manager. This has been shown to impact engagement and well-being, not just whilst at work but also outside the work situation including family and social life.

Our research has found that many line managers are initially given leadership roles because of their seniority or capability in team member roles. So, for example, a senior software engineer may end up as a team leader, not because they have been assessed as having any particular leadership capability, but because they are the most senior, or the most capable, software engineer. Organisations generally then provide training to try and instil these leadership capabilities through intensive training but, as we found in our recent major study with the Chartered Management Institute (Scott-Jackson et al. 2016), first line leadership training has some major issues. Of course, given the pyramid structure of virtually all organisations, there are far more of these 'first line' leaders than any other and they directly impact nearly all the employees. So, cumulatively, their effect on engagement and well-being is far greater than any of the more senior leaders in an organisation. In a study with a global oil company, we found that first line leaders tended to succeed or fail in the first two years (Fig. 6.14) due to failure in simple key leadership tasks, such as 'having a frank conversation' or 'allocating tasks'.

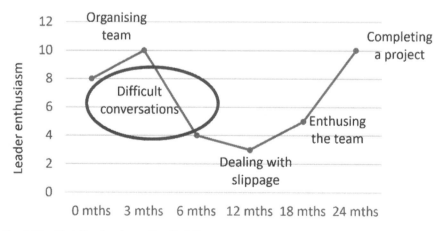

Fig. 6.14 First line leaders—the first 2 years

We found that most leadership training was too soon, i.e. had been forgotten by the time it was useful; too late, i.e. took place after it was first needed and/or too much, covering far too much detail with far too much theory and complexity. In addition, our study (Scott-Jackson et al. 2016) found that new technologies had generally been used to 'dump' the content of leadership programmes, rather than really exploiting the potential for immediate 'point of use' help and for collecting and utilising simple but effective data on, for example, team enthusiasm.

As a result of these various research studies, we investigated app or web-based tools that dealt with the key issues and effectively utilised the potential of personal mobile technology. In a project with Commercial Bank Qatar, the UK-based oil company and Cleveland Clinic in Abu Dhabi, we identified the top ten tasks (without worrying about whether they should be strictly defined as 'leadership' or 'management' tasks) that first line leaders found the most difficult, important and time-consuming (Fig. 6.15). There was considerable overlap despite the wide range of industries, countries and cultures. The top ten included frank conversations (most often 'pre-disciplinary'), running an effective meeting, organising tasks, delegating, managing emails (which was consistently raised by these first line leaders!), motivating teams, decision-making and delegating.

For each of these tasks, we asked the participants what exactly was difficult about them. In most cases, these difficulties did not involve complex psycho-social aspects of leadership (such as transformational or charismatic leadership) but could be solved by relatively straightforward processes which

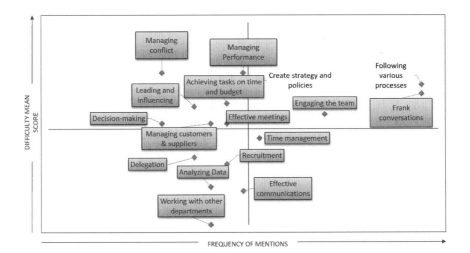

Fig. 6.15 Analysis of top ten leader issues in one organisation

implemented best practice as part of the process, rather than 'teaching' best practice as distinct concepts. It became clear that for each of these difficult, important and time-consuming tasks, it was possible to provide a straight-forward simple process which could help first line leaders to do these tasks more successfully without having to wait for training courses and without having to learn anything. Of course, training, experience and learning will no doubt increase leadership effectiveness, but to be a competent leader, and avoid the common pitfalls that lead to disengagement, anyone could simply follow the process and do (rather than learn) the task.

Having designed the processes, it also became clear that the ability to access these processes in real time on a smart phone would allow the leader to use them as true tools whilst carrying out the specific tasks. So, for example, the tool for 'frank conversation' could be used whilst preparing, organising, having the conversation and recording actions and the 'decision' tool can be used to make a decision between various options (Fig. 6.16), rather than just learning how to weight and evaluate options.

We also found that new leaders sometimes failed to register and act on the varying levels of engagement and productivity within their teams and individuals, and indeed, company-wide engagement measures tended to be carried out very infrequently (most often annually) when engagement, of course, varies daily and needs to be resolved daily. So, as well as the set of tools, we also provided a version for team members where they can record, on a simple slider, their view of the level of engagement and productivity of the team. Having tried questions reflecting best practice engagement surveys and so on, we found that two simple questions 'how engaged was the team today?' and 'how productive was the team today?' (Fig. 6.17). We originally asked 'how engaged were you today?' or 'How engaging was the team leader?' But both of

Fig. 6.16 iLeader toolMake a great decision

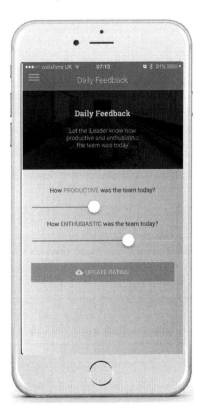

Fig. 6.17 How enthusiastic/productive was the team today?

these encouraged inaccurate answers aimed at appearing engaged or not criticising the leader (Fig 6.17).

The results of these questions are aggregated and analysed by iLeader to recommend actions for the leader, with, of course, the appropriate tool to help. So, if one person was 'red' on 'how enthusiastic was the team today', then the app might suggest having a frank conversation to find out why and to resolve any issues.

Lastly, especially for millennials, we found that many people find it easier to communicate some types of request for a discussion via smartphone, so we include a button which allows the team member to request a conversation to discuss an issue, idea or whatever.

Reference

Scott-Jackson, W., Owens, S., Saldana, M., Charles, L., Green, M., Woodman, P., & Plas, L. (2016). *Learning to lead*. London: Chartered Management Institute. http://www.oxfordstrategicconsulting.com/wp-content/uploads/2015/12/Learning-to-Lead-The-Digital-Potential-FINAL.pdf.

7

End Note—The Case of Dubai

Based on many years of research, this book has tried to help leaders of governments and organisations to maximise the engagement, happiness and well-being of their people by presenting a clear model of what these concepts actually mean and by providing a toolkit based on that clear understanding.

We propose that what countries, and in particular organisations, actually need is to maximise the active committed enthusiasm of their people, not just contentment or short-term emotions of happiness or to reduce 'ill-being'.

These tools have been discussed and validated with several large organisations and countries to ensure they have the potential to add real value.

The authors continue to research and advise government and organisational leaders and this topic is continually evolving so we are keen to continue the conversation and involvement of readers via the website www.PACEtools. org.

We also wanted to present a brief case study on one of the most advanced examples of a programme to maximise happiness, in the sense of active committed enthusiasm, in the world today, the Emirate of Dubai, where its ruler, H.H. Sheikh Mohammed bin Rashid Al Maktoum has stated that he intends Dubai to be the happiest city on earth, where this effort is spearheaded by Smart Dubai Office, with H.E. Dr Aisha bin Bishr as its Director General. Also, the United Arab Emirates, of which Dubai is an Emirate, has appointed one of the first Ministers of Happiness in the world, where H.E. Ohood Al Roumi has the task of maximising happiness and positivity across the UAE.

© The Author(s) 2018
W. Scott-Jackson and A. Mayo, *Transforming Engagement,*
Happiness and Well-Being, DOI 10.1007/978-3-319-56145-5_7

7.1   Dubai Happiness Agenda: Engineering the Happiest City on Earth

(Kindly contributed by Dr. Ali Al-Azzawi, City Experience Advisor, Smart Dubai Office)

The vision for Dubai is to become the 'Happiest City on Earth', as outlined by H.H Sheikh Mohammed Bin Rashid Al Maktoum, Vice-President and Prime Minister of UAE, and Ruler of Dubai. This vision is undoubtedly noble, with many technical, social and psychological challenges. This paper outlines the strategy, and the mechanisms employed to reach this vision, along with the technological and psychological tools used to ensure success, describing some actions taken to overcome such challenges, and data showing progress towards this vision.

The strategy opted for by the city's government is to focus efforts on transformation towards a world-class smart city, where Smart Dubai Office, led by H.E. Dr Aisha bin Bishr as Director General, is leading the orchestration of this transformation. Smart technologies are seen as enablers towards the goal of happiness. However, such a strategy also needs to be grounded in clear definitions, frameworks and activities, where excelling in their practice would eventually lead to the vision outlined above. There are various definitions of smart cities that include information and communication technologies (ICTs), quality of life, efficiency and competitiveness, while maintaining balance with respect to economic, social, environmental and cultural aspects. Within such a broad range of issues, there are dominant dimensions, such as the ones suggested by the European Union project aimed at ranking smart cities (Centre of Regional Science 2007): economy, living, mobility, governance, environment and people.

A primary step in this endeavour is to deal with the definition of 'happiness'. However, though at first this may seem challenging, with various philosophical and psychological theories, some dating back to ancient philosophers, this may be overcome by focusing on the well-being literature, and turning instead towards fulfilling the needs of city residents in such ways as to facilitate happiness. Starting with subjective well-being (SWB), it is equated to the sum of (A) Affective and (C) Cognitive needs (OECD 2013), though this equation ignores (B) Basic needs that address the prosaic aspects of life in the city, as well as the (D) Deeper and more profound eudaimonic needs, which are more about higher meaning and purpose. The model also includes (E) Enabling needs: internal (personal) and external (environmental). The internal enablers are about the personal skills and attitudes a person has, such as optimism and mindfulness, as well as their personality traits, such as openness and extraversion. The external enablers are about the environment around them, including physical like natural environment as well as social aspects such as fairness and trust. This view forms the basis of Smart Dubai Office's (SDO) ABCDE model of needs. SDO, therefore, aims to increase 'happiness' by satisfying and facilitating these needs towards a more complete and holistic positive experience in the city (Fig. 7.1).

The mechanism for fulfilling these needs is the Happiness Agenda, which aims to systematically address the needs of customers and increase happiness in a structured and methodical way. The Agenda has been designed to be fully aligned with the City Transformation Agenda, with its three impact axes: customer, financial and resources. The Happiness Agenda is composed of four portfolios: discover, change, educate and measure. Each portfolio is composed of programmes that are focused on achieving the strategic objectives of the portfolio, with each programme having a variety of specific projects to be executed. The projects within these portfolios are designed to find needs, create changes and interventions, create awareness so that other stakeholders may contribute to fixing issues proactively and innovate towards 'happiness' by satisfying these needs. In this way, psychological techniques and measures, combined with smart technologies, are used as the tools within the Happiness Agenda (Fig. 7.2).

The 'Discover' portfolio centres on finding out essential and baseline aspects of Happiness in Dubai. One of the first activities undertaken in this

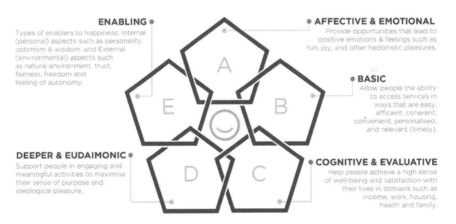

Fig. 7.1 Smart Dubai office ABCD model of needs

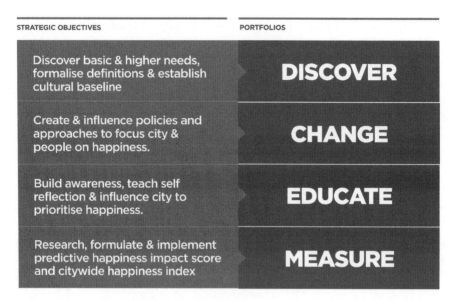

STRATEGIC OBJECTIVES

PORTFOLIOS

Discover basic & higher needs, formalise definitions & establish cultural baseline	**DISCOVER**
Create & influence policies and approaches to focus city & people on happiness.	**CHANGE**
Build awareness, teach self reflection & influence city to prioritise happiness.	**EDUCATE**
Research, formulate & implement predictive happiness impact score and citywide happiness index	**MEASURE**

Fig. 7.2 Smart Dubai office happiness agenda

portfolio was to take a 'snapshot' study of the levels of happiness in Dubai. This study was comprised of standard tools such as Cantril Ladder (Cantril 1965), Satisfaction with Life Scale (Diener et al. 1985), SPANE (Diener 2009), Portrait Values Questionnaire (Schwartz 2003) and Life Domain Satisfaction Measure (Biswas-Diener 2010; Frisch 2006). Taking such surveys, across a large sample within the city, gives a useful starting point of the different types of motivations and values of the residents, as well as their levels of satisfactions. Such data is then used to inform policy and interventions that have the highest positive impact on overall city happiness. However, a sector specific view (e.g. travel, trade, health) may be taken in order to establish the various customer journeys and ways of enhancing happiness along them. In this case, the top sectors in Dubai were chosen (prioritised by volume and economic impact) and preliminary reviews were undertaken, where insights were used to drive subsequent actions in the change portfolio.

The 'Change' portfolio focuses on interventions that directly facilitate increase in happiness. One example is the corporate happiness framework (CHF), developed in collaboration with Dubai Silicon Oasis and Oxford Strategic Consulting. This framework recognises the importance of happiness at work, as it accounts for significant aspect of people's lives in the city. In the corporate context, especially the objective is that employees, customers and other stakeholders should not just achieve contentment but should enjoy active committed enthusiasm (ACE) as described elsewhere in this book. The CHF is a 'needs impact tool' that makes use of the PACE model (process for active committed enthusiasm) as a way to measure the extent that employees are happy at work and allows for ways to diagnose, assess causality and act towards improving happiness in this context. Another example of activities in the change portfolio is running a Happiness Hackathon with a focus on the happiness of a particular segment, such as travellers. In this case, 'Happiness Hack DXB' was run at the arrivals hall of the busiest airport terminal in Dubai, where clear challenges were identified and specific solutions were prototyped in order to facilitate higher levels of happiness, within the ABCD model of needs.

The 'Educate' portfolio aims to build awareness and understanding of happiness and the needs underpinning it, as well as the methods that drive and facilitate it. In this case, an example of an activity within this portfolio is the Happiness Diploma that Smart Dubai Office has co-authored and co-delivered at RIT-Dubai University, with the aim of creating a shared understanding among the city workforce, in the private and public sector. Such a course also serves to ensure that happiness-related efforts are aligned within the Happiness Agenda, and thereby increasing overall chances of success.

The 'Measure' portfolio is used to close the feedback loop, and relies on the position that 'if you can't measure it, you can't improve it'. Here, the Happiness Meter forms the backbone of the measures within Dubai, which is a suit of types of measures, under a single umbrella. The Happiness Meter measures various types of ABCD needs, for example Basic needs where transaction satisfaction among city-wide services, as well as cognitive needs by collecting variables within existing city data that 'reveal' customer evaluations and satisfactions related to life domains, e.g. health, housing and education. These data are used within Machine Learning algorithms to estimate happiness scores.

Another way to assess the level of Happiness in Dubai is to evaluate the extent of organisational maturity in terms of adoption and execution of the Happiness Agenda. In this way, the Happiness Maturity Model (working in concert with the corporate happiness framework) is a project management tool and checklist that also helps organisations manage their internal processes in order to achieve increasing level of maturity to ultimately enhance happiness in the city.

References

Biswas-Diener, R. (2010). *Practicing positive psychology coaching: Assessment, activities and strategies for success.* New Jersey: Wiley.

Cantril, H. (1965). *The pattern of human concerns.* New Brunswick, NJ: Rutgers.

Centre of Regional Science. (2007). *Smart cities: Ranking of European medium-sized cities Final report.* Centre of Regional Science, Vienna University of Technology.

Diener, E. (2009). *Assessing well-being: The collected works of Ed Diener.* Dordrecht: Springer.

Diener, E., Emmons, R. A., Larson, R. J., & Griffin, S. (1985). The satisfaction with life scale. *Journal of Personality Assessment, 49,* 71–75.

Frisch, M. B. (2006). *Quality of life therapy: Applying a life satisfaction approach to positive psychology and cognitive therapy.* Hoboken, NJ: Wiley.

OECD. (2013). *OECD guidelines on measuring subjective well-being.* OECD Publishing.

Schwartz, S. H. (2003). *A proposal for measuring value orientations across nations.* Retrieved from https://www.europeansocialsurvey.org/docs/methodology/core_ess_questionnaire/ESS_core_questionnaire_human_values.pdf.

Index

© The Editor(s) (if applicable) and The Author(s) 2018
W. Scott-Jackson and A. Mayo, *Transforming Engagement, Happiness and Well-Being*, DOI 10.1007/978-3-319-56145-5

Druck

Canon Deutschland Business Services GmbH
Ferdinand-Jühlke-Str. 7
99095 Erfurt